Beyond Vibe Coding
From Coder to AI-Era Developer

Addy Osmani

O'REILLY®

Beyond Vibe Coding

by Addy Osmani

Printed in the United States of America.

Published by O'Reilly Media, Inc., 141 Stony Circle, Suite 195, Santa Rosa, CA 95401.

O'Reilly books may be purchased for educational, business, or sales promotional use. Online editions are also available for most titles (*http://oreilly.com*). For more information, contact our corporate/institutional sales department: 800-998-9938 or *corporate@oreilly.com*.

Acquisitions Editor: Louise Corrigan	**Indexer:** Ellen Troutman-Zaig
Development Editor: Sarah Grey	**Interior Designer:** David Futato
Production Editor: Katherine Tozer	**Cover Designer:** Susan Brown
Copyeditor: nSight, Inc.	**Cover Illustrator:** José Marzan Jr.
Proofreader: Piper Content Partners	**Interior Illustrator:** Kate Dullea

August 2025:   First Edition

Revision History for the First Edition

2025-08-18:   First Release

See *http://oreilly.com/catalog/errata.csp?isbn=9798341634756* for release details.

979-8-341-63475-6

LSI

Table of Contents

Part II. AI Coding in Practice

Part III. Trust and Autonomy

Preface

We're in the midst of a profound shift in how software is built. Professional *vibe coding*—the art of collaborating with AI to create software—is transforming developers from code artisans into product visionaries and orchestrators.

Vibe coding is about leveraging AI's prowess to handle the heavy lifting of coding, allowing developers to focus more on ideas, design, and high-level problem solving. As Andrej Karpathy quipped (*https://oreil.ly/7bnWe*), it's like "forget[ting] the code even exists" and simply building—describing what you need and letting the AI fill in the implementation details. This can lead to order-of-magnitude productivity gains, making the mythical "10x engineer" potentially a 100x reality (*https://oreil.ly/8UGID*).

Who This Book Is For

This book is written for three key audiences. The first is experienced developers and engineering leaders who want to multiply their impact. If you've been coding for years and feel the weight of repetitive tasks, this book will show you how to delegate the mundane to AI while elevating your role to architect and strategist. You'll learn to build faster without sacrificing the quality standards you've developed over your career.

Second, this book serves product-minded engineers who see code as a means to an end rather than an end itself. If you're frustrated by the gap between having a vision and implementing it, vibe coding can dramatically compress that distance. You'll discover how to rapidly prototype, iterate, and ship products that would have taken months with traditional approaches.

Here's the most counterintuitive thing I've discovered about AI tools: they help experienced developers more than beginners. This seems backward—shouldn't AI democratize coding?

The reality is that AI is like having a very eager junior developer on your team. They can write code quickly, but they need constant supervision and correction. The more you know, the better you can guide them.

This creates what I call the *knowledge paradox*: senior engineers and developers use AI to accelerate what they already know how to do, while juniors try to use it to learn *what* to do, and the results differ dramatically.

I've watched senior engineers use AI to:

- Rapidly prototype ideas they already understand
- Generate basic implementations they can then refine
- Explore alternative approaches to known problems
- Automate routine coding tasks

Meanwhile, juniors often:

- Accept incorrect or outdated solutions
- Miss critical security and performance considerations
- Struggle to debug AI-generated code
- Build fragile systems they don't fully understand

Third, this book addresses engineering managers and CTOs grappling with the implications of AI on their teams and processes. You'll gain insights into how to structure teams, evaluate talent, and maintain code quality in an era where a single engineer can produce what once required a team. The strategies here will help you navigate the transition while keeping your engineering culture intact.

What you *won't* find here is a beginner's guide to programming. While AI makes coding more accessible, wielding it effectively still requires judgment that comes from experience. Think of this book as advanced training for those ready to transcend traditional programming and embrace a new paradigm of software creation.

What to Expect

This book explores how the role of developers is evolving, from hands-on-keyboard programming to product engineering. This means using human judgment to guide AI, ensuring that quality, architecture, and user needs are met. We still provide the creativity, system thinking, and empathy that turn a functional program into a great product. AI doesn't replace us; it amplifies us—if we wield it wisely.

In Part I, I'll identify domains where vibe coding excels: spinning up new products, prototyping features, churning out standard CRUD apps or integration code—all areas where speed and pattern matching trump deep originality. Conversely, I'll also look at where we remain cautious about relying on AI: for truly complex, low-level, or novel algorithms where it might stumble. Recognizing the current limits of AI prevents frustration and failure; there's still plenty only human ingenuity can achieve.

The human element remains the linchpin. We ensure the architecture is sound, debug the tricky bugs, and judge the quality of code beyond "it runs." Critically, we infuse development with user-centric thinking—something an AI can't do. It's up to us to make sure the software not only works but works *for the users* in a meaningful way. In short, developers become curators and editors of AI output, always aligning it with real-world needs and high standards.

Part II looks at the practical aspects of vibe coding. Embracing new workflows is crucial. Techniques like "roll, not fix" remind us not to get bogged down—sometimes regenerating code is faster than debugging it. Parallel prompting lets us solve problems from multiple angles at once. We must balance rapid iteration with eventual refinement, ensuring we don't accumulate unsustainable mess. Best practices like modularizing AI code, thorough testing, and iterative refinement help keep the codebase clean and robust despite the speed of development.

As projects scale, we have to manage an accelerated influx of code and potential technical debt. AI can flood your repo with code; only discipline and good engineering practices (plus maybe AI-assisted refactoring) will keep it maintainable. On the people side, we'll hire and train engineers to be adept at using AI tools, valuing adaptability and system design skills. And we'll know when to dial back into traditional modes—like when solidifying a product for long-term maintenance or handling critical systems where caution trumps velocity.

Part III covers security and reliability, ethics, and an arsenal of tools that make vibe coding possible today: AI-augmented IDEs like Cursor and Windsurf that integrate models from Anthropic, Google's Gemini, and OpenAI to understand your entire codebase and assist at every turn. Knowing which tools and models to apply (Claude's variants for different tasks, ChatGPT for general Q&A) is part of the new developer skill set. They each have strengths: Cursor for interactive editing, Windsurf for context-heavy tasks, chat interfaces for brainstorming and troubleshooting, etc.

Looking to the future, I anticipate even more abstract ways of building software ("vibe designing" through GUIs and higher-level input), diminishing reliance on generic libraries as AI generates more bespoke code, and even software that evolves on its own based on AI feedback loops. In this future, success in software will lean heavily on human creativity, distribution savvy, and the ability to harness network effects, because the brute-force barrier of coding will be so low. New user experience paradigms may emerge, driven by AI's ubiquity—from conversational interfaces to adaptive UIs and beyond.

In all of this, one theme stands out: the fusion of human and AI strengths. Neither alone is as powerful as both together. AI brings speed, breadth of knowledge, and tireless execution. Humans bring direction, depth of understanding, and values. The optimal workflow of the future is a symbiosis—think of it as pairing a master craftsperson with a superpowered apprentice who can instantly fetch any tool or reference. The craftsperson's expertise is still crucial to create something truly excellent.

For developers reading this: it's time to embrace these tools and paradigms. This book will encourage you to experiment with an AI coding assistant on your next project, practice breaking problems down for an AI to solve parts of it, and cultivate that skill of crafting prompts and curating results. But it will also urge you to double down on what makes you uniquely valuable—your ability to design systems, empathize with users, and make judgment calls that align software with reality.

Conventions Used in This Book

The following typographical conventions are used in this book:

Italic
    Indicates new terms, URLs, email addresses, filenames, and file extensions.

`Constant width`
    Used for program listings, as well as within paragraphs to refer to program elements such as variable or function names, databases, data types, environment variables, statements, and keywords.

This element signifies a general note.

This element indicates a warning or caution.

O'Reilly Online Learning

O'REILLY® For more than 40 years, *O'Reilly Media* has provided technology and business training, knowledge, and insight to help companies succeed.

Our unique network of experts and innovators share their knowledge and expertise through books, articles, and our online learning platform. O'Reilly's online learning platform gives you on-demand access to live training courses, in-depth learning paths, interactive coding environments, and a vast collection of text and video from O'Reilly and 200+ other publishers. For more information, visit *https://oreilly.com*.

How to Contact Us

Please address comments and questions concerning this book to the publisher:

O'Reilly Media, Inc.
141 Stony Circle, Suite 195
Santa Rosa, CA 95401
800-889-8969 (in the United States or Canada)
707-827-7019 (international or local)
707-829-0104 (fax)
support@oreilly.com
https://oreilly.com/about/contact.html

We have a web page for this book, where we list errata and any additional information. You can access this page at *https://oreil.ly/BeyondVibeCoding*.

For news and information about our books and courses, visit *https://oreilly.com*.

Find us on LinkedIn: *https://linkedin.com/company/oreilly-media*.

Watch us on YouTube: *https://youtube.com/oreillymedia*.

PART I

Foundations

CHAPTER 1

Introduction: What Is Vibe Coding?

AI is reshaping how we build software, introducing new paradigms for coding that range from free-form prompting to structured assistance. Imagine writing software by simply *describing* what you want it to do—almost like talking to a teammate—while an AI translates those ideas into code. This is the essence of *vibe coding*, a prompt-first, exploratory approach where you describe what you want in natural language and let a large language model (LLM) fill in the blanks. The term was recently coined by AI pioneer Andrej Karpathy (*https://oreil.ly/Ot6CR*) to describe this new way of programming, where developers "fully give in to the vibes" of AI assistance.

In this book, I'll dive deeper into what vibe coding means for professional developers and how it compares with—and complements—what I call *AI-assisted engineering*, a more formal augmented coding process. I'll explore how the developer's role is evolving in this AI-first era, what tools and workflows can maximize your effectiveness, and how to address the unique challenges of letting an AI loose on your codebase. I'll also look at where vibe coding shines, where it struggles, and how to balance the speed of AI generation with the wisdom of human oversight. By the end, you should have a clear picture of how to harness "the vibes" in your own coding practice—responsibly and effectively—to become not just a faster coder but a more creative and impactful software product engineer in the age of AI.

In this chapter, we explore how the role of the developer is transforming from writing detailed instructions for machines to collaborating with AI by expressing intent (see Figure 1-1). We'll see why this "vibe shift" in programming is such a big deal, how it works at a high level, and what opportunities and challenges it brings.

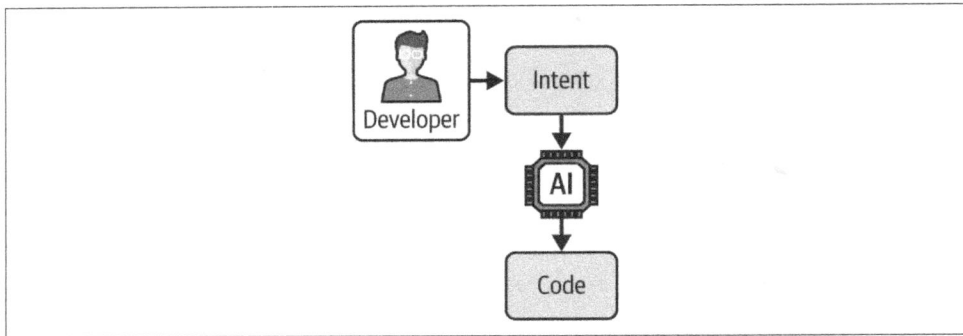

Figure 1-1. A conceptual illustration of programming with intent. The developer provides a high-level specification (the "intent"), and the AI translates it into code. This highlights the shift from writing code line by line to guiding code generation at a high level.

The AI Coding Spectrum: From Vibe Coding to AI-Assisted Engineering

Over the past year, I've observed a fascinating split in how developers—especially intermediate and advanced web developers—embrace AI in their workflow. On one end of the spectrum lies vibe coding. On the other end is what I'll call *AI-assisted engineering*: a disciplined method of weaving AI into each phase of software development, from design through testing, under clear constraints. Both approaches leverage powerful AI, but their goals, audiences, and expectations differ markedly. Throughout this book, I'll explore these two extremes and what they mean for modern web development.

The Vibe-Coding Approach: Code by Conversation

In vibe coding, you leverage powerful LLMs as coding partners, letting them handle the heavy lifting of code generation so you can focus on higher-level goals. As one *Business Insider* summary puts it (*https://oreil.ly/nvcFW*), vibe coding "means using AI tools...for the heavy lifting in coding to quickly build software." As NVIDIA's CEO Jensen Huang says, thanks to AI, "the hottest new programming language" is English, not Java or Python. Instead of manually typing out every function and bug fix, you interact with the AI in natural language—sketching out features, reviewing suggestions, and iterating based on the AI's output.

This approach represents a dramatic shift from traditional programming to AI-assisted development. Conventional coding demands careful planning, syntax precision, and often painstaking debugging. Vibe coding flips that script: "It's not really coding—I just see stuff, say stuff, run stuff, and copy-paste stuff, and it mostly works,"

Karpathy quipped to *Business Insider,* highlighting how AI can turn high-level instructions into working code with minimal manual effort.

Developers move from writing detailed instructions for computers to *orchestrating outcomes* with the help of AI. As an example, Karpathy describes (*https://oreil.ly/Ki6iJ*) building a web app by continually accepting the AI's suggestions: "I 'Accept All' always, I don't read the diffs anymore....When I get error messages, I just copy paste them in....Sometimes the LLMs can't fix a bug so I just work around it or ask for random changes until it goes away." The code "grows" beyond what he'd normally write himself, yet the project comes together quickly through iterative prompting and fixing. Essentially, vibe coding treats coding as an interactive conversation with your AI pair programmer rather than as a solo slog through syntax and stack traces. The goal is speed and exploration—to get a working solution with minimal friction.

Several trends converged to make vibe coding possible. First, modern AI coding assistants (like OpenAI's Codex, ChatGPT, Anthropic's Claude, etc.) have become astonishingly good at generating and correcting code. In the same post, Karpathy notes this is "possible because the LLMs...are getting too good"—they have ingested vast swaths of GitHub code and can produce plausible solutions for many tasks.

Second, new developer tools have emerged to integrate these models seamlessly into the coding workflow (more on these tools in a moment). Finally, the developer community's mindset is evolving to trust AI assistance for bigger and bigger chunks of work. It's no longer just autocomplete on steroids; it's handing over whole functions or files to the AI. In practical terms, vibe coding often feels like having an unlimited supply of eager junior developers to implement whatever you ask for—except they work at the speed of cloud computation.

One of the most eye-popping promises of vibe coding is the productivity boost. Early adopters report being able to create software features or prototypes ten to a hundred times faster than before. For instance, Codeium Windsurf engineer John Hoestje muses (*https://oreil.ly/_nfZn*), "Why be a 10x engineer when you could be a 100x engineer?" This suggests that, with the right AI-powered IDE, extraordinary productivity is within reach. Tools like Windsurf, an AI-enhanced IDE, "can dramatically accelerate development time, allowing you to achieve that 100x productivity." While 100x might be an extreme scenario, even more conservative studies find huge gains.

Developers can generate boilerplate code in seconds, fix bugs in the blink of an eye, and even have AI write tests or docs, compressing workflows that used to take days into mere hours. No longer limited by typing speed or memory, a single developer armed with AI can often prototype a full stack application in a weekend—something that might have taken a small team weeks to accomplish in the past. It's not just hype either; as I noted in a January 2025 blog post for *Pragmatic Engineer* (*https://oreil.ly/khEfs*), surveys show that *75% of developers* have already integrated some form of AI into their workflows, and many companies report double- or triple-digit percentage improvements in development velocity. In short, AI pair programmers are turning the mythical "10x engineer" into a very real (and reachable) 100x engineer phenomenon.

To understand how revolutionary this is, consider a concrete example. A developer wants to build a simple web app that counts words in a podcast script and estimates reading time. Instead of starting from scratch, they open an AI-powered coding environment and *tell* the AI their idea. Within minutes, the AI produces a working prototype. The developer then says, "Make the stats counters bright colors and add a PDF export," and the AI updates the code accordingly. The result is a functional tool, deployed with one click—all achieved in under 10 minutes. This real-world scenario (reported by a creator using Replit's AI (*https://oreil.ly/guqFZ*)) shows how vibe coding enables extremely rapid, iterative development driven by high-level requests. Similarly, nonengineers are jumping in: the same article describes one laid-off marketer with no coding background who used an AI coding assistant to build 100 simple web tools that collectively reached the top of Product Hunt. When the barrier to creating software drops this low, we're not just increasing productivity for seasoned developers—we're fundamentally expanding who can develop software in the first place.

However, vibe coding comes with serious caveats. Because you're deferring so much to the AI, you might end up with code that "works" in the happy path but hides a minefield of bugs or poor design decisions. Without a solid plan or constraints, an LLM might generate a solution that lacks proper error handling, security checks, or scalability. In fact, AI-generated code can sometimes be built on sand: it appears solid but has hidden issues that only surface under real-world conditions. I've seen cases where a developer vibed their way to a complete feature in record time, only to discover later that the code was inefficient and hard to maintain. This kind of "house of cards" code can collapse under pressure.

For example, imagine asking an AI to "whip up a user login system." The AI might produce a working authentication flow quickly, but perhaps it uses a simplified encryption method or a known vulnerable library. If you deploy that without deeper inspection, you're taking on faith that everything is sound. Seasoned engineers know that's risky: code running in production has to be understood and trusted. As one expert (*https://oreil.ly/ppXCf*) put it, "Vibe coding your way to a production codebase is clearly risky. Most of the work we do as software engineers involves evolving existing systems, where the quality and understandability of the underlying code is crucial." Vibe coding, at its extreme, can bypass those quality gates.

Another challenge is that vibe coding tends to downplay upfront planning. Traditional software engineering values designing for clarity and constraint-thinking through data models, choosing appropriate patterns, and writing out at least a minimal spec. Vibe coding flips this: it starts with *no scaffolding*, diving straight into implementation via prompts. That can lead to a meandering development process.

You might prompt your way into a corner—say the AI chooses a state management approach or library you didn't intend, and now you have to either steer it back or live with it. Without an initial blueprint, the final architecture might be haphazard. This is fine for a quick proof of concept, but it's troublesome in a larger codebase where consistency matters.

Vibe coding isn't inherently "bad." In fact, its emergence is part of the ongoing democratization of programming. It lowers the barrier to creating software, much like early low-code platforms or scripting languages did. A motivated nonengineer with a clear idea could potentially build a simple app through vibes alone. And for experienced developers, vibe coding can be a powerful brainstorming tool—it's like pseudo coding but with immediate, runnable results. The key is recognizing its limits. Speed without discipline can lead to brittle software, so vibe coding requires a vigilant human in the loop. I often remind developers (and myself) that "vibe coding is not an excuse for low-quality work." It should be the *start* of a solution, not the end.

The AI-Assisted Engineering Approach: Structure with an AI Partner

On the opposite end of our spectrum is *AI-assisted engineering*—a more structured, methodical way of building software with AI as a copilot at every step. Here, the developer remains very much in the driver's seat. AI-assisted engineering includes using AI across the traditional software development lifecycle (SDLC), such as AI-powered autocomplete, chat, code migrations, bug detection, test generation, and both granular (function, module, component) and full code generation (see Figure 1-2).

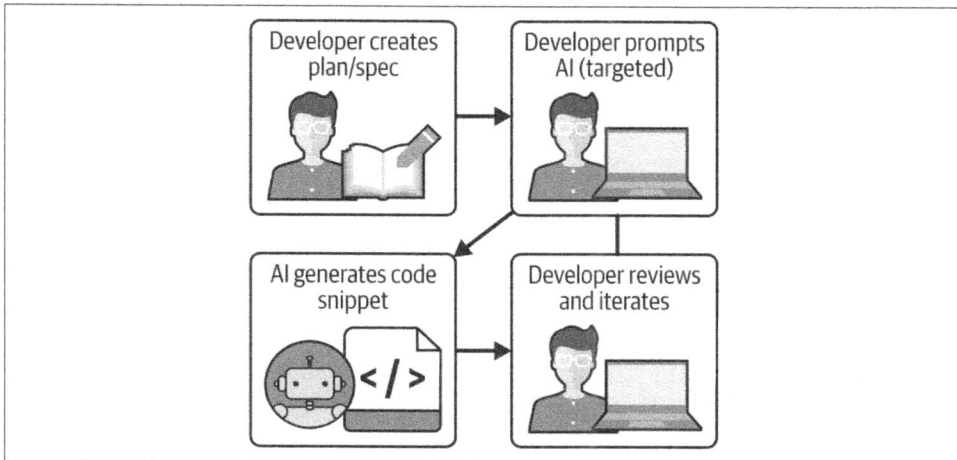

Figure 1-2. The plan-first AI-assisted engineering workflow: developers create specifications, provide targeted prompts to AI systems, review generated code snippets, and integrate approved solutions into their projects.

You begin with a plan (even if it's lightweight), outlining what you need to build and defining the constraints and acceptance criteria up front. Then you incorporate AI tools in a targeted manner to accelerate or enhance parts of that plan. In contrast to prompt-first vibe coding, we might call this "plan-first" development with AI support. This could be as formal as a mini-product requirements document (a short PRD for a feature) or as simple as a checklist of tasks. The crucial difference is that you ground the work in *clear intent and constraints* before letting the AI loose.

Consider a React developer tasked with creating a new interactive dashboard component. In an AI-assisted engineering approach, they might begin by writing down the component's responsibilities and API:

> Dashboard component shows a list of analytics cards, supports filtering by date range, and has refresh and export buttons. It should fetch data from our API (with proper error handling), and it must follow our design system for styling.

This outline is essentially a spec. The developer might even sketch a quick data model or identify existing utility functions to reuse. Only then do they bring in the AI: for instance, using an AI-enabled IDE or coding assistant to generate the skeleton of the component based on that description. The AI might provide a starting implementation of the React component with placeholders for data fetching and stubbed event handlers. Because the developer provided clear guidance, the AI's output is more likely to align with the project's needs (such as using the right design system classes or calling the correct API endpoints). The code isn't a surprise; it's the product of a well-formed request.

AI-assisted engineering doesn't stop at code generation for a single component. It permeates the entire development lifecycle in a controlled fashion. For routine coding tasks, an AI autocompletion tool like GitHub Copilot can suggest the next few lines as you type, saving keystrokes when you're implementing known patterns. For example, as you write a unit test, your AI helper might autosuggest assertions based on the function name. Speaking of tests, you might use AI to generate test cases once a feature is in place—feeding the component's spec or code into a prompt to get suggestions for edge cases you should check. The idea is to *augment* the engineer's work, not replace it. You're still thinking through the logic and verifying correctness; the AI just offloads some of the grunt work.

When it comes to code migration or refactoring, AI can be a godsend. Imagine needing to convert a class-based React component to a modern function component with hooks. Rather than doing it all manually, you could ask an AI assistant to transform the code or at least outline the steps. With a good understanding of the old and new patterns, an LLM can produce a draft of the refactored code, which you then review and polish. This structured use of AI tackles well-defined tasks (like "migrate this code from Redux to React Context API") one by one rather than handing the AI an open-ended "build whatever" mandate.

Perhaps the most dramatic form of AI-assisted engineering is using AI to generate a full mini-application or feature from a detailed specification. Several tools now allow you to input a description of an app, something akin to a mini-PRD, and get back a working codebase or prototype. For instance, a developer could supply a spec for:

> a to-do list app with React frontend and Node.js backend, supporting user authentication and real-time updates

The AI tool would scaffold the project, create the key components, and set up the database schema.

This isn't magic; it's an accelerated version of what a diligent engineer might do when starting a new project (setting up directories, choosing libraries, writing boilerplate code). The important thing is that the AI's creativity is *bounded by the constraints given in the spec.* The result is a minimum viable product (MVP) that adheres to the requirements you provide. An experienced developer, treating this output correctly, will not assume it's production-ready on the first generation. Instead, they'll treat it as a first draft. They'll run the app, write or regenerate tests to validate each feature, review the code for any inconsistencies or insecure configurations, and refine as needed. In short, they'll apply all their usual engineering rigor—just accelerated by an AI's ability to produce bulk code from a blueprint.

The goals of AI-assisted engineering are different from those of vibe coding. The aim here is not just to get *working* code quickly but to get *high-quality* code more efficiently. It's about boosting productivity while preserving (or even improving) the reliability of the outcome. A team practicing AI-assisted engineering might say, "We want to deliver this feature two times faster but with zero compromise on our standards."

The audience for this approach is typically professional developers and teams who have established processes (code review, testing, deployment pipelines) that they aren't willing to abandon. These are intermediate to senior engineers who see AI as a powerful new tool in their toolbox, not a replacement for the toolbox. They likely have seen what happens when you cut corners, so they value practices that keep software maintainable. (By way of comparison, the audience for vibe coding includes solo developers hacking together demos, product-minded folks with some coding knowledge, and even relatively new programmers who leverage AI to compensate for gaps in their expertise.)

The expectations in AI-assisted engineering are that humans remain in control of decisions, and the AI provides suggestions or accelerators. Code quality, performance, and security remain paramount, so every AI-generated piece is subject to the same scrutiny as if a junior developer wrote it. Treat the AI as your intern, not your replacement. You might delegate tasks to it, but you must review its work. Just as you'd never deploy code written by a human intern without a code review, you shouldn't deploy AI-written code without understanding it. This mindset keeps the engineering discipline front and center.

Different Mindsets, Different Expectations

Vibe coding and AI-assisted engineering are two distinct mindsets. Vibe coding is top-down and exploratory: you start with a broad idea and let the implementation emerge through interaction with the AI. It's a bit like improvisational jazz—minimal structure, lots of room for creative riffs, and you discover the shape of the song as you play. AI-assisted engineering is systematic and iterative: more like classical composition, where you begin with a theme or motif (your requirements) and methodically develop it, perhaps using some improvisation (AI suggestions) within the measures of a written score. Both can produce "music," but the process and the kind of result will differ.

For an intermediate or advanced web developer, your expectations for each approach are key. If you're vibe coding, you expect to be surprised. The AI might come up with an approach you wouldn't have written yourself—maybe it uses a different library or a programming idiom you're less familiar with. Part of the allure is learning from those surprises or quickly getting past things you find tedious. But you also need to expect hiccups. Vibe-coding enthusiasts should go in with eyes open that they'll be responsible for that tricky last stretch. The magic is real, but it's not total.

If you're practicing AI-assisted engineering, your expectations are more measured and arguably more realistic for long-term projects. You expect the AI to save you time and perhaps inspire a solution or two but not to do your whole job. In fact, a good AI-assisted engineer might use vibe-style prompting in *microdoses* within a larger framework. For example, while implementing a well-specified module, they might momentarily switch into "vibe mode" to ask, "Hey AI, generate a quick utility function to format these dates," then immediately switch back to engineer mode to integrate and check that function. The mindset is that AI is a collaborator that works under your guidance. You allocate tasks to it where it excels (like boilerplate, repetitive code, broad-stroke implementations), and you handle the rest yourself (critical logic, integration, final review).

Expectations here include improved productivity, fewer rote mistakes (an AI is less likely to misspell a variable name, for instance), and possibly a broader solution search space (the AI might suggest an algorithm you hadn't thought of). But you also expect to invest time in validation. Debugging AI-assisted code is still debugging: you run tests and step through the code in the debugger if needed. The difference is that you might find yourself debugging code the AI wrote for you, which is a new experience that comes with a learning curve. Chapter 5 will discuss this experience in detail.

The two approaches' goals highlight a fundamental difference between them: vibe coding optimizes for *velocity in the short term*, whereas AI-assisted engineering optimizes for *sustained velocity and reliability*. A vibe coder might say, "I need to get this app running by tonight to see if the idea works." An AI-assisted engineer would say, "I need to build this feature fast, but it should be robust enough to live in our codebase for years." The former is satisfied if the code basically functions; the latter cares that the code is clean enough for others to build upon.

These differences naturally appeal to different audiences. Less-experienced developers or those outside the engineering discipline might lean toward vibe coding because it lowers the barrier to entry and provides instant gratification. I've met product managers and designers dabbling in code via vibe prompts, treating the AI almost like a superpowered Stack Overflow that gives them full solutions. On the flip side, seasoned developers and engineering teams tend to favor AI-assisted engineering. They've been burned by fragile code before, so they start from a place of "let's do this right, even if we use new tools to go faster." They put in a bit more effort up front (writing that mini-PRD, setting up the project structure) in exchange for long-term payoffs.

Finding Your Place on the Spectrum

It's tempting to ask: which approach is better? The truth is, vibe coding and AI-assisted engineering aren't mutually exclusive categories: they represent two ends of a spectrum, and real-world workflows often blend elements of both. A developer might start a project with a burst of vibe coding to scaffold something novel, then switch into engineering mode to firm it up. Or they might generally follow an AI-assisted discipline but occasionally—for a trivial one-off script or a throwaway prototype—say, "You know what, I'll just vibe code this and see what I get." The key is understanding the trade-offs and using the right approach for the right context.

Think of vibe coding as a high-speed exploratory vehicle: it can take you off the beaten path quickly, and it's great for discovery. AI-assisted engineering is more like a reliable train on a track: you have to lay down rails first (plan), but it's a safer bet and more likely to reach a defined destination without derailing. Intermediate and advanced developers should be capable of driving both vehicles, but they'll choose based on the task at hand. If the goal is to innovate or ideate rapidly (say, in a hackathon or when validating an idea's feasibility), vibe coding provides momentum. Just remember to tighten things up if you plan to reuse that code. If the goal is to build a maintainable product feature in a professional setting, leaning toward AI-assisted engineering ensures you don't end up with a black-box chunk of code in your codebase that nobody truly understands.

One fascinating thing I've observed is that as developers gain experience with AI tools, their usage often naturally shifts from the vibe end toward the engineering end.

Initially, the novelty of having an AI generate entire blocks of code from a single prompt is alluring—who wouldn't want to try essentially "talking" an app into existence?

But after the honeymoon, pragmatism kicks in. Developers start to see where the AI shines and where it stumbles. They learn to break problems down and feed them to the AI in pieces rather than asking for the whole solution in one go. In effect, they move from being "prompt artists" to becoming AI "orchestra conductors"—still utilizing the AI's creative power but guiding it with a skilled hand and following a clear score. In my own practice, I've become more deliberate with prompts, often writing small pieces of pseudocode or comments and asking the AI to complete them instead of just asking open-ended questions. This way, I get the benefits of vibe-like fluidity but within a structure I control.

It's also worth noting that tooling is evolving to support the entire spectrum. On one side, we have chat-based interfaces and natural-language coding environments explicitly designed for vibe coding, where you might not even see the code until you ask for it. On the other, IDEs are adding AI features that seamlessly blend into traditional coding: for example, AI linters that suggest improvements, documentation generators that explain code, and version-control bots that can automatically create a pull request and suggest changes for review. These tools encourage an engineering mindset by fitting into the usual development workflow (edit, review, test, etc.) while still leveraging AI.

The distinction between vibe coding and AI-assisted engineering might even blur over time as best practices emerge. We may find that what today feels like "vibing" will gain more guardrails, and what feels like "structured engineering" will become more fluid. In fact, I'd argue that the ideal future is one where we can move up and down this spectrum effortlessly: exploring creative solutions with AI when we want to but always reining things in with solid engineering practices when it's time to harden and ship the software.

This spectrum of approaches represents a significant evolution in how we work with AI tools today. Yet even as we refine our techniques for collaborating with AI—whether through rapid vibe coding or structured engineering workflows—a more fundamental transformation is taking shape. The very nature of programming itself is changing. We're moving away from the traditional paradigm where developers must translate their ideas into explicit instructions and toward a future where we can express our intentions directly and let AI handle the translation into code.

This shift challenges our most basic assumptions about what it means to be a programmer. For generations, our value has been tied to our ability to think like machines—to break down problems into discrete, logical steps that computers can execute. But what happens when machines become capable of understanding what we *want*, not just what we tell them to do? This is where *programming with intent* enters the picture, representing not just a new tool or technique but a fundamental reimagining of the developer's role.

Beyond Lines of Code: Programming with Intent

For decades, programming has meant writing instructions: line after line of code telling the computer *how* to do something. Each function, loop, and conditional had to be carefully crafted by a human. Programming with intent flips this script. Instead of focusing on the low-level implementation, the developer focuses on the outcome or goal: what you want the program to accomplish. You express that intent in a high-level way (often in natural language), and the AI system figures out the code to fulfill it.

Think of it this way: traditional coding is like giving someone step-by-step directions, while intent-based coding is like telling them your destination and letting them figure out the best route. By focusing on the *what* instead of the *how*, developers can work at a higher level of abstraction. This approach isn't entirely new—tools like visual programming, low-code platforms, and code generators have long promised to raise the abstraction level. But today's AI advancements are finally making it practical to describe complex behaviors in plain language and get working code in return.

The Rise of the Prompt: From Instructions to Descriptions

At the heart of this shift is the humble prompt. A *prompt* is the input or question you give to an AI coding system. In essence, it's a description of what you want the program to do rather than an instruction for how to do it. This can feel very different from writing code. For example, instead of writing a loop to parse a file, you might prompt:

> Read this CSV file and extract the email addresses of all users older than 18.

The AI will attempt to generate code that accomplishes that description.

Why is this happening now? The rapid progress of LLMs in understanding and generating text, including programming languages, has been a game changer. These AI models have been trained on vast amounts of code and natural language text. They can interpret a prompt that looks like a description of software behavior and translate it into actual code that implements that behavior. In other words, they've learned the patterns of how humans describe tasks and how those tasks translate into code.

This rise of prompt-based development means that, as a developer, you increasingly write descriptions of features and logic in natural language or pseudocode and let the AI handle the heavy lifting of writing syntactically correct code. The prompt becomes your new unit of thought. It's a concise expression of intent. We've gone from telling the computer, "Do X, then Y, then Z" to saying, "I need X, Y, and Z done" and trusting the AI to fill in the blanks.

It's important to note that writing a good prompt is itself a skill (which we'll dive into in Chapter 3). A vague prompt can lead to incorrect or inefficient code, just as a vague requirement can confuse a human programmer. The better you can articulate your intent in the prompt, the better the AI's output will match your needs. This is why many are calling prompt writing the new programming literacy.

How It Works: The Iterative Cycle and AI's Role in Code Generation

So how does an AI go from your free-form description to actual, functioning code? The magic lies in LLMs' ability to interpret context and generate text. The *large* in "large language model" refers to the number of parameters (the internal configuration) it has, often billions or more, which enable it to capture the complexities of natural and programming languages. These models have been trained on public code repositories, forums, documentation, and Q&A sites, learning both the syntax of programming languages and the semantics of how code is used to solve problems. When you interact with an AI coder, you're tapping into this expansive learned knowledge. Let's break it down in simple terms:

Understanding the prompt
When you provide a prompt (for example, "Generate a function that checks if a number is prime"), the AI model analyzes the text of that prompt. Modern models from Google, OpenAI, and Anthropic have been trained on countless examples of language and code, so they use statistical patterns to infer what you're asking. Essentially, the AI tries to *predict* the most likely completion of the prompt with code that makes sense.

Leveraging context
These AI systems often take into account additional context beyond just the single-line prompt. For instance, if you're working in an IDE with an AI assistant, the model might also consider the current file content, your coding style, comments, and even related files. All this context helps the AI generate code that fits your project. It's similar to how a human developer reads surrounding code and documentation to understand what to do next.

Generating code
Once the model has understood (or at least made a best guess about) your intent, it proceeds to generate code. Under the hood, it does this one token at a time (a token is a piece of a word or code symbol) using probabilities learned during its training. The model doesn't "think" in the conventional sense; it doesn't have a compiler or runtime checking the code. It's simply very good at continuing text in a way that has a high chance of being correct code because it has seen so many

examples before. If the prompt and context are clear, the code it produces can be remarkably accurate and even follow best practices it has seen in its training data.

Validating with human oversight

Importantly, the AI doesn't run off and deploy your application for you. You remain in the loop. You review the generated code, test it, and can accept or modify it. In many cases, the AI might also offer an explanation of the code if asked, helping you understand the result. The AI's role is like an assistant that drafts the code for you—but you, the developer, are still the decision maker who ensures the code is correct and fits the project's needs.

What's truly impressive is that this process happens in seconds or less. The high-level overview is that your description (prompt) goes into a prediction engine (the LLM), which produces likely code as output. While the inner workings of models involve complex math and neural network layers, at the user level, it feels almost like collaborating with an expert who can instantly recall how to implement just about anything.

One of the key things to understand about vibe coding (intent-based programming) is that it's an iterative, collaborative process between the human and the AI. You don't just write one perfect prompt and then sit back as the AI writes an entire program flawlessly. In practice, you engage in a back-and-forth, a feedback loop that gradually takes a vague idea to polished code.

Here's how a typical cycle might look:

Step 1: You describe what you want

This is your initial prompt or request. For example:

Generate a function to calculate monthly loan payments given principal, interest rate, and term.

Step 2: AI provides an initial solution

The AI generates code for that function, complete with parameters and formula for loan payments. It might even include comments explaining the formula.

Step 3: You review and test

You look at the code. Does it make sense? Does it handle edge cases? You run a quick test: what if the interest rate is 0? Does it behave correctly? You notice it might not handle that scenario well.

Step 4: You refine your request or code

If the code isn't perfect (and often it won't be on the first try), refine it. Maybe you prompt the AI again ("Modify the function to handle a 0% interest rate gracefully"), or edit the code yourself and tell the AI, "Explain this part," if something is unclear. This guidance helps correct any misunderstandings.

Step 5: AI refines the solution

> The AI takes your feedback or new prompt and adjusts the code. Now the function checks for zero interest and handles it appropriately.

Step 6: Repeat as needed

> You continue this loop until satisfied. Perhaps next you ask the AI to also generate unit tests for this function to ensure it works correctly. It does so, and you run them to verify all is well.

This collaboration is much like a pair-programming scenario where one partner is the human and the other is an AI assistant. The human sets the direction and knows the high-level requirements, while the AI offers suggestions, writes boilerplate, and speeds up the tedious parts. Neither is effective alone for complex tasks: the AI relies on the human for direction and validation, and the human offloads some work to the AI to move faster.

Crucially, the iteration isn't just about fixing errors; it's also about evolving the solution. You might start with a very rough prompt and then progressively refine your intent as you see what the AI produces.

This encourages a mindset of experimentation. If the first attempt isn't right, you haven't wasted much time—just refine the prompt or tweak the code and try again. In traditional coding, writing a module only to throw it away can be frustrating, but with AI-generated code, the cost of a false start is low, encouraging exploration of different approaches.

Productivity, Accessibility, and the Changing Nature of Programming

Why is programming with intent such a big deal? This shift has several profound implications:

Boosting developer productivity

> Perhaps the most immediate benefit is speed. Developers can accomplish tasks faster when the AI handles the rote work. Routine code that might take hours to write by hand (like setting up database models, API endpoints, or data cleaning scripts) can often be generated in minutes. Early studies on AI coding assistants back this up: developers using tools like GitHub Copilot have been shown to complete tasks significantly faster (one study (*https://oreil.ly/4Ksmy*) found a 55% time reduction on a given task with Copilot assistance). When you multiply these gains across an entire project, it hints at a future where software development cycles shorten dramatically and teams can iterate more quickly.

Keeping developers "in the flow"

Beyond raw speed, there's a psychological benefit. Writing boilerplate or looking up syntax can break a programmer's flow and train of thought. With an AI handling many of those interruptions, developers can stay focused on the problem they're solving. Many users report (*https://oreil.ly/inQHR*) that with AI help, they feel less frustrated by tedious tasks and can concentrate on the creative and design aspects of coding. In other words, it can make coding more enjoyable by offloading the boring parts, which in turn can improve the quality of the work (a happier coder often produces better code).

Lowering the barrier to entry

Programming has traditionally required learning the exacting grammar of code and the quirks of various libraries and frameworks. With intent-based programming, some of that burden shifts to the AI. A newcomer might not remember the exact syntax to open a file or the parameters of a graphing function, but if they can describe what they want, the AI can fill in those details. This doesn't mean anyone can code complex systems with zero knowledge (you still need to understand what the program should do), but it does mean that the ramp-up to producing useful results is shorter. It's conceivable that domain experts (like a biologist or an economist) could write prototypes in their field by describing their needs, even if they're not professional developers. In this sense, programming becomes more accessible to people who have the ideas and intent but not deep coding skills.

Changing developer roles and skills

As AI takes on more code generation, the role of the human developer evolves. Skills like architectural design, problem decomposition, and validation become even more important. You might find yourself spending more time deciding *what* to build and reviewing *why* the code works (or doesn't) than typing out the syntax. The nature of "knowing how to code" may shift toward "knowing how to get the AI to code." This could democratize certain aspects of software development while also elevating the level at which professionals operate. We'll likely see new best practices centered around how to effectively guide AI (a topic I'll introduce in Chapter 3 and revisit throughout the book).

Productivity versus creativity

Interestingly, as AI handles more routine coding, human developers can focus on higher-level creative tasks like refining the user experience, brainstorming new features, or tackling tricky algorithmic problems that AI might not solve well on its own. In this ideal scenario, the AI increases productivity on the repetitive 80% of coding, freeing your mental energy for the inventive 20%. It's a shift in how we allocate our effort.

However, it's not all rainbows and sunshine. This new style of development also raises challenges:

Trust and correctness

Can you trust the code an AI writes? If you don't see every line, there's a risk of mistakes going unnoticed. Developers need to thoroughly test and review AI-generated code. The onus is on the human to ensure the output is correct, secure, and efficient. Blindly trusting AI output is risky, as we'll discuss.

Losing some low-level skills

If you rely on AI for routine coding, will you gradually lose your ability to write that code from scratch or debug issues deep in the weeds? It's a concern akin to overreliance on calculators weakening arithmetic skills. Developers will need to consciously balance convenience with maintaining a solid understanding of the fundamentals.

Shifting job landscape

As programming with intent becomes widespread, the industry might value different skills. There may be less demand for people who are good at just cranking out boilerplate logic, and more demand for those who can design systems, integrate components, and verify correctness. The nature of software jobs could shift, with AI handling more implementation and humans focusing on design and oversight.

Additionally, one of the most critical factors in "vibe coding" is context window size. Gemini offers the longest context window of all AI models, which can be game changing when working with large projects. Some models now support context windows of over a million tokens, allowing them to maintain awareness of entire applications. Developers can feed entire codebases to an AI for comprehensive understanding.

We'll delve into these trade-offs more at the end of the chapter. But first, let's familiarize ourselves with the emerging tools that enable this new way of coding.

A Glimpse of the Tools: The Emerging Ecosystem

Vibe coding may be a philosophy, but it's enabled by a new generation of AI-powered tools. Experienced developers who want to embrace this workflow will need to get acquainted with some key platforms and models that make AI-assisted coding effective.

This section is a quick tour of the essential tools in the vibe coder's toolkit. These include Visual Studio Code (VSCode) with its growing ecosystem of AI features and extensions, next-gen AI-integrated IDEs like Cursor and Windsurf, LLMs like Claude (in its various versions), and ChatGPT. This section does not cover background coding agents, but I discuss them in detail in Chapter 10.

As you read this section, don't worry about memorizing specific tool names or features; the landscape is evolving fast. The goal is to understand the types of solutions available.

VSCode + Copilot: Microsoft's Integrated AI Development Platform

VSCode (*https://code.visualstudio.com*) has transformed from the world's most popular code editor into a comprehensive AI-assisted development platform through its deep integration with GitHub Copilot. This evolution represents Microsoft's vision for keeping AI capabilities within the familiar VSCode environment that millions of developers already use daily.

GitHub Copilot is an AI-powered coding assistant integrated into VSCode. It provides code suggestions, explanations, and automated implementations based on natural language prompts and existing code context. What sets this integration apart is its seamless nature—Copilot isn't just an add-on but feels like a natural extension of the editor itself.

The core of VSCode's AI capabilities centers on three main modes of interaction. First, there's *inline code autocompletion*, where Copilot provides inline code suggestions as you type, ranging from single-line completions to entire function implementations. As you write code, ghost text appears with suggestions that you can accept with Tab or partially accept word by word.

Second, there's the *chat interface*, accessible through a sidebar panel where you can have conversations about your code, ask questions, or request specific implementations. Third, and perhaps most powerful, is the *agent mode* that uses tool calling to access a growing set of capabilities inside Visual Studio. When given a goal, it selects and executes the right tools step-by-step. This agent mode can analyze your codebase, propose edits across multiple files, run terminal commands, respond to build errors, and self-correct in a loop until the task is completed.

What makes VSCode's Copilot implementation particularly compelling is its support for the Model Context Protocol (MCP). MCP provides a standardized way for AI models to discover and interact with external tools, applications, and data sources. This means Copilot in VSCode can connect to databases, invoke APIs, access documentation, and integrate with your entire development ecosystem. For instance, with the GitHub MCP server enabled, you can ask Copilot to "create an issue for each bug we discussed," and it will interact directly with GitHub's API to create those issues. The extensibility through MCP transforms Copilot from a code generator into a comprehensive development assistant that understands not just your code but your entire workflow.

To leverage VSCode with Copilot effectively in professional development, start by exploring the different interaction modes based on your task complexity. For simple code completions and refactoring, rely on the inline suggestions and the sparkle icon that appears near errors—click it for AI-powered fixes.

For more complex tasks, switch to agent mode by opening the chat panel and selecting "Agent" from the drop-down. Agent mode is optimized for making autonomous edits across multiple files in your project. It is particularly useful for complex tasks that require not only code edits but also the invocation of tools and terminal commands. The combination of VSCode's familiar interface with Copilot's evolving AI capabilities offers a compelling option for teams that want enterprise-grade AI assistance without leaving their established development environment.

VSCode + Cline: The Open Source Autonomous Coding Agent

Before exploring purpose-built AI IDEs, it's worth examining how Cline (*https:// cline.bot*) (formerly Claude Dev) transforms VSCode into a powerful AI-assisted development environment. Cline represents a different philosophy from Microsoft's Copilot. Rather than being a tightly integrated assistant, it functions as an autonomous coding agent that can take on complex, multistep development tasks from start to finish. This open source extension brings capabilities to VSCode that often exceed those found in proprietary AI editors, all while maintaining the flexibility and extensibility that VSCode users expect.

What distinguishes Cline is its truly agentic approach to software development. When you give Cline a high-level request like "Create a REST API for user management with authentication," it doesn't simply generate boilerplate code. Instead, it analyzes your project structure, plans the implementation across multiple files, creates proper folder hierarchies, installs necessary dependencies, and can even run tests to verify the implementation. Throughout this process, Cline maintains transparency by showing you each planned action—file creations, modifications, and terminal commands—and giving you the opportunity to approve or modify each step. This *human-in-the-loop* design provides the perfect balance between automation and control, allowing developers to leverage AI's capabilities while maintaining oversight of their codebase.

Cline's technical capabilities extend far beyond code generation. It can use *browser automation* to research API documentation, debug complex issues by analyzing error traces across multiple files, and even interact with external services through its MCP support. For debugging, you can paste an error message, and Cline will trace through your codebase to identify the root cause, propose a fix, implement it, and add appropriate error handling to prevent similar issues. Its MCP integration means Cline can connect to your database to understand schemas before generating queries, access your project management tools to align implementations with requirements, or interact with any other MCP-compatible service. This extensibility transforms Cline from a code generator into a comprehensive development partner that understands your entire technical ecosystem.

For teams, Cline offers several compelling advantages. Being open source, teams can inspect its code, contribute improvements, or fork it for custom needs—crucial for organizations with specific security or compliance requirements. It supports multiple AI providers including Anthropic's Claude, OpenAI's models, Google's Gemini, and even local models through Ollama, giving teams flexibility in model selection based on performance, cost, or data residency requirements.

To use Cline effectively, craft detailed prompts that include project context and constraints, leverage its ability to analyze your entire codebase before making changes, and take advantage of its iterative development capabilities. After Cline implements a feature, you can immediately test it and request refinements in the same conversation context. The combination of VSCode's mature ecosystem with Cline's autonomous capabilities offers teams a powerful, flexible, and cost-effective path to AI-assisted development without abandoning their existing tools and workflows.

Cursor: The AI-Driven Code Editor

One of the flagship tools of the vibe-coding movement is Cursor, an AI-enhanced IDE that has quickly gained popularity among developers seeking a more fluid coding experience. Cursor is essentially an AI-first code editor (a fork of VSCode, in fact) that builds state-of-the-art code generation and understanding right into your development environment.

Its tagline is "The AI Code Editor," and it's designed to let you write and modify code using plain language instructions. For example, you can highlight a function and ask Cursor to "optimize this function" or "add error handling here," and it will instantly suggest the code changes. Cursor's AI is project-aware—it indexes your codebase and understands the context of your files, so it can make more relevant suggestions (far beyond a simple autocomplete). Cursor IDE integrates LLM capabilities into its core interface. It's ChatGPT that knows your codebase.

Under the hood, Cursor leverages advanced language models (often Anthropic's Claude or OpenAI's models, depending on your setup) to power its features. It has a chat sidebar where you can have conversations about your code, and even a "Composer" mode for multistep code generation. Andrej Karpathy himself has used Cursor's Composer with a model called "Sonnet" in his vibe-coding experiments (*https://oreil.ly/aFqAO*). This setup allowed him to literally *talk* to the editor (using voice-to-text via "SuperWhisper") and have code appear, which he would then accept or refine.

Cursor can not only generate code but also *edit existing code* when instructed. For example, you can ask:

Could you make it easier to switch certificates in the transport listener?

Cursor will understand you're referring to your code and propose direct edits in the relevant file or read from relevant files, such as a specification markdown file (see Figure 1-3). In the free version, it often provides the diff in the chat for you to approve; in the pro version, it can auto-apply changes to your workspace.

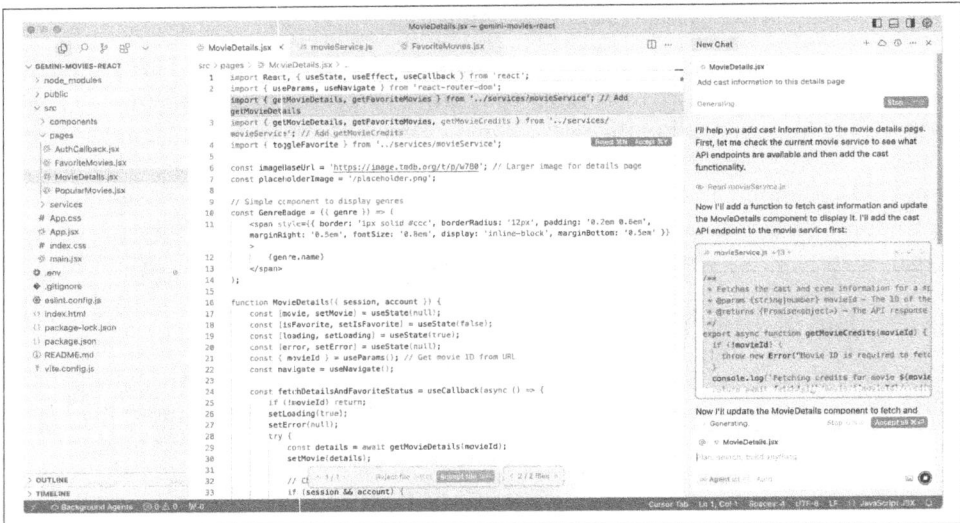

Figure 1-3. Cursor's interface exemplifies the newer breed of IDEs integrating AI. By indexing your project and iterating on prompts, tools like Cursor enable "leaving your editor running, grabbing coffee, and coming back to fully working features," delivering exponential productivity gains.

To use Cursor effectively in a professional workflow, you should take advantage of its capabilities systematically. Start by opening a chat in Cursor and describe the feature or fix you want. For instance: add a user login form with email and password, including validation and error messages. Cursor will generate the needed code (creating new files or modifying existing ones) in a draft state. You can review these changes (it shows a diff or preview) and then hit "Apply" to merge them into your codebase. Many developers follow this loop: prompt → review → accept. If the suggestion isn't perfect, you can refine your prompt (for instance, "Use Tailwind CSS for styling the form") or just ask Cursor to fix any issues you spot ("Now, handle the case where the email is already registered"). In essence, you converse with your code until it looks good.

Cursor also excels at understanding errors and logs. If you run your code and get a traceback or error message, you can paste it into the Cursor chat, and often the AI will analyze it and suggest a fix. This turns debugging into a cooperative experience (*https://oreil.ly/aFqAO*): rather than you manually searching Google or Stack Overflow, Cursor's AI can often pinpoint the problem and even write the patch. That said, it's wise to verify the fixes, as the AI might not always get it right on the first try.

Another pro tip: use Cursor's ability to take multiple files into account. You can select a set of files (or let it know about project context in the prompt) so that it considers your whole codebase when generating code. For example: add a new API endpoint in the backend to support the login form, and connect it to the frontend form we just made. Cursor will recall the frontend code it just wrote and help craft the corresponding backend logic. This project-wide context is a game changer compared to earlier coding assistants that only worked file by file.

In summary, Cursor is like having an AI pair programmer *inside* your IDE, 24/7. It's intuitive (you chat with it in plain language), and it can update your code directly. The more you practice breaking down tasks and prompting Cursor with clear instructions, the more you'll find you can accomplish in a short time. It's particularly great for iterative development: you build a bit, run and see output, then immediately ask Cursor to adjust or extend the code, and repeat.

Windsurf: An AI-Powered IDE with Full Codebase Indexing

Another rising star in the vibe-coding toolbox is Windsurf, an AI-driven development environment that takes code understanding to the next level. Windsurf is built by the team behind Codeium (*https://windsurf.com*), and it differentiates itself by indexing your entire codebase and using retrieval techniques to feed the relevant pieces to the AI model as you work. In practical terms, this means Windsurf is extremely good at handling large projects where the answer to your question might be spread across many files. Its core uses something called *retrieval-augmented generation* (RAG), which is a fancy way of saying it looks up the parts of your code that are relevant to your prompt and provides that context to the AI so that its suggestions are consistent with your existing code.

What does this look like for a developer? Let's say you're new to a big codebase and need to add a feature. With Windsurf, you can ask in natural language:

> Where in the codebase is the user authentication logic handled?

It will search through the index and point you to the right file or even function. Then, you might open a chat (Windsurf calls it the "Cascade" view, triggered by Cmd+L) and say:

> Add a phone-based two-factor authentication to the login flow.

Because Windsurf has the context of your auth logic, it can generate changes spanning multiple files (database, API, frontend) to implement this, making informed choices that line up with how your system is structured.

Windsurf's Write mode can boldly apply changes for you: it will create new files or edit existing ones automatically rather than just suggesting diffs in a sidebar. This can be a huge time-saver: instead of copy-pasting from suggestions, you see your project evolving in place. Windsurf essentially tries to take actions on your behalf when it's confident, behaving like an autonomous junior dev implementing features across the codebase. (Cursor's philosophy is a bit more conservative, asking for confirmation, although its Pro version has an "auto-apply" feature too.)

To leverage Windsurf effectively, it helps to understand its strengths:

Codebase Q&A
You can query your codebase in plain English, almost like a custom Stack Overflow for your project. This is great for large legacy projects where finding where something is defined can take hours. Windsurf will answer in seconds by pulling from the indexed code.

Global context suggestions
Because it feeds relevant files into the model, Windsurf can handle tasks like "Refactor the payment module to use the new logging utility we wrote" very well, as it knows about both the payment module and the logging utility.

Modes of operation
Windsurf has multiple modes (Autocomplete, Chat, Command, and Cascade, as mentioned). The Cascade is like a superchat, where it can consider a broader context. The Write mode (within chat) actually executes changes. You, as the engineer, can decide how much autonomy to give it.

For a team, Windsurf can be integrated into daily development much like Cursor. When picking between them, some developers prefer Windsurf for its speed and boldness (noting that it feels faster to generate and apply changes) and for working with very large projects due to its indexing. On the other hand, Cursor's interface might feel more familiar to VSCode users. It's not necessarily an either/or choice— some engineers keep both handy, or teams might standardize on one.

In sum, Windsurf is an excellent tool if you want an AI coding assistant that truly "reads the docs/code" before writing. It minimizes the chances of hallucinated functions or misnamed variables because it can look things up. To get the most out of it, feed it clear instructions and let it rip in Write mode for big tasks, but also feel free to use it in a more controlled fashion for delicate changes. Always review the changes it makes (it will show them to you), especially for critical code. Windsurf is smart, but it's not infallible. Used wisely, it's like a hyperintelligent IDE that knows your entire project and can implement ideas across it, giving a serious boost to your throughput.

AI Models: The Landscape for Code Generation

The AI coding landscape has transformed dramatically, with multiple powerful models now competing for developers' attention, including models from the Claude, Gemini, and OpenAI families. Where once a single model might have dominated, today's ecosystem offers a rich selection of options, each with distinct strengths that make them suitable for different coding scenarios.

Understanding Model Categories

Today's coding models generally fall into several categories based on their approach and strengths:

Speed optimized
> These prioritize quick responses and are ideal for real-time code completion and rapid iteration. They typically offer lower latency at the cost of slightly reduced accuracy on complex tasks.

Deep reasoning
> These take more time to "think through" problems but excel at complex debugging, architectural decisions, and multistep problem solving. Models with advanced reasoning capabilities can break down complex bugs step-by-step.

Multimodal powerhouses
> Some models can process not just code and text but also images, diagrams, and even video content. This makes them particularly valuable for understanding visual documentation or working with UI/UX elements.

Open source alternatives
> DeepSeek stands out by offering a comparable level of AI power to closed-source models without requiring payment or sign-up, though it may lack some features like image generation or web browsing capabilities.

Choosing the Right Model for Your Task

Rather than seeking a single "best" model, successful developers now match models to specific tasks:

- For rapid prototyping and general coding, models optimized for speed and broad language support work well.
- For complex debugging and system design, deep reasoning models that can trace through logic methodically are a good choice.

- For working with large codebases, choose models with extensive context windows that can maintain project-wide awareness.

- For budget-conscious teams, open source models provide excellent value without subscription costs.

Many tools now support multiple AI models, including OpenAI, Claude, and Gemini variants, along with proprietary models, allowing developers to switch between them based on the task at hand.

Practical Tips for Any Model

Regardless of which AI model you choose, certain practices consistently improve results. First, provide rich context. Don't just ask for "a payment processing function." Instead, share your data models, existing code patterns, error-handling approaches, and any specific requirements. The more context you provide, the better the output will align with your codebase.

Most modern coding models excel at reviewing their own output. After receiving generated code, ask the model to check for potential issues, suggest improvements, or explain its reasoning. This self-critique often catches subtle bugs or suggests optimizations.

Use the model's ability to maintain conversation context. Start with a basic implementation, then progressively refine it through follow-up requests. This iterative approach often yields better results than trying to specify everything up front.

Each model has subtle differences in how it approaches problems. Some are more verbose in their explanations, while others are more concise. Some default to newer syntax, while others play it safe. Learning these tendencies helps you craft better prompts.

Major Models

The AI coding landscape evolves monthly, with new models regularly challenging established leaders. The competition has become so intense that developers benefit from unprecedented choice and capability improvements. What matters most isn't picking the "perfect" model but understanding how to leverage the strengths of whatever tools are available.

Many development teams now use a portfolio approach—leveraging fast models for routine tasks, powerful models for complex challenges, and specialized models for specific domains like database optimization or frontend development. Some IDEs even allow seamless switching between models midtask.

Success comes from understanding these options and strategically applying them to accelerate your development workflow.

Google Gemini: The Multimodal Coding Powerhouse

Google's Gemini (*https://gemini.google.com*) family represents a fundamental shift in AI-assisted development through its native multimodal capabilities. Unlike models that were primarily trained on text and code, Gemini was architected from the ground up to seamlessly understand and work across text, code, images, video, and other data formats. This makes it exceptionally powerful for modern development workflows where visual context matters as much as textual information.

The multimodal nature of Gemini proves particularly valuable in web development scenarios. Developers can share screenshots of design mockups, and Gemini can generate pixel-perfect implementations that match the visual style. It excels at understanding charts, diagrams, and UI elements, making it an ideal partner when translating visual designs into functional code. This capability extends beyond simple image recognition: Gemini can reason about visual elements, understand design patterns, and maintain aesthetic consistency across an entire project.

Gemini's integration with development workflows through popular editors (VSCode, Cursor, Windsurf) and plug-ins like Cline and Code Assist offers developers powerful customization options that scale from individual preferences to team-wide standards. Developers can create custom commands for repetitive tasks, establish rules that apply to every code generation, and maintain consistent coding patterns across large codebases. The generous free tier makes it accessible to students, hobbyists, and startups, while enterprise features support complex organizational requirements.

What distinguishes Gemini in the coding landscape is its ability to think deeply about problems while maintaining practical speed. The model can alternate between quick responses for simple tasks and extended reasoning for complex challenges, adapting its approach based on the problem at hand. This flexibility, combined with its visual understanding capabilities, makes it particularly effective for full stack development where both backend logic and frontend aesthetics matter equally.

Claude: The Reasoning Virtuoso

Anthropic Claude's approach (*https://anthropic.com/claude*) to coding assistance centers on transparency and deep reasoning capabilities. The Claude family, particularly the Sonnet models, has established itself as exceptionally capable at complex software engineering tasks that require careful analysis and step-by-step problem solving. What sets Claude apart is its ability to show its thinking process, allowing developers to follow along with its reasoning and verify its logic before implementing solutions.

The Artifacts feature represents a paradigm shift in how developers interact with AI coding assistants. Rather than simply providing code in a chat interface, Claude creates a dedicated workspace where code can be viewed, edited, and previewed in real time. This interactive environment is particularly powerful for frontend development, data visualization, and any scenario where immediate visual feedback accelerates the development process. Developers can iterate on designs, test functionality, and refine implementations all within the same conversation.

Claude demonstrates exceptional performance on real-world software engineering benchmarks, consistently ranking among the top models for tasks like bug fixing, feature implementation, and code refactoring. Its strength lies not just in generating code but in understanding the broader context of software projects. Claude can analyze existing codebases, identify patterns and antipatterns, suggest architectural improvements, and maintain consistency with established coding styles. This makes it invaluable for both greenfield projects and legacy system maintenance.

The model's approach to memory and context management enables it to build understanding over extended coding sessions. When working with large projects, Claude can extract and retain key information about the codebase structure, design decisions, and project-specific patterns. This accumulated knowledge allows it to provide increasingly relevant and contextual suggestions as development progresses, making it feel more like a team member who grows familiar with the project over time rather than a stateless assistant.

ChatGPT: The Versatile Coding Companion

ChatGPT (*https://oreil.ly/hZdNC*) has established itself as the Swiss Army knife of AI coding assistants, valued not for specialized features but for its remarkable versatility and broad knowledge base. Its position in the developer toolkit is unique. While other models might integrate directly into IDEs or offer specialized coding environments, ChatGPT serves as an always available programming consultant that developers keep open in their browsers throughout the workday.

The conversational interface of ChatGPT makes it exceptionally effective for exploratory problem solving and learning. Developers regularly use it for rubber-duck debugging, pasting in problematic code and thinking through issues in natural conversation. Its extensive training enables it to recognize patterns across virtually every programming language, framework, and tool in common use. Whether debugging a regex expression, understanding an obscure error message, or exploring unfamiliar library documentation, ChatGPT can provide relevant insights drawn from its comprehensive knowledge base.

ChatGPT's strength lies in its ability to bridge the gap between human intent and code implementation. It excels at *bidirectional translation*—converting natural language descriptions into working code and explaining complex code in plain English.

This makes it invaluable for documentation, code reviews, and knowledge transfer within teams. Developers can paste unfamiliar code and receive clear explanations of its functionality, or describe desired behavior and receive appropriate implementations across multiple programming paradigms.

The model's versatility extends beyond traditional programming languages to configuration files, scripts, data formats, and domain-specific languages. While specialized coding tools excel within their focused domains, ChatGPT provides valuable assistance across the entire spectrum of software development tasks. This breadth makes it particularly useful when working at the boundaries between different technologies or when encountering problems that span multiple domains. Its ability to maintain context across extended conversations allows developers to explore complex problems iteratively, refining solutions through collaborative dialogue.

Choosing the Right Model for Your Needs

The availability of these powerful AI coding assistants represents a fundamental shift in software development practices. Rather than viewing them as competing options, successful developers recognize that each model family brings unique strengths to different aspects of the development process. Google's Gemini excels when visual context and multimodal understanding are crucial, particularly in UI/UX development and when working with design specifications. Anthropic's Claude shines in scenarios requiring deep reasoning, complex refactoring, and transparent problem-solving approaches. The OpenAI family of models provides unmatched versatility and broad knowledge, making it ideal for learning, debugging, and cross-domain challenges.

Many development teams now employ a portfolio approach, leveraging different models for different tasks within the same project. A typical workflow might involve using Gemini to translate design mockups into initial implementations, Claude for complex architectural decisions and code reviews, and ChatGPT for general problem solving and documentation. This multimodel approach maximizes productivity by matching each tool's strengths to specific development challenges.

As these models continue to evolve, the key to effective AI-assisted development lies not in choosing a single "best" option but in understanding how to orchestrate multiple AI assistants to accelerate and enhance every aspect of the software development lifecycle.

This ecosystem is young and rapidly changing. New players and capabilities are emerging every few months. The key takeaway is that you don't have to build your own AI from scratch to leverage programming with intent—there are plenty of tools that bring this power to your fingertips. Throughout this book, I'll discuss various platforms and how they fit into the vibe-coding workflow.

The Benefits and Limitations of Vibe Coding: A Nuanced View

It's important to recognize the scenarios where AI-assisted development truly shines—and where it might still fall flat. Let's explore some ideal use cases where vibe coding excels, as well as situations where today's AI still struggles or requires heavy human intervention.

Ideal Use Cases for Vibe Coding

Just as certain architectures are suited for certain problems, vibe coding has its "sweet spots" in the software development landscape.

Zero-to-one product development

Vibe coding is a game changer for getting a brand-new project off the ground. The term *zero to one* (popularized by Peter Thiel) refers to creating something new from scratch. With AI, you can go from a blank canvas to a functional prototype at lightning speed. Need to stand up a web app that's never existed before? You can generate boilerplate code for your frontend, backend, database schema, and even deployment scripts in one frenetic session of prompting. This is perfect for startups or hackathon projects where the goal is to validate an idea quickly. Instead of spending weeks setting up the "scaffolding" of a project (all the repetitive setup code), you can have the AI do it in minutes.

Many developers have recounted how they built an MVP over a weekend with the help of AI pair programmers—something that might have taken them a month working solo before. By quickly materializing the idea into a working product, you can start testing it with users or stakeholders much sooner. The AI is great at the generic stuff (setting up routing, basic UI components, standard CRUD operations), which frees you to focus on the novel aspects of your product.

However, once your MVP gains traction and moves toward production, your approach must shift. This is where AI-assisted engineering becomes essential. While vibe coding has helped you explore and validate quickly, scaling now requires more deliberate practices. You'll need to refactor that rapidly generated code with proper error handling, add comprehensive test coverage, and establish clear architectural boundaries. The transition from prototype to product marks the natural evolution from vibe coding's exploratory freedom to engineering's structured discipline. Smart teams recognize this inflection point and adjust their AI usage accordingly—maintaining velocity while introducing the guardrails necessary for sustainable growth.

Feature prototyping and CRUD applications

A lot of software engineering, especially in business apps, involves CRUD—create, read, update, delete—functionality around data. This is formulaic work that AI is exceptionally good at because it's seen countless examples. If you need to add, say, a new "Inventory" module to your system with CRUD screens and APIs, vibe coding will handle that extremely well. It can produce database migrations, ORM models, API endpoints, and UI forms with validation—basically the full stack—largely error-free because these patterns are so common in its training data. Even if your app has custom rules, you can specify those in a prompt and get a decent first pass. The result: what used to be a week-long task of boring wiring-up becomes an afternoon of prompting and testing. For internal tools or admin panels (which are essentially big CRUD apps), you might almost entirely lean on AI to generate them, given how straightforward yet time-consuming they normally are.

The engineering approach becomes crucial when these CRUD operations involve complex business logic, data validation rules, or integration with existing systems. While vibe coding can generate the basic structure quickly, AI-assisted engineering ensures that your inventory module properly handles edge cases like concurrent updates, maintains referential integrity, and follows your organization's established patterns. For instance, you might use vibe coding to generate the initial CRUD scaffolding, then switch to engineering mode to implement domain-specific rules like inventory threshold alerts, multiwarehouse allocation logic, or integration with your existing authentication and authorization systems. The key is recognizing when to transition from rapid generation to careful refinement.

Glue code and integration

Need to integrate two services or APIs together? That often involves reading docs and writing code to transform data from one format to another. AI models have often been trained on API documentation and code examples, meaning they can expedite integration work. Ask ChatGPT to show how to call Service A's API from Language B—chances are it will produce example code with the right endpoints and maybe even an auth example. Combining multiple systems (like hooking up a payment gateway with your order system or connecting a third-party analytics SDK) becomes easier when the AI can suggest the boilerplate and edge cases to handle. It excels at these standard integration patterns.

Modern framework utilization

AI coding assistants have effectively read the manuals on all popular frameworks: React, Angular, Django, Rails, Node/Express, Flutter—you name it. This means that if you're using well-known frameworks, the AI can generate idiomatic code for those frameworks. For instance, it can spit out a new React component with hooks and state management or a new Django model with the proper admin class and serializer.

The benefit is you don't have to remember every little detail—the AI fills in the gaps. Vibe coding performs especially well with modern web development tasks like generating HTML/JSX with the right classes or hooking up controller endpoints, because these are tasks AI models have seen over and over. It's like having a framework expert always by your side to write the boilerplate while you decide on the specifics of what the feature should do.

Repetitive code generation

Sometimes you need to create lots of similar code (like many similar endpoints or classes for each type in some schema). This can be tedious and error-prone for a human. AI, on the other hand, loves repetitive structures—once you show it one or two examples, it can churn out the rest consistently. This bulk code generation can save a ton of time. For instance, if you're writing data model classes for 50 types of records, you can prompt one example and ask the AI to generate classes for all 50 types following that pattern. It will likely do so flawlessly and in seconds. The result: you avoid a whole day of monotonous coding.

When AI-assisted engineering should take precedence

While vibe coding excels in certain scenarios, AI-assisted engineering becomes indispensable in others. Understanding these situations helps developers choose the right approach from the start, avoiding costly rewrites or technical debt. Complex algorithmic implementations require the engineering approach. When you're building sophisticated data structures, implementing performance-critical algorithms, or solving novel computational problems, you need precise control over every aspect of the implementation.

Here, AI serves as a knowledgeable assistant rather than a code generator. You might ask it to explain algorithmic approaches or review your implementation for correctness, but you maintain direct control over the architecture and optimization decisions. The AI helps you think through problems rather than solving them wholesale.

Mission-critical systems demand engineering rigor from the outset. Financial transactions, healthcare applications, security infrastructure, and other high-stakes domains cannot afford the exploratory nature of vibe coding. In these contexts, every line of code needs careful consideration, comprehensive testing, and often regulatory compliance. AI assists by suggesting best practices, identifying potential vulnerabilities, and helping ensure compliance with standards, but the developer maintains tight control over the implementation.

The cost of failure in these systems far outweighs any speed advantages from rapid generation. Legacy system integration presents unique challenges where engineering discipline proves essential. When working with decades-old codebases, proprietary protocols, or systems with extensive technical debt, vibe coding's pattern matching often fails. These scenarios require deep understanding of existing constraints, careful planning of integration points, and methodical refactoring. AI can help by explaining legacy code patterns or suggesting modernization strategies, but the actual implementation requires the precision that only structured engineering provides.

Performance optimization represents another domain where engineering trumps vibing. While AI can generate functional code quickly, it rarely produces optimal solutions for performance-critical paths. Tasks like memory management, cache optimization, parallel processing, and latency reduction require deep understanding of hardware, operating systems, and algorithmic complexity. Here, AI serves best as a research assistant, helping you explore optimization techniques or benchmark different approaches, while you make the informed decisions about implementation.

In these scenarios, AI's pattern recognition and speed align perfectly with the task. Essentially, vibe coding thrives on tasks that are well-trodden territory in programming (like CRUD or typical web app structures) and tasks that benefit from rapid trial and error (prototypes, new ideas). It's like having a junior developer who has read every GitHub repo and can instantly recall how it's usually done and write it for you to review. That's incredibly powerful for getting things moving quickly.

Recognizing the transition points

The art of modern AI-enhanced development lies not in choosing one approach over the other but in recognizing *when to transition between them*. Successful developers develop an intuition for these inflection points. Starting a new feature? Begin with vibe coding to explore possibilities quickly. Notice the code becoming complex or touching critical systems? Shift to engineering mode. Building a proof of concept for a client demo? Vibe coding gets you there fast. Converting that proof of concept into a production system? Time for engineering discipline.

This fluidity—the ability to move seamlessly between rapid exploration and careful construction—distinguishes truly effective AI-augmented developers. They understand that vibe coding and AI-assisted engineering are complementary tools in their toolkit, each suited for different phases of the development lifecycle. The goal isn't to pick a side but to leverage both approaches strategically, maximizing both velocity and quality throughout the software development process.

Where AI Still Struggles

As impressive as current AI coding tools are, they are not magic. There are classes of problems that remain difficult for AI to handle reliably, often requiring human insight or traditional coding techniques. Knowing these limitations helps set the right expectations and lets you plan when to lean in versus when to take back the reins.

The limitations include the following:

Deeply complex systems
> If you're dealing with very complex algorithms or novel problems that the AI likely hasn't seen, it may flounder. For example, writing a brand-new algorithm from a research paper or doing something like writing a compiler or highly concurrent system—these involve intricate logic that requires true understanding and often creative leaps. AI can try, but it might get things subtly wrong.
>
> In complex domains like these, the AI's tendency to make approximately correct but not exactly correct code can lead to a lot of back-and-forth. As Chapters 3 and 4 will discuss, the final 30% or so of correctness is very hard for the AI to nail down. This is related to what I call the *70% problem*—AI gets you most of the way quickly, but the last part is tough. An experienced developer might use AI to generate skeletons or helper functions for such complex tasks but do the core logic themselves.

Low-level optimizations and systems programming
> Current AI models are primarily trained on high-level languages and abstractions. If you need to do low-level bit-twiddling, write highly optimized C code for a specific microcontroller, or generate vectorized SIMD instructions, the AI might not be reliable. It might produce code that looks plausible but isn't truly optimal, or even correct, on a hardware level.
>
> Similarly, for things like memory management or real-time constraints, the AI doesn't have a real concept of those (it doesn't simulate a CPU cache in its head). So for performance-critical code, you'll want to either thoroughly test AI suggestions or write those parts manually. That said, AI might still help by providing a starting template or explaining assembly, but you cannot blindly trust it in these scenarios.

Unique or niche frameworks
> If you're using a very new or obscure framework that wasn't around during the AI's training, it won't know about it. In such cases, the AI might try to generalize or might produce code that looks like it fits but actually call functions that don't exist (hallucinations) or use outdated versions of the API. For example, if a new web framework version came out last month with breaking changes, the AI won't know about those changes. It might give you code for the old version. In these cases, you have to fall back on documentation and perhaps even help train the AI by feeding it context from the docs within your prompt (basically teaching it on the fly).

Creative UI/UX design
> If you ask AI to design a completely novel user interface or experience, it's not great at that creative leap. It can generate UI code for known patterns (like a

standard form or a dashboard), but if you want an innovative UI that doesn't have clear precedents, the AI might not give you something inspiring. It might just stitch together familiar components. Human designers and frontend devs are still very much needed to dream up new user experiences. In coding terms, AI can make you a standard-looking interface quickly, but for that special custom feel, you'll guide it or hand-tweak.

Interpreting intent and requirements

Sometimes AI struggles when requirements are implicit or contradictory. It has no true understanding of the end goal beyond what you explicitly tell it. If requirements are vague ("make it efficient"—what does that precisely mean?), the AI might guess incorrectly what you care about (memory versus speed, for instance). Humans are better at clarifying intent, especially with nontechnical stakeholders. AI can also misinterpret instructions, especially if there's domain-specific context it's unaware of (like business rules). It might produce a logically correct solution that doesn't actually solve the real problem because the nuance was lost in translation.

A good example scenario combining these: imagine developing a new 3D graphics engine (complex system) in Rust (system-level, performance critical). You have novel algorithms for rendering (unique problems). AI could maybe help write some boiler-plate, but you'd largely rely on human ingenuity for the core. The AI might get you started with setting up a window and a basic render loop (common tasks), but for the bespoke parts, you'd proceed with traditional careful coding and perhaps get some algorithmic help from AI in pseudocode form. And if you asked it to optimize a hot loop in assembly, you'd have to verify every instruction.

AI also lacks true problem-solving insight. At the end of the day, it's pattern matching. So if your problem requires an *aha!* insight, the AI might just flail around, presenting things that look like code but don't solve it. This is where a human stepping back, thinking abstractly, or drawing on real experience can save the day. Once you have the insight, you can then use the AI to implement it quickly.

Understanding these strengths and weaknesses ensures you'll deploy vibe-coding techniques in the right situations. To maximize success, leverage the AI for what it's good at (the known patterns), and apply your creativity to the unique parts of your application. Be ready to intervene in those areas where AI is known to struggle. For instance, do a careful review of any security-sensitive code it writes, because it might miss an edge case or two.

Use AI to complement human strengths: let it handle breadth (lots of code, boiler-plate) while you handle depth (complex logic, architecture). Use it as a booster where it excels, and don't be afraid to take the wheel on those tougher stretches of the road. This plays to the strengths of both and yields the best outcome. Knowing when to use

AI and when to rely on human skill is what will make you a highly effective developer in this new era.

Every new technology comes with its advantages and its caveats. As we embrace the productivity and creativity boost from AI-assisted development, it's important to approach it with a nuanced understanding of its limitations and trade-offs. Key benefits include:

Faster development cycles
Projects can move from concept to prototype to finished product more quickly. AI can generate scaffolding code (like setting up the boilerplate for a new project) in a flash, so you spend more time on the unique parts of your application.

Enhanced prototyping and experimentation
Because the cost of trying something is lower (just describe what you want to the AI and get a quick draft), developers may feel freer to experiment. You can prototype multiple approaches to a problem by prompting the AI in different ways, then pick the best one. This iterative ideation can lead to more creative solutions.

Knowledge at your fingertips
LLMs are trained on a vast corpus of programming knowledge. It often "knows" obscure APIs or error message solutions. In practice, it can surface solutions or ideas you might not have thought of, making you a more effective problem solver.

Consistency and standardization
In team settings, an AI assistant can help enforce coding standards and best practices by generating code in a consistent style. If configured with your project's style guide, it could ensure everyone's code follows similar patterns. Even without explicit training, AI models often produce idiomatic code (since they learned from millions of examples). This can reduce the effort involved in code reviews, since its functions may look familiar and adhere to common conventions by default.

Some of the limitations and trade-offs to consider include:

Variable output quality
These models are not infallible. They might produce code that looks correct but has subtle bugs or inefficiencies. They might choose an outdated approach because their training data included a lot of older code. As a developer, you must remain vigilant. Just as you wouldn't copy-paste code from the internet without understanding it, you shouldn't accept AI code thoughtlessly. Part II of this book will discuss techniques to validate and test AI-generated code thoroughly.

Ambiguity in prompts leads to ambiguity in code

If your prompt is underspecified, the AI has to guess your intent—and it might guess wrong. For example, if you tell it to "sort a list of names," it might default to alphabetical sorting, but maybe you meant something else (like sorting by the length of the name). The AI won't know the difference unless you clarify it. This is why specificity in prompts (Chapter 2's topic) is vital—you'll learn to anticipate what details you need to spell out.

Overreliance and skill atrophy

If new developers always rely on AI to write their code, will they develop the same depth of understanding of algorithms and debugging? There's a risk of skill atrophy, similar to how relying on GPS for navigation might weaken your own sense of direction. To mitigate this, it's important to use AI as a learning tool (pay attention to the code it provides and ask why) and sometimes practice coding without it to ensure you retain your fundamental skills.

Privacy and security concerns

Using cloud-based AI coding tools often means sending your code (which might be proprietary or sensitive) to a third-party service for analysis. Companies need to consider this. Many tools are addressing it by allowing on-premises models or giving assurances about not storing code, but it's still a consideration. Also, there's a risk that AI might inadvertently generate code that is very similar to something in its training data, which could be under an open source license (like GPL). While unlikely (and measures are in place to prevent verbatim long outputs), it highlights the need to review and understand what the AI produces before integrating it. Chapter 8 dives into questions of security and reliability.

Bias in AI output

AI models can reflect biases present in their training data. In a coding context, this might be as benign as preferring certain variable names or as significant as using examples that assume particular user attributes. For instance, it might use `foo`/`bar` for every example variable (because many examples did), or it might assume things about user locales. It's usually not a huge issue in code generation compared to other AI applications, but it's worth being aware of this possibility. More subtly, the AI might be biased toward solutions it saw more often, even if those aren't the best for your case. Chapter 9 discusses bias and other ethical considerations.

Human factors and trust

Not all developers are immediately comfortable with this style of work. Coding has a certain pleasure and artistry to it, and some may feel that is diminished by AI involvement. There can also be an initial lack of trust—"Did it really do this right?"—which only good practices and time can overcome. Teams adopting AI should allow a period of adjustment and encourage sharing of experiences and tips. Over time, as with any tool, most will find a balance where the AI's contributions are valued and human expertise focuses on what humans do best.

Summary and Next Steps

The vibe shift toward programming with intent offers tremendous potential to make software development faster, more accessible, and in many ways more enjoyable. But realizing that potential means understanding the new dynamics: how to communicate with AI effectively, how to verify its output, and how to integrate it responsibly into your development process.

My perspective, forged from working with these tools and observing many projects, is that AI's best use lies in combining the creative "vibe" with solid engineering hygiene. Encourage the wild ideas and rapid drafts that AI can offer—those are the new superpowers at our disposal. But channel them with the wisdom that software development has accumulated over decades: the importance of planning, testing, and understanding what you build.

When we strike that balance, we get the best of both worlds. We get software that is built faster and potentially more imaginatively but also software that we trust, maintain, and grow with confidence. That, ultimately, is how we elevate our craft in the age of AI: not by choosing vibes over engineering, or vice versa, but by mastering the whole spectrum between.

Next, Chapter 2 explores the art of crafting prompts and collaborating with AI. With the foundational concepts from this chapter in mind, you're ready to explore the practical side of this new programming era. This will set the stage for hands-on examples and deeper prompting techniques in subsequent chapters.

The Art of the Prompt: Communicating Effectively with AI

In vibe coding, prompts are the new source code.

The way you communicate your intent to the AI has a direct impact on the quality of the code it generates. Writing a good prompt is both an art and a science, often called *prompt engineering*. This chapter will equip you with techniques to get the most out of your AI coding assistant. We'll start with some fundamentals about why prompts matter and then delve into a toolbox of prompting techniques, from simple to advanced. By learning how to craft effective prompts and how to iteratively refine them (Figure 2-1), you'll be able to cocreate with AI more efficiently and accurately.

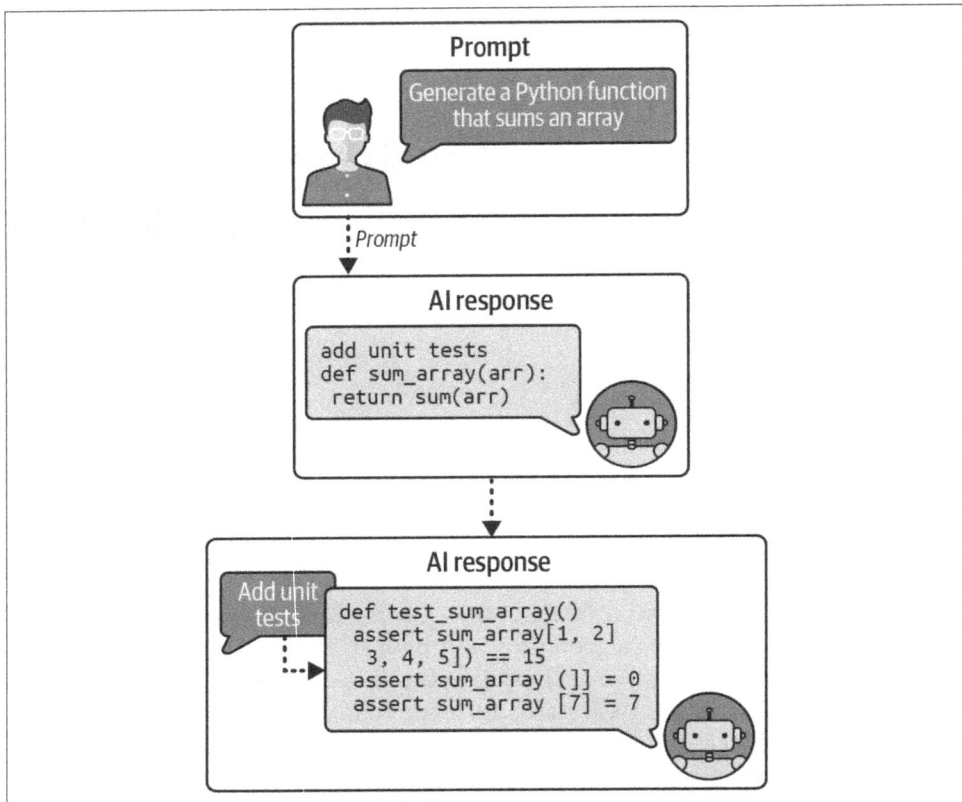

Figure 2-1. An illustration of a chatbot assisting with coding. The developer and AI engage in a dialogue: the developer provides instructions or questions (prompts), and the AI responds with code or answers. Communicating effectively with the AI through well-crafted prompts is key to getting accurate and useful code generation.

Prompt Engineering Fundamentals

If vibe coding is a conversation between you and an AI model, *prompt engineering* is the skill of speaking the AI's language to get the best results. A well-crafted prompt can be the difference between an irrelevant or buggy code suggestion and a perfect solution. Mastering prompt engineering means understanding how to guide the AI effectively, how to provide context, and how to iterate with the AI when the first answer isn't quite right.

When you program with an AI, you are essentially programming *through* the AI using natural language. The prompt you provide is like a high-level programming language that the AI interpreter then translates into actual code. Just as a compiler's output is only as good as the source code fed to it, an AI's output is only as good as the prompt.

Why are prompts so important? LLMs, despite their sophistication, are not mind readers. They respond only to the input they're given. Ambiguous or poorly worded prompts can lead to irrelevant or incorrect code, while a clear and specific prompt can yield a spot-on solution on the first try. In traditional coding, you spend time thinking about algorithms and writing code; in vibe coding, you spend time thinking about how to convey your requirements to the AI. It's a shift in what "writing code" means: you might write a paragraph instead of a function, but you still need to be precise and logical.

Think of writing prompts as being like writing documentation or user stories for a very literal and pedantic junior developer, one who will do exactly (and only) what the documentation says, and who has a lot of knowledge but no common sense beyond patterns they have seen. If your instructions (prompts) leave room for interpretation, the AI might fill the gaps in ways you didn't intend. Thus, learning to *communicate* with the AI is as crucial as learning a programming language's syntax used to be.

Another reason prompts are crucial is reproducibility and future-proofing. If you discover a prompt that reliably generates good code for a certain pattern or task, that prompt becomes a valuable piece of knowledge (almost like a snippet or template). You might save it or reuse it in similar contexts. In teams, developers might share effective prompt patterns with each other, similar to how they share coding best practices.

Finally, as models get better and more integrated, they may allow more complex interactions. Being good at prompting will let you harness new capabilities quickly. For instance, some advanced systems allow you to attach extensive instructions or provide entire reference documents as part of the context for the model. Knowing how to structure that input is key to leveraging such power.

So treat prompt writing as a new essential skill. In many ways, prompting *is* programming. The main difference is you're writing in a language (like English) that the AI then converts into code. But you still have to be clear, logical, and anticipate edge cases in your description.

Specificity and Clarity: Writing Prompts That Deliver

One of the golden rules of prompting (which I'll lay out more fully in Chapter 3) is to be specific and clear about what you want. Unlike a human collaborator, an AI doesn't truly understand your goal beyond the words you provide. A common mistake is giving the AI a very high-level prompt like "Make a website" and expecting magic. The AI works better with concrete details.

Always assume it knows nothing about your project beyond what you provide. Include relevant details such as the programming language, framework, and libraries, as well as the specific function or snippet in question. If there's an error, provide the exact error message and describe what the code is supposed to do. Any vagueness or room for interpretation can lead to unintended outputs.

For example, instead of "Write a sorting function," you could say:

> Write a Python function sort_by_lastname(customers) that takes a list of customer records (each with a first_name and last_name field) and returns a list sorted by last_name alphabetically. Include a brief docstring and handle the case of missing last names by treating them as empty strings.

This prompt sets clear expectations about the language (Python), the function name and purpose, the input structure, the sort key, additional requirements (docstring), and an edge case. It's likely to produce exactly what you need or very close to it. Essentially, think like a spec writer: the more precisely you specify the task, the less guesswork the AI has to do and the fewer revisions you'll need.

Strategies for specificity include:

Mention the language or environment
    If you want a solution in JavaScript, say so: "Write a JavaScript function..." versus just "Write a function..." If you want it for a specific framework or version, include that ("Using React Hooks..." or "in Python 3...").

Define the scope of the output
    Do you want just a single function? A full file or module? Tests included? For example, "Provide only the function implementation" and "Provide a complete runnable script" can yield different responses.

Include requirements and constraints
    In the login example, we specified password length and attempt limit. Think of edge cases or constraints and put them in the prompt. If you need the code to be optimized for performance or use a certain algorithm, say so: "using $O(n)$ time and $O(1)$ space" or "using a binary search approach."

Avoid ambiguous references
    Don't use words like *it* without a clear antecedent. Instead of "Process it and return the result," say, "Process the array and return the resulting array."

Name your desired output format
    If you want the AI to output just code or code with comments or an explanation, you can instruct that: "Give only the code, no explanation" or "Provide code and a brief comment for each step."

A clear prompt sets the AI up for success. If you find the AI's answers often need a lot of correction, examine whether your prompts might be underspecified.

Here's what not to do:

Don't write a whole novel
> Long-winded prompts that include irrelevant info can confuse the model or cause it to focus on the wrong thing. Be concise but complete in your description. For instance, you usually don't need to preface with "You are a world-class programmer..." in a coding context (some people do that in general ChatGPT usage, but for coding tasks, it's often unnecessary and could add noise).

Don't assume the AI will fill in details by itself correctly
> If something is important (like thread safety, handling of special characters, etc.), mention it. If it's not mentioned, assume the AI might not handle it.

Avoid open-ended "creative" prompts when you need deterministic outputs
> For example, saying, "Write some code to analyze data" might cause the AI to guess what analysis you want. Instead, specify:
>
> Calculate the average and standard deviation of a list of numbers.

In summary, *say exactly what you mean*. The more the AI "knows" about what you truly want, the better it can deliver. If you find yourself having to correct the AI multiple times, ask: could my initial prompt have been clearer?

Iterative Refinement: The Feedback Loop with the AI

Even with clear prompts, you won't always get the perfect answer on the first try. Think of interacting with the AI as a conversation or an iterative development process. This is the feedback loop I touched on in Chapter 1.

When the AI gives you code, review it critically, just as you would code written by a human. Does it meet the requirements? If not, identify what's missing or wrong. Then provide feedback or a refined prompt. This can be done in a conversational AI by simply continuing the dialogue, or in an editor by writing another comment for the AI to respond to.

By providing feedback to the AI, you steer it closer to your desired outcome. In a sense, you are *training* it on the fly for your specific problem. Advanced prompt engineering is like the loop in Figure 2-2: Prompt → AI output → Review → Refine prompt → AI output →...until satisfied. Keeping each iteration's changes small is useful; if you overhaul the prompt too much, you may lose some good parts of the previous output.

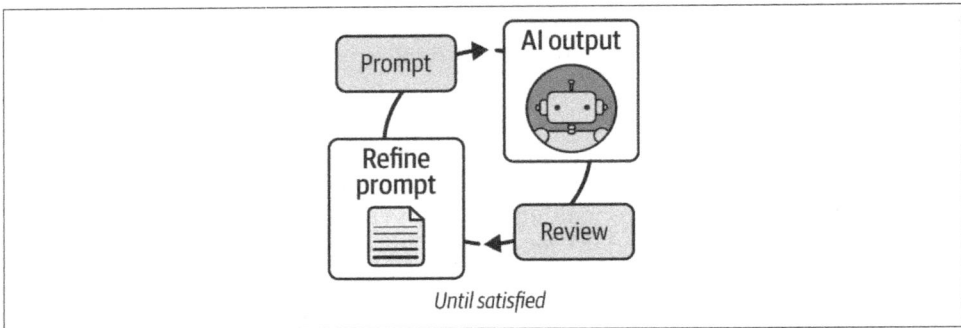

Figure 2-2. Advanced prompt engineering loop.

For example, you might prompt:

> Write a function that takes a list of integers and returns their sum.

The AI then returns a function, but its code assumes a non-empty list and doesn't handle an empty list well. You could then reply:

> That looks good. However, please modify it to return 0 if the list is empty.

The AI would then update the function accordingly. In this way, you didn't have to prompt from scratch; you just told the AI to make an adjustment. The AI already had the context of the previous code it gave.

If you're using an inline assistant, refinement might look like editing the code and perhaps writing a comment like `# TODO: handle empty list` and then seeing if the AI suggests a fix for that.

Another refinement approach is reprompting with more info if the first output wasn't right. Suppose you said, "Sort a list of names," and it gave code sorting case-sensitively but you wanted case-insensitive. You could rephrase:

> Sort a list of names case-insensitively.

Or even:

> The previous code sorts case-sensitively. Modify it to be case-insensitive.

In debugging, for more complex logic bugs (where no obvious error message is thrown but the output is wrong), you can prompt the AI to walk through the code's execution. For instance:

> Walk through this function line by line and track the value of total at each step. It's not accumulating correctly—where does the logic go wrong?

This is an example of a "rubber duck" debugging prompt: you're essentially asking the AI to simulate the debugging process a human might do with prints or a debugger.

Such prompts often reveal subtle issues like variables not resetting or incorrect conditional logic, because the AI will spell out the state at each step. If you suspect a certain part of the code, you can zoom in:

> Explain what the filter call is doing here and if it might be excluding more items than it should.

Engaging the AI in an explanatory role can surface the bug in the process of explanation.

After the explanation, it's often effective to directly ask for what you need:

> What might be causing this issue, and how can I fix it?

This invites the AI to both diagnose and propose a solution. If the AI's first answer is unclear or partially helpful, don't hesitate to ask a follow-up question:

> That explanation makes sense. Can you show me how to fix the code? Please provide the corrected code.

In a chat setting, the AI has the conversation history, so it can directly output the modified code. If you're using an inline tool like Copilot in VSCode or Cursor without a chat, you might instead write a comment above the code:

```
// BUG: returns NaN, fix this function and see how it autocompletes
```

In general, though, the interactive chat yields more thorough explanations.

Another follow-up pattern: if the AI gives a fix but you don't understand why, ask:

> Can you explain why that change solves the problem?

This way, you learn for next time, and you double-check that the AI's reasoning is sound.

LLMs thrive on examples and corrections. If you point out what's wrong or give a quick example, the AI can incorporate it:

> If input is [], it should return 0, but now it errors.

This iterative process is normal. In fact, trying to cram every detail into one prompt might be less effective than a couple of back-and-forth turns. Use that to your advantage.

Be patient and specific in your feedback. Instead of saying, "No, that's wrong," say what's wrong or what's needed:

> This code doesn't handle negative numbers correctly. It should treat them as 0 in the sum.

Also, if the AI goes off track, you can steer it back: sometimes resetting or rephrasing is easier than trying to salvage a very incorrect attempt. Use your judgment. If the AI output shows that it is completely misunderstanding you, clarify your prompt from scratch.

As you refine, you'll also learn how the AI interpreted your prompt. This can inform how you write future prompts. You might realize, "Oh, it took 'login system' to mean an entire UI. Next time I'll specify backend only."

Think of it like debugging code: if the AI output is wrong, the "bug" might be in your prompt, not in the AI's processing. Just as you'd examine and fix your code when it produces incorrect results, you should refine your prompts when the AI generates unexpected or incorrect output. The conversation between you and the AI is like a debugging session where each exchange helps you pinpoint and fix the issue.

Comparing Two Prompts

Imagine you have a simple Node.js function meant to convert a list of user objects to a lookup map by user ID. However, it's throwing an error. Here's the buggy code:

```
// Buggy function: converts array of users to a map by ID
function mapUsersById(users) {
  const userMap = {};
  for (let i = 0; i <= users.length; i++) {
    // Note: using <= will go out of bounds on the last iteration
    const user = users[i];
    userMap[user.id] = user;
  }
  return userMap;
}

// Example usage:
const result = mapUsersById([{ id: 1, name: "Alice" }]);
```

This code is supposed to iterate through the user's array and build an object where keys are user IDs. However, there is a bug: the loop uses i <= users.length instead of i < users.length. This will cause users[i] to be undefined on the last iteration, likely leading to a runtime error (like attempting to access the property ID of undefined). Let's see how an AI assistant might respond to two different prompts about this issue (see Figure 2-3).

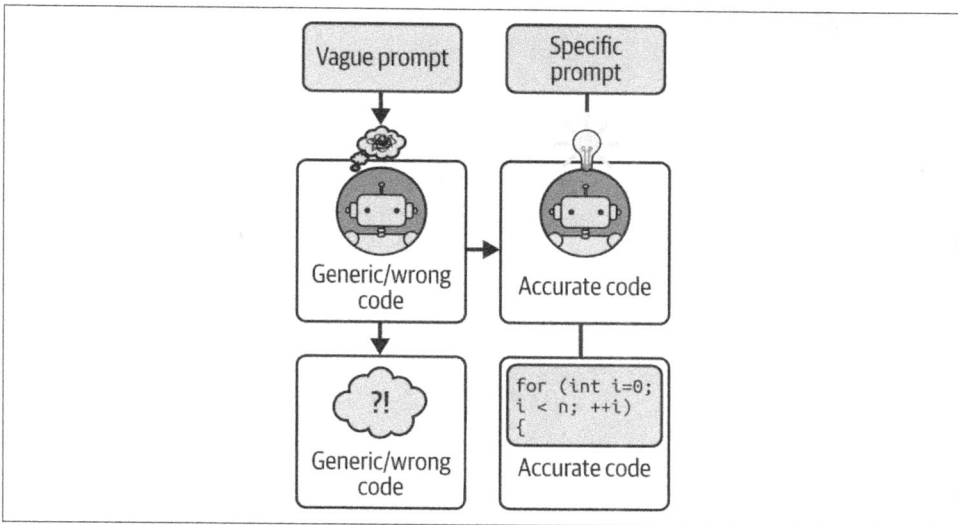

Figure 2-3. Prompt quality impact comparison: vague prompts produce generic or incorrect code, while specific, well-structured prompts generate accurate, contextually appropriate solutions.

Poor prompt

Here's an example of a poor prompt:

> Why isn't my mapUsersById function working?

AI's response to the poor prompt (simulated):

> It's hard to say without more information. Are you sure the function is being called with a proper array of users? Perhaps the issue is that users is empty or not an array, causing the loop not to execute properly. It could also be that there's an error when setting the property on userMap. Make sure that each user has an id property. If users is undefined or null, that would also cause it to not work.

This answer is quite vague. The prompt gave no details except the function name, so the AI is guessing at generic causes ("Maybe the array is empty or not an array," "Make sure each user has an ID"). It did not identify the actual bug.

This is the kind of response you get when the question is underspecified—the model can only regurgitate common debugging tips. If you're a developer, this isn't very helpful because it doesn't address the real mistake. The lack of context and specificity in the prompt yields a generic answer: essentially, the AI equivalent of "Have you tried turning it off and on again?" This aligns with the community advice that vague prompts lead to irrelevant or generic answers.

Improved prompt

Let's try this again:

I have a JavaScript function `mapUsersById` that should convert an array of user objects into a `map` (`object`) keyed by user ID. However, it throws an error when I run it. For example, when I pass [{id: 1, name: "Alice"}], I get `TypeError: Cannot read property 'id' of undefined`. Here is the function code:

```
function mapUsersById(users) {
  const userMap = {};
  for (let i = 0; i <= users.length; i++) {
    const user = users[i];
    userMap[user.id] = user;
  }
  return userMap;
}
```

It should return { "1": {id: 1, name: "Alice"} }. What is the bug and how can I fix it?

The AI's response to the improved prompt (simulated):

The error Cannot read property `'id'` of undefined suggests that at some point, user is undefined, and then you try to access user.id. Looking at your loop, the issue is with the loop bounds. You are using `i <= users.length`. If `users.length` is 1 (for one user in the array), the loop runs with `i = 0` and `i = 1`. When `i` is 1, `users[1]` is undefined (since the only index in the array is 0). Thus user becomes undefined on that iteration, and `user.id` throws a `TypeError`. The fix is to change the loop condition to `i < users.length` so that `i` goes from 0 to `users.length-1`. For example:

```
for (let i = 0; i < users.length; i++) {
  const user = users[i];
  userMap[user.id] = user;
}
```

This way, `i` will be 0 for the first (and only) element, and then the loop stops. With that change, your function will no longer hit an undefined user and should work as expected, returning {"1": {id: 1, name: "Alice"}} for the given input.

This response directly pinpoints the bug (using <= in the loop) and explains why it causes the user to be undefined. It then provides the correct code solution (i < users.length) and confirms the expected outcome. The improved prompt succeeded because it followed our principles: it specified the language (JavaScript), described the function's purpose, included the exact error message and a sample input, and even provided the code snippet in question.

Notice how the AI used the error message as a clue to focus on the loop bounds—a targeted prompt enabled the AI to engage in true problem solving, effectively simulating how a human debugger would think: "Where could undefined come from?

Likely from the loop indexing." This is a concrete demonstration of the benefit of detailed prompts.

Prompting Techniques: A Toolbox for Effective Communication

Now let's get into specific techniques that can supercharge your prompting skills. These are like patterns or recipes you can use when a straightforward instruction isn't enough or when you want to guide the AI in a certain way.

By mastering these techniques, you can handle an array of situations: instructing the AI in plain English, giving it examples, making it explain or structure its output, or setting it into different mindsets or roles. All of these help you guide the AI to produce exactly what you need.

Prompting techniques are not mutually exclusive; you will often use several together for best results, especially on complex tasks.

A Note on Style

When you use these techniques, adapt your tone to the model. Many models respond well to polite or neutral instructions. You don't need to use archaic or overly formal language. Direct but polite often works: "Please do X" or "Let's do Y." For example, with chain-of-thought (CoT) prompting, a popular phrase is "Let's think step-by-step." Models like GPT-4 recognize this as a cue to show reasoning.

Zero-Shot Prompting

Zero-shot prompting is simply asking the model to do something without providing any examples or additional guidance beyond the instruction. Essentially, the model is solving the task from "zero" examples.

When to use: This is the most common scenario: you just ask for what you want in plain language. If the task is standard and the prompt is clear, this is often sufficient.

Example:

Write a Python function that checks if a number is prime.

This is zero shot. The AI will likely produce a prime-checking function using a loop or trial division.

Pros: It's quick and relies on the model's learned knowledge. Modern models are surprisingly good at zero-shot responses for many programming tasks, especially if they're common (like prime checking, sorting, or string manipulation).

Cons: If the task is unusual or output format is specific, zero shot might yield a result that doesn't quite match what you need on the first try, because the model might have multiple ways to interpret it.

Usually, it's a good idea to try zero shot first for simple things. If the result is off, you may then shift to refining or other techniques.

One-Shot and Few-Shot Prompting

One-shot prompting means you provide exactly one example of what you want (input and desired output) as part of the prompt; *few-shot* prompting means providing a few examples (typically two to five) before asking the model to perform the task on a new input.

This is like showing the model, "Here's how I solve one instance. Now you do the next one similarly."

When to use: This type of prompting is useful when the model might not know exactly the format or style you need or when the task is a bit unusual. By giving examples, you reduce ambiguity.

Example (one shot): Suppose you're using a language or a certain style that the model might not have seen as much. Let's say you want pseudocode in a specific format. Your prompt might be:

Convert the following English instructions to Python-like pseudocode.

Example instruction: "Calculate the factorial of n":

```
Example pseudocode:

function factorial(n):

    if n <= 1:

        return 1

    else:

        return n * factorial(n-1)

Instruction: "Find the largest number in a list"

Pseudocode:
```

You've provided one example (factorial) and the format you want. Now the model is more likely to produce pseudocode for the "largest number" instruction in a similar format (with a function, with if/else or loop logic as needed).

Example (few shot): Let's say you want the AI to use a specific algorithm. You might give it a smaller example of that algorithm in action as a hint. Or if the task has multiple correct answers but you prefer a certain one, an example can push it toward that.

Few-shot prompting is powerful for formatting; for instance:

> Convert The Following English Statements To SQL Queries.\N1."Get All Employees Hired After 2020" → Select * From Employees Where Hire_Date > '2020-01-01';\N2. "List Customer Names Who Made A Purchase In The Last Month" → Select Name From Customers Join Purchases On ... Where Purchase_Date > ...;\N3. "Count Of Products That Are Out Of Stock" →

Here, once you give two examples of English-to-SQL, the AI is likely to answer the third query correctly by following the pattern. Few-shot examples can be applied to coding too: show the AI the style you want in a small sample and then ask for more. It's like giving it a minitraining dataset within your prompt.

Pros: You can achieve outputs in very specific styles. This technique also helps the model handle tasks that involve following a pattern or applying a concept repetitively.

Context Window

The term *context window* refers to the maximum amount of text (measured in tokens) that a language model can process in a single interaction, including both the input prompt and the generated response. This represents a limitation of current AI models—once you reach this threshold, the model cannot process additional information. When you're crafting prompts, everything you include (instructions, examples, data, and the space needed for the response) must fit within this fixed capacity.

Cons: Few-shot prompting in particular makes the prompt longer (which uses up context window). For very large/complex examples, it might "eat" a lot of the model's capacity. But usually a small example or two is fine.

Tip: If you want the model to strictly adhere to a certain output structure, giving an example can nearly guarantee it matches that structure rather than offering a free-form reply that you have to parse.

Chain-of-Thought Prompting

Chain-of-thought (CoT) prompting involves asking the model to think step-by-step or show its reasoning before giving the final answer. In other words, you encourage the model to break down the problem.

When to use: This is useful for complex problems that involve reasoning and multi-step computations, or when you suspect the model might make a mistake if it jumps straight to the answer. It's also useful if you want an explanation in the output.

Combinatorial Math

Combinatorial math deals with counting, arranging, and selecting objects according to specific rules or constraints. Common problems include calculating permutations (arrangements where order matters), combinations (selections where order does not matter), and other counting principles. Key notation includes "n choose k" (written as C(n,k) or nCk), which represents the number of ways to choose k items from n total items, calculated using the formula n!/(k!(n-k)!). These calculations frequently appear in probability, statistics, and discrete mathematics applications.

Example: Instead of just asking a combinatorial math problem (*https://oreil.ly/vI3V5*) like "What is 12 choose 4?" and getting an answer, you might say:

> Solve 12 choose 4 step-by-step.

The model might then outline:

```
12 choose 4 = 12!/(4!*8!) = ... = 495
```

In coding, CoT can be useful for tricky algorithmic tasks. You might try the following prompt:

> Explain step-by-step how to merge two sorted lists, then provide the Python code.

The model would first outline something like:

> We will use two pointers starting at the heads of each list, compare the elements, append the smaller to a result list, and move that pointer, and so on...

Then it might give the code. This ensures it has structured the solution correctly before coding.

Another use is debugging or understanding output:

> Walk through the logic to determine if the number 19 is prime, then give the result.

The model might list divisions by primes, then conclude:

> 19 is prime.

Pros: Improves correctness on tasks requiring reasoning. There's research evidence (*https://oreil.ly/t7flF*) that prompting the model to "think out loud" can lead to better results on math and logic tasks. It also gives you insight into the model's process, which can be instructive or help you trust the answer more.

Cons: The output is longer (which might not be what you want in final code). Also, some interfaces (like typical code completions) aren't set up to show reasoning separate from code. This technique is more common in Q&A or chat scenarios. However, you can instruct the model to include the reasoning as comments in the code, which is a neat way to get thoroughly commented code.

Role Prompting

Role prompting means you ask the AI to assume a certain identity or role that might influence how it responds.

When to use: This is useful when you want to influence the style or detail of the answer or get a certain perspective. For instance, an AI taking on an "expert" role might give a more advanced solution or more explanation, while a "beginner" role might make it explain more basic concepts.

Examples:

- You are a Python instructor. Explain the following code and then modify it to be more Pythonic.
- Act as a security analyst. Here's some code. Identify any security vulnerabilities.
- Pretend you are a linter that checks code for style issues.

This can significantly affect the response. Assigning the AI a security analyst role might make it focus on things it otherwise wouldn't mention (like data validation, secure coding practices, or potential vulnerabilities). An instructor role might make it provide clearer explanations and perhaps not assume prior knowledge.

In coding, you might say before asking for code:

> You are an expert C++ programmer well-versed in optimization, instructing a junior developer.

The result will likely use more advanced C++ features and explain why certain choices were made, balancing technical sophistication with educational clarity.

Pros: This technique steers the tone and depth of the answer. This can tailor the solution to a certain level of complexity or thoroughness. It's useful if you want either a very simple solution (tell it to act as a novice and maybe it'll avoid complex tricks) or a very optimized one (tell it to act as a performance guru).

Cons: Sometimes the model might focus more on the persona than needed (an "instructor" might start explaining things you already know). Also, some AI safety systems are more sensitive to certain role descriptions—particularly those that might suggest deception, authority impersonation, or potentially harmful activities—though straightforward technical and professional roles like "data analyst" or "software engineer" typically work without issues.

Contextual Prompting

Contextual prompting means giving the AI additional context or information beyond the immediate task description. AI models don't have persistent memory of your entire project unless you provide it in the prompt (or through some integrated context window in advanced IDE integrations). So if you want the AI to write code that fits into your existing codebase, give it that context. Basically, you supply relevant data or background as part of the prompt.

When to use: Use when solving a problem requires knowing certain data or definitions that the model might not know or might not recall correctly from training. Or use when you want to ensure consistency with some external info (like an API spec or previous part of conversation).

Examples:

If you have a data structure and you want code that works with it, you might paste its definition:

```
Given the class below, implement the function X.

class Node:

    def __init__(self, value, next=None):

        self.value = value

        self.next = next

# Now write a function to count the nodes in a linked list starting at head.
```

By including the class definition, you make the AI much more likely to use `Node.value` and `Node.next` properly in its code.

If you want to use a specific API, include a snippet of the documentation in the prompt:

```
Using the requests library, fetch the data from the API. (The API returns JSON with format: {...})
```

If you include even a short example of API usage from docs, the AI can mimic it.

For disambiguation:

```
Using the term student to refer to high school students, write a function that...
```

If *student* could be ambiguous in context, you've clarified it.

Pros: You're grounding the AI in the context you care about. It's less likely to make wrong assumptions if you supply the facts. This is extremely helpful if the AI otherwise might not remember or know your specific use-case details.

Cons: This technique makes prompts longer. Also, the model might occasionally regurgitate the provided context into the answer (like copying lines from a documentation snippet into the code if not careful). But usually it uses it appropriately.

Tip: If you have a large context (like a big schema or many lines of code), sometimes it's better to summarize the key elements for the model rather than including everything verbatim. This approach helps you stay within context limits while ensuring the model receives the most relevant information. However, if the content is small enough, just include it raw.

Constraints are also useful to mention: performance constraints ("Optimize for O(n log n) or better"), compatibility constraints ("Must run on Python 3.8"), or library choices ("Use standard library only, no external dependencies"). These act like guardrails and ensure the AI doesn't suggest something outside acceptable bounds.

Metaprompting

Metaprompting is giving instructions about the output itself, not just what the solution should do. It's like telling the AI how to format or approach the solution.

When to use: Useful when you need the answer in a specific format or style or when you want to control how the AI works through the problem.

Examples:

> First, explain the approach in two sentences, then provide the code.

This ensures the AI doesn't launch straight into code:

> Do not use any libraries in the solution.

This places a constraint on the solution:

> Format the output as JSON.

This is useful if you're using the AI to produce data, not code:

> Only provide the function body, without the definition line.

This is handy if you want to insert the function into existing code:

> If the input is invalid, instead of error, return None.

This is not exactly the output format, but it's instructing the AI how to behave for certain cases.

Pros: You get exactly what you need, how you need it, without extra editing. This is crucial for some scenarios. If you plan to automatically use the AI's output in a pipeline, then you really want consistent formatting.

Cons: If the instructions conflict with the model's default style, sometimes it might partially follow them or you have to emphasize them. For instance, even if you say "only code, no explanation," occasionally the model might include a tiny comment or so. Usually, phrasing it as a direct imperative helps:

> Do not include any explanation; output only code inside a single code block.

Models like GPT follow that quite well.

Self-Consistency (Multiple Outputs and Majority Voting)

Self-consistency is more of a strategy than a prompt style. The idea is to get multiple outputs for the same prompt and then decide on the best or most common one. As Sander Schulhoff of Learn Prompting notes (*https://oreil.ly/fHABW*), self-consistency leverages the notion that if you ask the model multiple times (with slight randomness) and many of its answers agree, that consensus is likely correct.

When to use: This is useful for complex problems where you're unsure the model's first answer is correct, especially if you can't verify it easily yourself, or if you want a confidence check from the AI by seeing whether it gives the same answer repeatedly.

How to use manually: On some platforms (like ChatGPT), you can click "Regenerate answer." Or you can copy the prompt into a new session and see if it gives the same result. If you get three answers and two are the same and one is different, you might trust the two (assuming the problem has a single correct answer).

In programming context, if it's generating code for something deterministic, usually it will give very similar code each time (with small variations in variable names or style). But if it's an algorithmic question (like "What's the output of this code?"), you could check multiple runs.

This technique is more powerful in noncoding tasks (like logic puzzles) but worth noting.

Another angle—ensemble prompting: You can actually ask the model within one prompt to consider multiple possibilities:

> Give two different solutions to this problem.

Then perhaps you can see which one you like or test both. This is like self-consistency in one shot because you get multiple answers.

Pros: This technique can increase confidence in the solution if multiple attempts converge. Also, you might get variety (which is good if you want to choose the most elegant solution among many).

Cons: It's time-consuming to do multiple calls and compare outputs.

In practice, if I'm unsure about an answer, I'll often repose the question differently to see if I get the same answer. If I do, I'm more confident it's correct.

ReAct (Reason + Act) Prompting

ReAct is a more advanced prompting technique that combines *reasoning* and *acting* (*https://arxiv.org/abs/2210.03629*). It gets the model not only to think, like CoT does, but also to take actions like making a calculation, calling an API, or using a tool. (See the ReAct Prompt Engineering Guide (*https://oreil.ly/P_KIV*) for more). In current practice, this is often used with frameworks like LangChain, where the AI can output a special format that a program interprets as an action (like a command to execute or a query to run), then feed the result back.

For our scope (without such an execution environment in the loop), you can still do a form of ReAct by instructing the AI to first outline a plan, then output the result. It's similar to CoT but specifically oriented to using tools or performing subtasks.

Example:

> Using Python, determine the current weather in Paris and print it.

Unless the AI has browsing capabilities, it cannot truly get the current weather. A ReAct approach would have the AI first reason through the problem by stating:

> I need to access current weather data for Paris, which requires calling a weather API.

The AI would then attempt to use an available tool to make this API call. If successful, it would receive actual weather data; if no such tool is available, it might acknowledge the limitation or work with hypothetical data. Finally, the AI would write the Python code to display the weather information, incorporating whatever data it was able to obtain through this reasoning and action process.

Without external tool access, ReAct might not be particularly relevant for simple prompting tasks. However, when evaluating AI tools for your organization, determining whether they can access current information from the internet represents a critical capability assessment. Many AI models operate with knowledge cutoffs, meaning their training data only extends to a specific date, which can result in outdated information for rapidly changing topics.

If you are using an environment where the AI can execute code (such as Jupyter integrations or similar platforms), you could implement ReAct by instructing the system:

First write a test for this function, run it, then adjust the code accordingly.

This demonstrates the ReAct pattern through a reasoning step (writing the test), followed by an action (executing the test), and then code adjustment based on the results. However, orchestrating such workflows through pure prompts requires advanced prompting techniques and appropriate technical infrastructure.

Simpler use: You can simulate a Q&A where the AI has intermediate steps that mimic actions:

Think step-by-step and if you need to, do calculations.

It's effectively CoT but with a more imperative tone.

Pros: When available, it can solve problems that require external info or iterative trial (like the AI can correct itself by actually running code). In debugging contexts, an AI that can execute code to test it is fantastic.

Cons: This technique is not widely accessible without specific tooling. And if you just prompt that way in plain ChatGPT, it will either imagine the actions or just do CoT.

For our purposes in prompt writing, keep in mind that some systems (like OpenAI's tool-using agents or others) exist, but in vanilla prompting we mostly do CoT, and we ourselves handle actions like running the code or tests.

Advanced Prompting: Combining Techniques and Handling Complexity

Prompting techniques can be combined. For instance, you might do a few-shot prompt that also demonstrates CoT in the examples. Or you might combine a role with CoT:

As a senior engineer, think step-by-step through the problem, then give the code.

Now that we've explored various prompting techniques, let's see them in action with a scenario or two, then discuss how to review and refine the AI's output (which leads into the next chapter about understanding and owning the generated code).

Imagine you have a function that isn't working. You might use a combination of role and CoT prompting:

You are a Python debugger. Let's think step-by-step to find the bug in the following code.

This would be followed by the code. The AI might respond with an analysis of each line and pinpoint the bug.

Or let's say you want to generate code for a somewhat complex algorithm, ensure it's well commented, and also get test cases for it. A combined prompt might look like this:

> You are an expert Python developer. Let's solve this step-by-step. We need a function `merge_sorted_lists(list1, list2)` that merges two sorted lists into one sorted list. First, explain the approach, then provide the Python code with comments. After that, give 2–3 example tests in code to demonstrate it works.

This single prompt is quite comprehensive. The first sentence sets a role. The second requests step-by-step reasoning. The third gives the main task. The fourth sentence asks for code with explanatory comments, and the fifth even asks for tests.

The AI might then output an explanation, then the code with inline comments, then some test cases at the end. This is an advanced use, but it shows how you can direct the AI through a multifaceted response.

Know the Model's Limits

Prompt engineering also involves knowing what *not* to ask and how to avoid pitfalls. If a prompt is getting too large or includes too many instructions, the model might get confused or truncate some output. If you find it starts ignoring parts of your prompt, you might need to simplify or do it in parts. If an AI model sometimes produces incorrect facts or code (it "hallucinates"), you learn to double-check and not use it as a factual oracle. If you find it tends to give overly verbose code, you can pre-empt that with "Make the solution as concise as possible." If it sometimes uses functions that don't exist, you might instruct, "Use only the API functions listed below" and list them. The better you understand the AI's behavior, the more you can mold your prompts to get around any weaknesses.

If a task is very complex, you can also break it into subtasks for the AI. For example, you might first prompt:

> List the steps to implement a basic compiler for a simple arithmetic expression language.

Once the AI gives the steps, you tackle each step with separate prompts, maybe even in separate files or sessions:

> Now implement step 1: tokenization.

This is like doing system design with the AI: you can outline then refine each piece. It leverages the AI's ability to assist in planning (not just coding).

Stateful Conversation Versus One-Shot Prompting

In a chat setting, you have a conversation history, known as *state*. You can build up context by discussing with the AI. In an IDE completion setting, the context is mostly your file content and comments. Both allow cumulative context in different ways. Use conversation if you need the AI to remember what was said (like refining an answer). Use fresh prompts or file context if you want to ensure it's focusing only on what's relevant now. Sometimes wiping away the context prevents the model from sticking to a potentially wrong earlier assumption.

By practicing with these techniques on various examples, you'll become adept at knowing which approach to use and when:

- If output format is important, give examples (few shot) or explicit formatting instructions.
- If logic is tricky, use CoT or step-by-step.
- If the solution can vary in quality, set a role (like "seasoned engineer") to get a better style.
- If the model isn't complying, maybe break your prompts into pieces, simplify them, or use stronger wording for constraints.

Common Prompt Antipatterns and How to Avoid Them

Not all prompts are created equal. By now, we've seen numerous examples of effective prompts, but it's equally instructive to recognize antipatterns—common mistakes that lead to poor AI responses. This section covers some frequent prompt failures and how to fix them.

The vague prompt

This is the classic "It doesn't work, please fix it" or "Write something that does X" without enough detail. The question "Why isn't my function working?" will generally get a useless answer. Vague prompts force the AI to guess the context and often result in generic advice or irrelevant code.

The fix is straightforward: add context and specifics. If you find yourself asking a question and the answer feels like a Magic 8–Ball response ("Have you tried checking X?"), stop and reframe your query with more details (error messages, code excerpt, expected versus actual outcome, etc.). A good practice is to read your prompt and ask, "Could this question apply to dozens of different scenarios?" If the answer is yes, it's too vague. Make it so specific that it could only apply to your scenario.

The overloaded prompt

This is the opposite issue: asking the AI to do too many things at once. For instance:

> Generate a complete Node.js app with authentication, a frontend in React, and deployment scripts.

Or even, on a smaller scale:

> Fix these 5 bugs and also add these 3 features in one go.

The AI might attempt it, but you'll likely get a jumbled or incomplete result, or it might ignore some parts of the request. Even if it addresses everything, the response will be long and harder to verify.

The remedy is to split the tasks. Prioritize: do one thing at a time, as we emphasized earlier. This makes it easier to catch mistakes and ensures the model stays focused. If you catch yourself writing a paragraph that uses "and" multiple times in the instructions, consider breaking it into separate prompts or sequential steps.

Missing the question

Sometimes users will present a lot of information but never clearly ask a question or specify what they need, like dumping a large code snippet and just saying, "Here's my code." This can confuse the AI—it doesn't know what you want.

Always include a clear ask:

- Identify any bugs in the above code.
- Explain what this code does.
- Complete the to-dos in the code.

A prompt should have a purpose. If you just provide text without a question or instruction, the AI might make incorrect assumptions (like summarizing the code instead of fixing it, etc.). Make sure the AI knows why you showed it some code. Even a simple addition like "What's wrong with this code?" or "Please continue implementing this function" gives it direction.

Vague success criteria

This is a subtle one. Sometimes you might ask for an optimization or improvement, but you don't define what success looks like—for example, "Make this function faster." Faster by what metric? If the AI doesn't know your performance constraints, it might micro-optimize something that doesn't matter or use an approach that's theoretically faster but practically negligible. Or "Make this code cleaner": "cleaner" is subjective. We dealt with this by explicitly stating goals like "reduce duplication" or "improve variable names," etc.

The fix: quantify or qualify the improvement:

- Optimize this function to run in linear time (current version is quadratic).
- Refactor this to remove global variables and use a class instead.

Basically, be explicit about what problem you're solving with the refactor or feature. If you leave it too open, the AI might solve a different problem than the one you care about.

Ignoring AI's clarification or output

Sometimes the AI might respond with a clarifying question or an assumption:

- Are you using React class components or functional components?
- I assume the input is a string—please confirm.

If you ignore these and just reiterate your request, you're missing an opportunity to improve the prompt. The AI is signaling that it needs more info. Always answer its questions or refine your prompt to include those details.

Additionally, if the AI's output is clearly off (like it misunderstood the question), don't just retry the same prompt verbatim. Take a moment to adjust your wording. Maybe your prompt had an ambiguous phrase or omitted something essential. Treat it like a conversation: if a human misunderstood, you'd explain differently; do the same for the AI.

Inconsistency

If you keep changing how you ask or mixing different formats in one go, the model can get confused. Two examples include switching between first person and third person in instructions or mixing pseudocode with actual code in a confusing way.

Try to maintain a consistent style within a single prompt. If you provide examples, ensure they are clearly delineated (use Markdown triple backticks for code, quotes for input/output examples, etc.). Consistency helps the model parse your intent correctly. Also, if you have a preferred style (say, ES6 versus ES5 syntax), consistently mention it; otherwise, the model might suggest one way in one prompt and another way later.

Vague references like "the above code"

When using chat, if you say "the above function" or "the previous output," be sure the reference is clear. If the conversation is long and you say, "Refactor the above code," the AI might lose track or pick the wrong code snippet to refactor.

It's safer to either quote the code again or specifically name the function you want refactored. Models have a limited attention window, and although many LLMs can refer to prior parts of the conversation, giving it explicit context again can help avoid confusion. This is especially true if some time (or several messages) passed since the code was shown.

Summary and Next Steps

The art of prompting is iterative and creative. As models evolve, prompt best practices might change (for instance, future models might better understand intent with less wording). But the underlying principle remains: communicate effectively, and the AI will serve you better.

In essence, mastering prompt engineering is like mastering a new programming language—the language of instructions for AI. It's a blend of technical writing, foresight, and interactive debugging of the *prompt* itself. But once you get good at it, the AI truly starts to feel like an extension of your own mind, because you can reliably extract the solutions you envision (or even those you don't fully envision yet but can guide the AI to discover) with minimal friction. This skill will likely become as fundamental as knowing how to google things or how to use a debugger—it's part of the modern developer's skill set in the age of vibe coding.

If AI can solve about 70% of a problem, how do you approach it as a partner in coding? Chapter 3 looks at how developers *really* use AI and sets out some "golden rules" for vibe coding.

PART II

AI Coding in Practice

The 70% Problem: AI-Assisted Workflows That Actually Work

AI-based coding tools are astonishingly good at certain tasks.[1] They excel at producing boilerplate, writing routine functions, and getting projects *most of the way* to completion. In fact, many developers find that an AI assistant can implement an initial solution that covers roughly 70% of the requirements.

Peter Yang perfectly captured what I've been observing in the field in a post on X (*https://oreil.ly/i9qwq*):

> Honest reflections from coding with AI so far as a non-engineer:
>
> It can get you 70% of the way there, but that last 30% is frustrating. It keeps taking one step forward and two steps backward with new bugs, issues, etc.
>
> If I knew how the code worked I could probably fix it myself. But since I don't, I question if I'm actually learning that much.

Nonengineers using AI for coding find themselves hitting a frustrating wall. They can get 70% of the way there surprisingly quickly, but that final 30% becomes an exercise in diminishing returns.

This "70% problem" reveals something crucial about the current state of AI-assisted development. The initial progress feels magical: you can describe what you want, and AI tools like v0 or Bolt will generate a working prototype that looks impressive. But then reality sets in.

---

1 This chapter is based on an essay originally published on my Substack newsletter. See Addy Osmani, "The 70% Problem: Hard Truths About AI-Assisted Coding" (*https://oreil.ly/aRKIJ*), *Elevate with Addy Osmani*, December 4, 2024.

The 70% is often the straightforward, patterned part of the work—the kind of code that follows well-trod paths or common frameworks. As one *Hacker News* commenter observed (*https://oreil.ly/Ff3Ts*), AI is superb at handling the "accidental complexity" of software (the repetitive, mechanical stuff), while the "essential complexity"—understanding and managing the inherent complexity of a problem—remains on human shoulders. In Fred Brooks's classic terms, AI tackles the incidental but not the intrinsic difficulties of development.

Where do these tools struggle? Experienced engineers consistently report a "last mile" gap. AI can generate a plausible solution, but the final 30%—covering edge cases, refining the architecture, and ensuring maintainability—"needs serious human expertise."

For example, an AI might give you a function that technically works for the basic scenario, but it won't automatically account for unusual inputs, race conditions, performance constraints, or future requirements unless explicitly told. AI can get you most of the way there, but that final crucial 30% (edge cases, keeping things maintainable, and solid architecture) needs serious human expertise.

Moreover, AI has a known tendency to generate convincing but incorrect output. It may introduce subtle bugs or "hallucinate" nonexistent functions and libraries. Steve Yegge wryly likens (*https://oreil.ly/hjv8f*) today's LLMs to "wildly productive junior developers"—incredibly fast and enthusiastic but "potentially whacked out on mind-altering drugs," prone to concocting crazy or unworkable approaches.

In Yegge's words (*https://oreil.ly/yPMPO*), an LLM can spew out code that looks polished at first glance, yet if a less-experienced developer naively says, "Looks good to me!" and runs with it, hilarity (or disaster) ensues in the following weeks. The AI doesn't truly *understand* the problem; it stitches together patterns that *usually* make sense. Only a human can discern whether a seemingly fine solution hides long-term landmines. Simon Willison echoed this (*https://oreil.ly/sLzFY*) after seeing an AI propose a bewitchingly clever design that *only a senior engineer with deep understanding of the problem* could recognize as flawed. The lesson: AI's confidence far exceeds its reliability.

Crucially, current AIs do not create fundamentally new abstractions or strategies beyond their training data (*https://oreil.ly/HkwVF*). They won't invent a novel algorithm or an innovative architecture for you—they remix what's known. They also won't take responsibility for decisions. As one engineer noted, "AIs don't have 'better ideas' than what their training data contains. They don't take responsibility for their work."

All of this means that creative and analytical thinking—deciding *what* to build, *how* to structure it, and *why*—firmly remains a human domain. In summary, AI is a force multiplier for developers, handling the repetitive 70% and giving us a "turbo boost" in productivity. But it is *not* a silver bullet that can replace human judgment. The remaining 30% of software engineering—the hard parts—still requires skills that only trained, thoughtful developers can bring. Those are the durable skills to focus on, and Chapter 4 is dedicated to them. As one discussion (*https://oreil.ly/QXYsj*) put it: "AI is a powerful tool, but it's not a magic bullet.…Human judgment and good software engineering practices are still essential."

How Developers Are Actually Using AI

I've observed two distinct patterns in how teams are leveraging AI for development. Let's call them the "bootstrappers" and the "iterators." Both are helping engineers (and even nontechnical users) reduce the gap from idea to execution (or MVP).

First, there are the *bootstrappers*, who are generally taking a new project from zero to MVP. Tools like Bolt, v0, and screenshot-to-code AI are revolutionizing how these teams bootstrap new projects. These teams typically:

- Start with a design or rough concept
- Use AI to generate a complete initial codebase
- Get a working prototype in hours or days instead of weeks
- Focus on rapid validation and iteration

The results can be impressive. I recently watched a solo developer use Bolt to turn a Figma design into a working web app in next to no time. It wasn't production-ready, but it was good enough to get very initial user feedback.

The second camp, the *iterators*, uses tools like Cursor, Cline, Copilot, and Windsurf for their daily development workflow. This is less flashy but potentially more transformative. These developers are:

- Using AI for code completion and suggestions
- Leveraging AI for complex refactoring tasks
- Generating tests and documentation
- Using AI as a "pair programmer" for problem solving

But here's the catch: while both approaches can dramatically accelerate development, they come with hidden costs that aren't immediately obvious.

When you watch a senior engineer work with AI tools like Cursor or Copilot, it looks like magic. They can scaffold entire features in minutes, complete with tests and documentation. But watch carefully, and you'll notice something crucial: they're not just accepting what the AI suggests. They're constantly refactoring the generated code into smaller, focused modules. They're adding comprehensive error handling and edge-case handling the AI missed, strengthening its type definitions and interfaces, and questioning its architectural decisions. In other words, they're applying years of hard-won engineering wisdom to shape and constrain the AI's output. The AI is accelerating their implementation, but their expertise is what keeps the code maintainable.

Common Failure Patterns

Junior engineers often miss these crucial steps. They accept the AI's output more readily, leading to what I call "house of cards code"—it looks complete but collapses under real-world pressure.

Two steps back

What typically happens next follows a predictable antipattern I call the "two steps back" pattern (shown in Figure 3-1):

- You try to fix a small bug.
- The AI suggests a change that seems reasonable.
- This fix breaks something else.
- You ask AI to fix the new issue.
- This creates two more problems.
- Rinse and repeat.

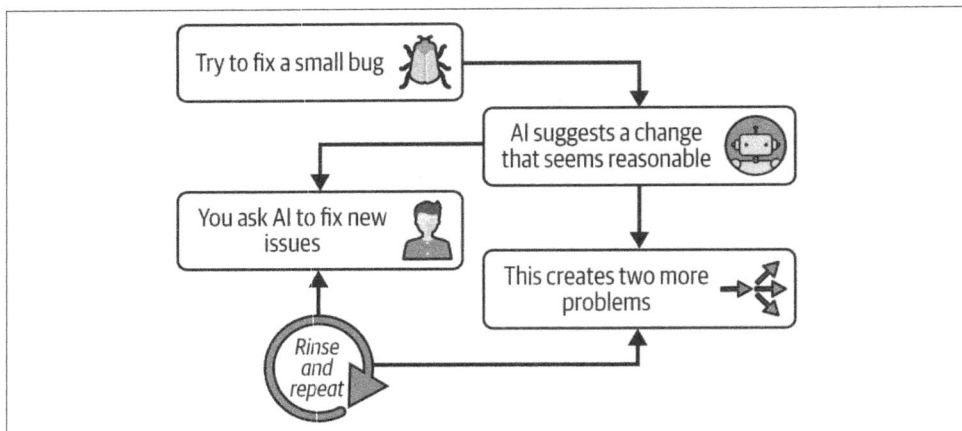

Figure 3-1. The "two steps back" antipattern.

This cycle is particularly painful for nonengineers because they lack the mental models to understand what's actually going wrong. When an experienced developer encounters a bug, they can reason about potential causes and solutions based on years of pattern recognition. Without this background, you're essentially playing whack-a-mole with code you don't fully understand. This is the "knowledge paradox" I mentioned back in this book's preface: senior engineers and developers use AI to accelerate what they already know how to do, while juniors try to use it to learn *what to do*.

This cycle is particularly painful for nonengineers using AI in a "bootstrapper" pattern, because they lack the mental models needed to address these issues building their MVP. However, even experienced "iterators" can fall into this whack-a-mole trap if they overly rely on AI suggestions without deep validation.

There's a deeper issue here: the very thing that makes AI coding tools accessible to nonengineers—their ability to handle complexity on your behalf—can actually impede learning. When code just "appears" without you understanding the underlying principles, you don't develop debugging skills. You miss learning fundamental patterns. You can't reason about architectural decisions, and so you struggle to maintain and evolve the code. This creates a dependency where you need to keep going back to the AI model to fix issues rather than developing the expertise to handle them yourself.

This dependency risk enters a new dimension with the emergence of autonomous AI coding agents—a topic I explore in depth in Chapter 10. Unlike current tools that suggest code snippets, these agents represent a fundamental shift in how software can be developed. As I write this, we're witnessing the early deployment of systems that can independently plan, execute, and iterate on entire development tasks with minimal human oversight.

This evolution from assistive to autonomous AI introduces profound questions about developer expertise and control. When an AI system can handle complete development workflows, from initial implementation through testing and deployment, the risk of skill atrophy becomes acute. Developers who rely heavily on these agents without maintaining their foundational knowledge may find themselves unable to effectively audit, guide, or intervene when the AI's decisions diverge from intended outcomes.

The challenge compounds when we consider how these autonomous systems make cascading decisions throughout a project. Each individual choice might appear reasonable in isolation, yet the cumulative effect could steer development in unintended directions. Without the expertise to recognize and correct these trajectory shifts early, teams risk building increasingly complex systems on foundations they don't fully understand.

As we'll examine more thoroughly later, the advent of autonomous coding agents doesn't diminish the importance of software engineering fundamentals—it amplifies it. The more powerful our AI tools become, the more critical it is that we maintain the expertise to remain architects of our systems rather than mere operators. Only through deep understanding of software principles can we ensure these remarkable tools enhance our capabilities rather than erode them.

The demo-quality trap

It's becoming a pattern: teams use AI to rapidly build impressive demos. The happy path works beautifully. Investors and social networks are wowed. But when real users start clicking around? That's when things fall apart.

I've seen this firsthand: error messages that make no sense to normal users, edge cases that crash the application, confusing UI states that never got cleaned up, accessibility completely overlooked, and performance issues on slower devices. These aren't just low-priority bugs—they're the difference between software people tolerate and software people love.

Creating truly self-serve software—the kind where users never need to contact support—requires a different mindset, one that's all about the lost art of polish. You need to be obsessing over error messages; testing on slow connections and with real, non-technical users; making features discoverable; and handling every edge case gracefully. This kind of attention to detail (perhaps) can't be AI-generated. It comes from empathy, experience, and caring deeply about craft.

What Actually Works: Practical Workflow Patterns

Before we dive into coding in Part II of this book, we need to talk about modern development practices and how AI-assisted coding fits within a team workflow. Software development is more than writing code, after all—it's a whole workflow that includes planning, collaboration, testing, deployment, and maintenance. And vibe coding isn't a standalone novelty—it can be woven into agile methodologies and DevOps practices, augmenting the team's productivity while preserving quality and reliability.

In this section, we'll explore how team members can collectively use vibe-coding tools without stepping on each other's toes, how to balance AI suggestions with human insight, and how continuous integration/continuous delivery (CI/CD) pipelines can incorporate AI or adapt to AI-generated code. I'll also touch on important considerations like version-control strategies.

After observing dozens of teams, here are three patterns I've seen work consistently in both solo and team workflows:

AI as first drafter
> The AI model generates the initial code and developers then refine, refactor, and test it

AI as pair programmer
> Developer and AI are in constant conversation, with tight feedback loops, frequent code review, and minimal context provided

AI as validator

> Developers still write the initial code and then use AI to validate, test, and improve it (see Figure 3-2)

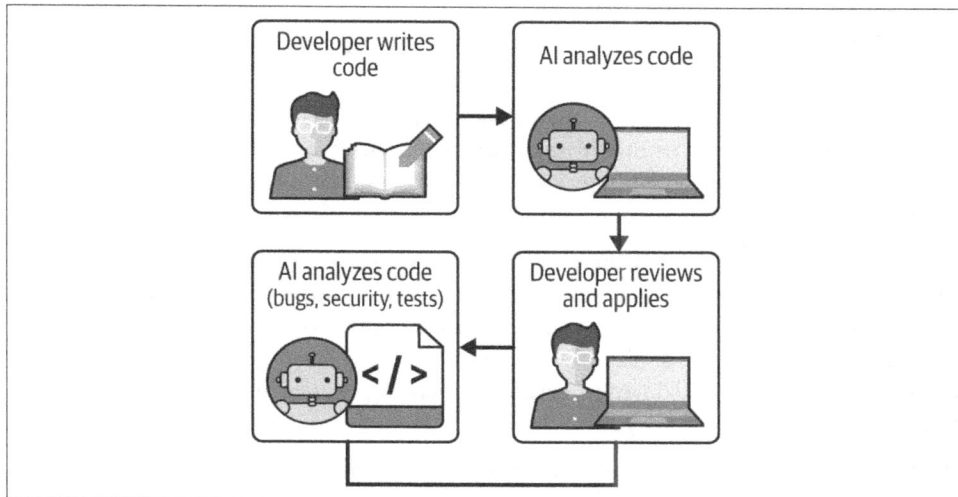

Figure 3-2. AI validation workflow: developers write initial code; AI systems analyze for bugs and security issues, then suggest improvements; and developers review and apply recommended changes.

In this section, I'll walk you through each pattern in turn, discussing workflows and tips for success.

AI as first drafter

It's important to ensure everyone on the team is on the same page before you ask your AI model to draft any code. Communication is key so that developers don't ask their AI assistants to do redundant tasks or generate conflicting implementations.

In daily stand-ups (a staple of agile workflows), it's worth discussing not just what you're working on but also whether you plan to use AI for certain tasks. For example, two developers might be working on different features that both involve a utility function for date formatting. If both ask the AI to create a `formatDate` helper, you might end up with two similar functions. Coordinating up front ("I'll generate a date utility we can both use") can prevent duplication.

Teams that successfully integrate AI tools often start by agreeing on coding standards and prompting practices. For example, the team might decide on a consistent style (linting rules, project conventions) and even feed those guidelines into their AI tools (some assistants allow providing style preferences or example code to steer outputs). As noted in Codacy's blog (*https://oreil.ly/FeEN_*), by familiarizing the AI with the team's coding standards, you get generated code that is more uniform and easier for everyone to work with. On a practical level, this could mean having a section in your project README for "AI Usage Tips," where you note things like "We use functional components only" or "Prefer using Fetch API over Axios," which developers can keep in mind when prompting AI.

Another practice is to use your tools' *collaboration features*, if available. Some AI-assisted IDEs allow users to share their AI sessions or at least the prompts they use. If Developer A got a great result with a prompt for a complex component, sharing that prompt with Developer B (perhaps via the issue tracker or a team chat) can save time and ensure consistency.

As for using version control, the fundamentals remain—with a twist. Using Git (or another version control system) is nonnegotiable in modern development, and that doesn't change with vibe coding. In fact, version control becomes even more crucial when AI is generating code rapidly. Commits act as the safety net to catch AI missteps; if an AI-generated change breaks something, you can revert to a previous commit.

One strategy is to commit more frequently when using AI assistance. Each time the AI produces a significant chunk of code (like generating a feature or doing some major refactoring) that you accept, consider making a commit with a clear message. Frequent commits ensure that if you need to bisect issues or undo a portion of AI-introduced code, the history is granular enough.

Also, try to isolate different AI-introduced changes. If you let the AI make many changes across different areas and commit them all together, it's harder to disentangle if something goes wrong. For example, if you use an agent to optimize performance and it also tweaks some UI texts, commit those separately. (Your two commit messages might be "Optimize list rendering performance [AI-assisted]" and "Update UI copy for workout completion message [AI-assisted]"). Descriptive commit messages are important; some teams even tag commits that had heavy AI involvement, just for traceability. It's not about blame but about understanding the origin of code—a commit tagged with "[AI]" might signal to a reviewer that the code could use an extra thorough review for edge cases.

Essentially, the team should treat AI usage as a normal part of the development conversation: share experiences, successful techniques, and warnings about what not to do (like "Copilot suggests using an outdated library for X, so be careful with that").

Review and refinement are crucial to this pattern. Developers should manually review and refactor the code for modularity, add comprehensive error handling, write thorough tests, and document key decisions as they refine the code. The next chapter goes into detail about these processes.

AI as pair programmer

Traditional pair programming involves two humans collaborating at one workstation. With the advent of AI, a hybrid approach has emerged: one human developer working alongside an AI assistant. This setup can be particularly effective, offering a blend of human intuition and machine efficiency.

In a human-AI pairing, the developer interacts with the AI to generate code suggestions while also reviewing and refining the output. This dynamic allows the human to leverage the AI's speed in handling repetitive tasks, such as writing boilerplate code or generating test cases, while maintaining oversight to ensure code quality and relevance.

For instance, when integrating a new library, a developer might prompt the AI to draft the initial integration code. The developer then reviews the AI's suggestions, cross-referencing with official documentation to verify accuracy. This process not only accelerates development but also facilitates knowledge acquisition, as the developer engages deeply with both the AI's output and the library's intricacies.

Let's compare this to traditional human-human pair programming:

- *Human-AI pairing* offers rapid code generation and can handle mundane tasks efficiently. It's particularly beneficial for solo developers or when team resources are limited.
- *Human-human pairing* excels in complex problem-solving scenarios, where nuanced understanding and collaborative brainstorming are essential. It fosters shared ownership and collective code comprehension.

Both approaches have their merits, and your choice between them can be guided by the project's complexity, resource availability, and the specific goals of the development process.

Best practices for AI pair programming

To maximize the benefits of AI-assisted development, consider the following practices:

Initiate new AI sessions for distinct tasks
This helps maintain context clarity and ensures the AI's suggestions are relevant to the specific task at hand.

Keep prompts focused and concise
Providing clear and specific instructions enhances the quality of the AI's output.

Review and commit changes frequently
Regularly integrating and testing AI-generated code helps catch issues early and maintains project momentum.

Maintain tight feedback loops
Continuously assess the AI's contributions, providing corrections or refinements as needed to guide its learning and improve future suggestions.

AI as validator

Beyond code generation, AI can serve as a valuable validator, assisting in code review and quality assurance. AI tools can analyze code for potential bugs, security vulnerabilities, and adherence to best practices. For example, platforms like DeepCode and Snyk's AI-powered code checker can identify issues such as missing input sanitization or insecure configurations, providing actionable insights directly within the development environment. Platforms such as Qodo and TestGPT can automatically generate test cases, ensuring broader coverage and reducing manual effort. And many AI tools can assist in monitoring application performance, detecting anomalies that might indicate underlying issues.

By integrating AI validators into the development workflow, teams can enhance code quality, reduce the likelihood of defects, and ensure compliance with security standards. This proactive approach to validation complements human oversight, leading to more robust and reliable software. These tools enhance the efficiency and effectiveness of the quality assurance (QA) process by handling repetitive and time-consuming tasks, allowing human testers to focus on more complex and nuanced aspects of QA.

Incorporating AI into the development process, whether as a pair programmer or validator, offers opportunities to enhance productivity and code quality. By thoughtfully integrating these tools, developers can harness the strengths of both human and artificial intelligence.

To maximize the benefits of both AI and human capabilities in QA, I recommend a few best practices:

- Use AI for initial assessments and preliminary scans to identify obvious issues.
- Prioritize human review for critical areas, such as complex functionalities, user experience, and AI limitations.
- Foster an environment of continuous collaboration, where AI tools and human testers work in tandem, with ongoing feedback loops to improve both AI performance and human decision making.

The Golden Rules of Vibe Coding

While vibe coding offers unprecedented speed and creative freedom in software development, its very flexibility demands a structured approach to ensure consistent quality and team cohesion. The rapid, intuitive nature of AI-assisted development can quickly lead to chaos without clear guidelines that balance creative exploration with engineering discipline.

These golden rules emerged from collective experience across teams who have successfully integrated vibe coding into their workflows. They represent hard-won insights about where AI excels, where it stumbles, and how human judgment remains essential throughout the process. Rather than constraining creativity, these principles create a framework within which teams can confidently experiment while maintaining the standards necessary for production-ready software.

The rules address three critical dimensions of vibe coding: the interaction between human and AI, the integration of AI-generated code into existing systems, and the cultivation of team practices that support sustainable AI-assisted development. By following these guidelines, teams can harness the transformative power of vibe coding while avoiding common pitfalls that lead to technical debt, security vulnerabilities, or unmaintainable codebases:

Be specific and clear about what you want
> Clearly articulate your requirements, tasks, and outcomes when interacting with AI. Precise prompts yield precise results.

Always validate AI output against your intent
> AI-generated code must always be checked against your original goal. Verify functionality, logic, and relevance before accepting.

Treat AI as a junior developer (with supervision)
> Consider AI outputs as drafts that require your careful oversight. Provide feedback, refine, and ensure quality and correctness.

Use AI to expand your capabilities, not replace your thinking
> Leverage AI to automate routine or complex tasks, but always remain actively engaged in problem solving and decision making.

Coordinate up front among the team before generating code
> Align with your team on AI usage standards, code expectations, and practices before starting AI-driven development.

Treat AI usage as a normal part of the development conversation
> Regularly discuss AI experiences, techniques, successes, and pitfalls with your team. Normalize AI as another tool for collective improvement.

Isolate AI changes in Git by doing separate commits
> Clearly identify and separate AI-generated changes within version control to simplify reviews, rollbacks, and tracking.

Ensure that all code, whether human or AI-written, undergoes code review
> Maintain consistent standards by subjecting all contributions to the same rigorous review processes, enhancing code quality and team understanding.

Don't merge code you don't understand
> Never integrate AI-generated code unless you thoroughly comprehend its functionality and implications. Understanding is critical to maintainability and security.

Prioritize documentation, comments, and ADRs
> Clearly document the rationale, functionality, and context for AI-generated code. Good documentation ensures long-term clarity and reduces future technical debt.

Share and reuse effective prompts
> Document prompts that lead to high-quality AI outputs. Maintain a repository of proven prompts to streamline future interactions and enhance consistency.

Regularly reflect and iterate
> Periodically review and refine your AI development workflow. Use insights from past experiences to continuously enhance your team's approach.

By adhering to these golden rules, your team can harness AI effectively, enhancing productivity while maintaining clarity, quality, and control.

Summary and Next Steps

The 70% problem defines the current state of AI-assisted development: these tools excel at generating boilerplate and routine functions but struggle with the final 30% that includes edge cases, architectural decisions, and production readiness. We've identified two main usage patterns—bootstrappers who rapidly build MVPs, and iterators who integrate AI into daily workflows—along with common failure patterns like the "two steps back" antipattern and the "demo-quality trap" where impressive prototypes fail under real-world pressure.

Three proven workflow patterns have emerged: AI as first drafter (generate then refine), AI as pair programmer (continuous collaboration), and AI as validator (human-written code with AI analysis). The golden rules of vibe coding provide essential guardrails, emphasizing clear communication, thorough validation, team coordination, and the nonnegotiable requirement to understand all code before merging it.

Individual developers should choose one workflow pattern to experiment with systematically while implementing the golden rules in daily practice. Focus on developing the durable skills covered in Chapter 4: system design, debugging, and architecture—rather than competing with AI on code generation.

Teams need to establish standards for AI usage, create shared repositories of effective prompts, and integrate AI considerations into existing agile practices. Regular knowledge sharing about successes and pitfalls will help teams avoid common traps while maximizing AI's benefits.

As autonomous AI coding agents emerge, the human role will shift toward architectural oversight and strategic decision making. The next chapter explores how to maximize this irreplaceable human contribution, helping engineers at every level thrive as partners to increasingly capable AI systems rather than competitors.

CHAPTER 4

Beyond the 70%: Maximizing Human Contribution

You've seen how AI coding assistants like Cursor, Cline, Copilot, and Windsurf have transformed how software is built, shouldering much of the grunt work and boiler-plate—about 70%.[1] But what about that last "30%" of the job that separates a toy solution from a production-ready system? This gap includes the hard parts: understanding complex requirements, architecting maintainable systems, handling edge cases, and ensuring code correctness. In other words, while AI can generate *code*, it often struggles with *engineering*.

Tim O'Reilly, reflecting on decades of technology shifts (*https://oreil.ly/BYrNh*), reminds us that each leap in automation has changed *how* we program but not *why* we need skilled programmers. We're not facing the end of programming but rather "the end of programming as we know it today," meaning developers' roles are evolving, not evaporating.

The challenge for today's engineers is to embrace AI for what it does best (the first 70%) while doubling down on the durable skills and insights needed for the remaining 30%. This article dives into expert insights to identify which human skills remain crucial. We'll explore what senior and midlevel developers should continue to leverage and what junior developers must invest in to thrive alongside AI.

This chapter's goal, then, is to offer you pragmatic guidance for maximizing the value of that irreplaceable 30%, with actionable takeaways for engineers at every level.

---

[1] This chapter is based on two essays I first published on my Substack newsletter: Addy Osmani, "Beyond the 70%: Maximizing the Human 30% of AI-Assisted Coding" (*https://oreil.ly/PMFsp*), *Elevate with Addy Osmani*, March 13, 2025; and Addy Osmani, "Future-Proofing Your Software Engineering Career" (*https://oreil.ly/1EoW8*), *Elevate with Addy Osmani*, December 23, 2024.

Senior Engineers and Developers: Leverage Your Experience with AI

If you're a senior engineer, you should see the advent of AI coding tools as an opportunity to amplify your impact—if you leverage your experience in the right ways. Senior developers typically possess deep domain knowledge, intuition for what could go wrong, and the ability to make high-level technical decisions.

These strengths are part of the 30% that AI can't handle alone. This section looks at how seasoned developers can maximize their value.

Be the Architect and the Editor in Chief

Let AI handle the first draft of code while you focus on architecting the solution and then refining the AI's output. In many organizations, Steve Yegge (*https://oreil.ly/QtJ7_*) writes that we may see a shift where teams need "only senior associates" who "(a) describe the tasks to be done; i.e., create the prompts, and (b) review the resulting work for accuracy and correctness." Embrace that model. As a senior dev, you can translate complex requirements into effective prompts or specifications for an AI assistant, then use your critical eye to vet every line produced. You are effectively pair programming with the AI—it's the fast typer, but you're the brain.

Maintain high standards during review: ensure the code meets your organization's quality, security, and performance benchmarks. By acting as architect and editor, you prevent the "high review burden" from overwhelming you. (A cautionary note: if junior staff simply throw raw AI output over the wall to you, push back—instill a process where they must verify AI-generated work first, so you're not the sole safety net.)

Use AI as a Force Multiplier for Big Initiatives

Senior engineers often drive large projects or tackle hairy refactors that juniors can't approach alone. AI can supercharge these efforts by handling a lot of mechanical changes or exploring alternatives under your guidance. Yegge introduced the term *chat-oriented programming* (CHOP) (*https://oreil.ly/QtJ7_*) for this style of working—"coding via iterative prompt refinement," with the AI as a collaborator. Leverage CHOP to be more ambitious in what you take on.

Having AI assistance lowers the bar for when a project is worth investing time in at all since what might have taken days can now be done in hours. Senior devs can thus attempt those "Wouldn't it be nice if…?" projects that always seemed slightly out of reach.

The key is to remain the guiding mind: you decide which tools or approaches to pursue, and you integrate the pieces into a cohesive whole. Your experience allows you to sift the AI's suggestions—accepting those that fit, rejecting those that don't.

Mentor and Set Standards

Another crucial role for senior engineers is to coach less-experienced team members on effective use of AI and on the timeless best practices. You likely have hard-won knowledge of pitfalls that juniors may not see, like memory leaks, off-by-one errors, and concurrency hazards.

With juniors now potentially generating code via AI, it's important to teach them how to self-review and test that code. Set an example by demonstrating how to thoroughly test AI contributions, and encourage a culture of questioning and verifying machine output. Some organizations (including even law firms) have instituted rules that if someone uses an AI to generate code or writing, they must *disclose it and verify the results themselves*—not just assume a senior colleague will catch mistakes.

As a senior engineer, champion such norms on your team: AI is welcome, but diligence is required. By mentoring juniors in this way, you offload some of the oversight burden and help them grow into that 30% skill set more quickly.

Continue to Cultivate Domain Mastery and Foresight

Your broad experience and context are more important than ever. Senior developers often have historical knowledge of why things in the company are built a certain way or how an industry operates. This domain mastery lets you catch AI's missteps that a newcomer wouldn't.

Continue investing in understanding the problem domain deeply. That might mean staying up-to-date with the business's needs, user feedback, or new regulations that affect the software. AI won't automatically incorporate these considerations unless you tell it to. When you combine your domain insight with AI's speed, you get the best outcomes.

Also, use your foresight to steer AI. For instance, if you know that a quick fix will create maintenance pain down the line, you can instruct the AI to implement a more sustainable solution. Trust the instincts you've honed over the years—if a code snippet looks "off" or too good to be true, dig in. Nine times out of ten, your intuition has spotted something that the AI didn't account for. Being able to foresee the second- and third-order effects of code is a hallmark of senior engineers; don't let the convenience of AI blunt that habit. Instead, apply it to whatever the AI produces.

Hone Your Soft Skills and Leadership

With AI shouldering some coding, senior developers can spend more energy on the human side of engineering: communicating with stakeholders, leading design meetings, and making judgment calls that align technology with business strategy. Tim O'Reilly and others (*https://oreil.ly/rbIKm*) suggest that as rote coding becomes easier, the value shifts to deciding *what* to build and *how to orchestrate* complex systems.

Senior engineers are often the ones orchestrating and seeing the big picture. Step up to that role. Volunteer to write that architecture roadmap, to evaluate which tools (AI or otherwise) to adopt, or to define your org's AI coding guidelines. These are tasks AI can't do—they require experience, human discretion, and, often, cross-team consensus building. By amplifying your leadership presence, you ensure that you're not just a code generator (replaceable by another tool) but an indispensable technical leader guiding the team.

In short, continue doing what seasoned developers do best: seeing the forest for the trees. AI will help you chop a lot more trees, but someone still needs to decide *which* trees to cut and *how* to build a stable house from the lumber. Your judgment, strategic thinking, and mentorship are now even more critical. A senior developer who harnesses AI effectively can be dramatically more productive than one who doesn't—but the ones who truly excel will be those who apply their human strengths to amplify the AI's output, not just let it run wild.

As one Redditor observed (*https://oreil.ly/HulC9*), "AI is a programming force multiplier" that "greatly increases the productivity of senior programmers." The multiplier effect is real, but it's your expertise that's being multiplied. Keep that expertise sharp and at the center of the development process.

Midlevel Engineers: Adapt and Specialize

Midlevel engineers face perhaps the most significant pressure to evolve. Many of the tasks that traditionally occupied your time—implementing features, writing tests, debugging straightforward issues—are becoming increasingly automatable.

This doesn't mean obsolescence; it means elevation. The focus shifts from writing code to more building specialized knowledge, which the following sections explore.

Learn to Manage Systems Integration and Boundaries

As systems become more complex, understanding and managing the boundaries between components becomes crucial. This includes API design, event schemas, and data models—all requiring careful consideration of business requirements and future flexibility. Deepen your computer science fundamentals, including gaining an advanced understanding of disciplines like:

- Data structures and algorithms
- Distributed-systems principles

- Database internals and query optimization
- Network protocols and security

This knowledge helps you understand the implications of AI-generated code and make better architectural decisions.

Learn to handle edge cases and ambiguity too. Real-world software is rife with oddball scenarios and changing requirements. AI tends to solve the general case by default. It's up to the developer to ask "What if...?" and probe for weaknesses.

The durable skills here are critical thinking and foresight—enumerating edge cases, anticipating failures, and addressing them in code or design. This might mean thinking of null input, network outages, unusual user actions, or integration with other systems.

Build Your Domain Expertise

Understanding the business context or the user's environment will reveal edge cases that a generic AI simply doesn't know about. Experienced engineers habitually consider these scenarios. Practice systematically testing boundaries and questioning assumptions. Specialize in complex domains where human understanding remains crucial. Generic domains include:

- Financial systems with regulatory requirements
- Healthcare systems with privacy concerns
- Real-time systems with strict performance requirements
- Machine learning infrastructure

Software-engineering-specific domains include frontend and backend engineering, mobile development, DevOps, and security engineering, to name a few. Domain expertise provides context that current AI tools lack and helps you make better decisions about where and how to apply them.

Master Performance Optimization and DevOps

While LLMs can suggest basic optimizations, identifying and resolving system-wide performance issues requires a deep understanding of the entire stack, from database query patterns to frontend rendering strategies. Understanding how systems run in production becomes more valuable as code generation becomes more automated.

Focus on fields like the following:

- Monitoring and observability
- Performance profiling and optimization

- Security practices and compliance
- Cost management and optimization

Focus on Code Review and Quality Assurance

With AI writing lots of code, the ability to rigorously review and test that code becomes even more critical. "Everyone will need to get a lot more serious about testing and reviewing code," Yegge emphasizes (*https://oreil.ly/QtJ7_*). Treat AI-generated code as you would a human junior developer's output: you are the code reviewer responsible for catching bugs, security flaws, or sloppy implementations. This means strengthening your skills in unit testing, integration testing, and debugging.

Writing good tests is a durable skill that forces you to understand the spec and verify correctness. It's wise to assume nothing works until proven otherwise. AI often yields functional but unoptimized code until you guide it through iterative improvement. This can be due to a number of reasons, including that the training data coding models are trained on don't reflect all best practices as completely as they could.

Cultivate a testing mindset: verify every critical logic path, use static analysis or linters, and don't shy away from rewriting AI-given code if it doesn't meet your quality bar. Even if you're following the "AI as validator" pattern discussed in the previous chapter, quality assurance is not an area to simply outsource to AI—it's where human diligence shines. When software doesn't work as expected, you need real problem-solving chops to diagnose and fix it. AI can assist with debugging (for example, by suggesting possible causes), but it lacks true understanding of the specific context in which your application runs. Human testers possess domain-specific knowledge and an understanding of user expectations that AI currently lacks. This insight is vital when assessing the relevance and impact of potential issues. Diagnosing complex bugs often requires creative problem solving and the ability to consider a broad range of factors—skills that are inherently human. And evaluating the ethical implications of software behavior, such as fairness and accessibility, requires human sensitivity and judgment.

Being able to reason through a complex bug—reproducing it, isolating the cause, understanding the underlying systems (OS, databases, libraries)—is a timeless engineering skill. This often requires a strong grasp of fundamentals (how memory and state work, concurrency, etc.) that junior developers must learn through practice. Use AI as a helper (it might explain error messages or suggest fixes), but *don't rely on it thoughtlessly*. The skill to methodically troubleshoot and apply first principles when debugging sets great developers apart. It's also a feedback loop: debugging AI-written code will teach you to prompt the AI better next time or avoid certain patterns.

Learn Systems Thinking

Software projects are not just isolated coding tasks; they exist within a larger context of user needs, timelines, legacy code, and team processes. AI has no innate sense of the big picture, like your project's history or the rationale behind certain decisions (unless you explicitly feed all that into the prompt, which is often impractical). Humans need to carry that context.

The durable skill here is systems thinking—understanding how a change in one part of the system might impact another, how the software serves the business objectives, and how all the moving pieces connect.[2] This holistic perspective lets you use AI outputs appropriately. For example, if an AI suggests a clever shortcut that contradicts a regulatory requirement or company convention, you'll catch it because you know the context. Make it a point to learn the background of your projects and read design docs, so you can develop your judgment about what fits and what doesn't.

Be Adaptable—and Never Stop Learning

Finally, a metaskill: the ability to learn new tools and adapt to change. The field of AI-assisted development is evolving rapidly. Engineers who keep an open mind and learn how to effectively use new AI features will remain ahead of the curve—Tim O'Reilly suggests that (*https://oreil.ly/BYrNh*) developers who are "eager to learn new skills" will see the biggest productivity boosts from AI. Invest in learning the *fundamentals* deeply and staying curious about new techniques. This combination enables you to harness AI as a tool without becoming dependent on it.

It's a balancing act: use AI to accelerate your growth, but also occasionally practice without it to ensure you're not skipping core learning (some developers do an "AI detox" (*https://oreil.ly/XFPqu*) periodically to keep their raw coding skills sharp). In short, be the engineer who learns constantly—that's a career-proof skill in any era.

Get Good at Cross-Functional Communication

The ability to translate between business requirements and technical solutions becomes more valuable as implementation time decreases. Engineers who can effectively communicate with product managers, designers, and other stakeholders will become increasingly valuable. Good areas of focus here include:

- Requirements gathering and analysis
- Technical writing and documentation

---

2 To learn more about systems thinking, check out Donella H. Meadows, *Thinking in Systems: A Primer*, 2nd edition (Rizzoli, 2008); and Peter M. Senge, *The Fifth Discipline: The Art and Practice of the Learning Organization* (Crown, 2010).

- Project planning and estimation
- Team leadership and mentoring

Learn System Design and Architecture

Instead of spending days implementing a new feature, midlevel engineers might spend that time designing robust systems that gracefully handle scale and failure modes. This requires deep understanding of distributed systems principles, database internals, and cloud infrastructure—areas where LLMs currently provide limited value.

Practice designing systems that solve real-world problems at scale. These skills remain valuable regardless of how code is generated, as they require understanding business requirements and engineering trade-offs.

Designing a coherent system requires understanding trade-offs, constraints, and the "big picture" beyond writing a few functions. AI can generate code but won't automatically choose the best architecture for a complex problem.

The overall design—how components interact, how data flows, how to ensure scalability and security—is part of that 30% that demands human insight; this includes the following:

- Load balancing and caching strategies
- Data partitioning and replication
- Failure modes and recovery procedures
- Cost optimization and resource management

Senior developers have long honed this skill, and midlevel and junior devs should actively cultivate it. Think in terms of patterns and principles (like separation of concerns and modularity)—these guide an AI-generated solution toward maintainability. Remember, *solid architecture doesn't emerge by accident*; it needs an experienced human hand on the wheel.

Use AI!

Remember that AI should be an integral part of your workflow—it's not something to resist. Practical ways to incorporate AI into your daily work include:

- Scaffolding initial code structures
- Quick prototypes and proof of concepts
- Pair programming for faster debugging and problem solving
- Suggesting optimizations and alternative approaches

- Handling repetitive code patterns while you focus on architecture and design decisions

Venture into UI and UX Design

There's a growing narrative that midlevel software engineers should "just quit"—that pure engineering skills will become obsolete as AI handles the implementation details. While the conclusion is overstated, the discourse about the importance of skills beyond engineering (like design) deserves examination. In a representative exchange on X in December 2024, @fchollet wrote (*https://oreil.ly/BokTH*):

> We'll soon be in a world where you can turn test-time compute into competence—for the first time in the history of software, marginal cost will become critical.

To which @garrytan replied:

> UX, design, actual dedication to the craft will take center stage in this next moment.

Actually make something people want. Software and coding won't be the gating factor. It is the ability to be a polymath and smart/effective in many domains together that creates great software.

Successful software creation has always required more than just coding ability. What's changing is not the death of engineering but rather the lowering of pure implementation barriers. This shift actually makes engineering judgment and design thinking more crucial, not less.

Consider what makes applications like Figma, Notion, or VSCode successful. It's not just technical excellence—it's the deep understanding of user needs, workflows, and pain points. This understanding comes from the following:

- User experience design thinking
- Deep domain knowledge
- Understanding of human psychology and behavior
- System design that considers performance, reliability, and scalability
- Business model alignment

The best engineers have always been more than just coders. They've been problem solvers who understand both technical constraints and human needs. As AI tools reduce the friction of implementation, this holistic understanding becomes even more valuable.

However, this doesn't mean every engineer needs to become a UX designer. Instead, it means developing stronger product thinking abilities and building better collaboration skills with designers and product managers. It means thinking more about users, understanding their psychology and behavior patterns, and learning to make technical decisions that support user experience goals. You're at the point of achieving technical elegance: now balance it out with close attention to practical user needs.

Tan went on to post:

> UX, design, actual dedication to the craft will take center stage in this next moment.

Actually make something people want. Software and coding won't be the gating factor. It is the ability to be a polymath and smart/effective in many domains together that creates great software.

The future belongs to engineers who can bridge the gap between human needs and technical solutions—whether that's through developing better design sensibilities themselves or through more effective collaboration with dedicated designers.

Junior Developers: Thrive Alongside AI

If you're a junior or less-experienced developer, you might feel a mix of excitement and anxiety about AI. AI assistants can write code that you might not know how to write yourself, potentially accelerating your learning. Yet there are headlines about the "death of the junior developer" (*https://oreil.ly/QtJ7_*), suggesting entry-level coding jobs are at risk. Contrary to popular speculation, while AI is significantly changing the early-career experience, junior developers *are not obsolete*.

You need to be proactive in developing skills that ensure you're contributing value beyond what an AI can churn out. The traditional path of learning through implementing basic CRUD applications and simple features will evolve as these tasks become increasingly automated.

Consider a typical junior task: implementing a new API endpoint following existing patterns. Previously, this might have taken a day of coding and testing. With AI assistance, the implementation time might drop to an hour, but the crucial skills become:

- Understanding the existing system architecture well enough to specify the requirement correctly
- Reviewing the generated code for security implications and edge cases
- Ensuring the implementation maintains consistency with existing patterns
- Writing comprehensive tests that verify business logic

These skills can't be learned purely through tutorial following or AI prompting—they require hands-on experience with production systems and mentorship from senior engineers.

This evolution presents both challenges and opportunities for early-career developers. The bar for entry-level positions may rise, requiring stronger fundamental knowledge to effectively review and validate AI-generated code. However, this shift also means junior engineers can potentially tackle more interesting problems earlier in their careers.

Here's how to invest in yourself to handle that 30% gap effectively.

Learn the Fundamentals—Don't Skip the "Why"

It's tempting to lean on AI for answers to every question ("How do I do X in Python?") and never truly absorb the underlying concepts. Resist that urge. Use AI as a tutor, not just an answer vending machine. For example, when AI gives you a piece of code, ask *why* it chose that approach, or have it explain the code line by line.

Make sure you understand concepts like data structures, algorithms, memory management, and concurrency without always deferring to AI. The reason is simple: when the AI's output is wrong or incomplete, you need your own mental model to recognize and fix it. If you're not actively engaging with why the AI is generating certain code, you might actually learn less, hindering your growth. So take time to read documentation, write small programs from scratch, and solidify your core knowledge. These fundamentals are durable; they'll serve you even as the tools around you change.

Practice Problem Solving and Debugging Without the AI Safety Net

To build real confidence, sometimes you have to fly solo. Many developers advocate doing an "AI-free day" or otherwise limiting AI assistance periodically. This ensures you can still solve problems with just your own skills, which is important for avoiding skill atrophy. You'll find it forces you to truly think through a problem's logic, which in turn makes you better at using AI (since you can direct it more intelligently).

Additionally, whenever you encounter a bug or error in AI-generated code, jump in and debug it *yourself* before asking the AI to fix it. You'll learn much more by stepping through a debugger or adding print statements to see what's going wrong.

Consider AI suggestions as hints, not final answers. Over time, tackling those last tricky bits of a task will build your skill in the very areas AI struggles—exactly what makes you valuable.

Focus on Testing and Verification

As a junior dev, one of the best habits you can develop is writing tests for your code. This is doubly true if you use AI to generate code.

When you get a chunk of code from an LLM, don't assume it's correct—challenge it. Write unit tests (or use manual tests) to see if it truly handles the requirements and edge cases. This accomplishes two things: it catches issues in the AI's output, and it trains you to think about expected behavior before trusting an implementation.

You might even use the AI to help write tests, but *you* define what to test. Yegge's advice (*https://oreil.ly/QtJ7_*) about taking testing and code review seriously applies at all levels. If you cultivate a reputation for carefully verifying your work (AI-assisted or not), senior colleagues will trust you more, and you'll avoid the scenario where they feel you're just "dumping" questionable code on them.

In practical terms, start treating testing as an integral part of development, not an afterthought. Learn how to use testing frameworks, how to do exploratory manual testing, and how to systematically reproduce bugs. These skills not only make you better at the 30% work, but they also accelerate your understanding of how the code really works.

Remember: if you catch a bug that the AI introduced, *you* just did something the AI couldn't—that's added value.

Build an Eye for Maintainability

Junior devs often focus on "getting it to work." But in the AI era, getting a basic working version is easy—the AI can do that. The harder part (and what you should focus on) is making code that's readable, maintainable, and clean.

Start developing an eye for good code structure and style. Compare the AI's output with best practices you know of; if the AI code is messy or overly complex, take the initiative to refactor it. For instance, if an LLM gives you a 50-line function that does too many things, you can split it into smaller functions. If variable names are unclear, rename them.

Essentially, pretend you're reviewing a peer's code, and improve the AI's code as if a peer wrote it. This will help you internalize good design principles. Over time, you'll start prompting the AI in ways that yield cleaner code to begin with (because you'll specify the style you want). Software maintainers (often working months or years later) will thank you, and you'll prove that you're thinking beyond just "make it run"—you're thinking like an engineer. Keeping things maintainable is exactly in that human-driven 30%, so make it your concern from the start of your career.

Develop Your Prompting and Tooling Skills (Wisely)

There's no denying that "prompt engineering"—the skill of interacting with AI tools effectively—is useful. As a junior dev, you should absolutely learn how to phrase questions to AI, how to give it proper context, and how to iterate on prompts to improve the output (Chapter 2 of this book is a good place to start). These are new skills that can set you apart (many experienced devs are still figuring this out too!). However, remember that prompting well is often a proxy for understanding the problem well. If you find you can't get the AI to do what you want, it might be because *you* need to clarify your own understanding first. Use that as a signal.

One strategy is to outline a solution in plain English yourself before asking the AI to implement it. Also, experiment with different AI tools (Copilot, Claude, etc.) to see their strengths and weaknesses. The more fluent you are with these assistants, the more productive you can be—but never treat their output as infallible. Think of AI like a super-charged Stack Overflow: an aid, not an authority.

You might even build small personal projects using AI to push your limits ("Can I build a simple web app with AI's help?"). Doing so will teach you how to integrate AI into a development workflow, which is a great skill to bring into a team. Just balance it with periods of working without the net, as mentioned earlier.

Seek Feedback and Mentorship

Lastly, one durable skill that will accelerate your growth is the ability to seek out feedback and learn from others. An AI won't get offended if you ignore its advice, but your human teammates and mentors are invaluable for your development—especially when it comes to soft skills, leadership, communication, and navigating office politics.

Don't hesitate to ask a senior developer why they prefer one solution over another, especially if it differs from what an AI suggested. Discuss design decisions and trade-offs with more experienced colleagues—these conversations reveal how seasoned engineers think, and that's gold for you. In code reviews, be extra receptive to comments about your AI-written code. If a reviewer points out that "this function isn't thread-safe" or "this approach will have scaling issues," take the time to understand the root issue. These are exactly the kinds of things an AI might miss, and you want to learn to catch them. Over time, you'll build a mental checklist of considerations.

Additionally, find opportunities to pair program (even if remotely). Perhaps you can "pair" with a senior who uses AI in their workflow—you'll observe how they prompt the AI and how they correct it. But even more important, you'll see how they communicate, lead discussions, and handle delicate team dynamics. Being open to feedback and actively asking for guidance will help you mature from doing tasks that an AI could do to performing the high-value tasks that only humans can do. In a sense, you're trying to acquire the wisdom that usually comes with experience, as efficiently as you can. That makes you more than just another coder in the room—it makes you the kind of engineer teams are eager to keep and promote.

Communicate and Collaborate

Building software is a team sport. AI doesn't attend meetings (thank goodness)—humans still must talk to other humans to clarify requirements, discuss trade-offs, and coordinate work. Strong communication skills are as valuable as ever. Practice asking good questions and describing problems clearly (both to colleagues and to AI).

Interestingly, prompting an AI is itself a form of communication; it requires you to precisely express what you want. This overlaps with a core engineering skill: *requirements analysis*.[3] If you can formulate a clear prompt or spec, it means you've thought through the problem.

Additionally, sharing knowledge, writing documentation, and reviewing others' code are collaborative skills that AI cannot replace. In the future, as developers work "with" AI, the human-to-human collaboration in a team—making sure the right problems are being solved—stays vital. One emerging trend is that developers may focus more on high-level design discussions (often with AI as a participant) and on coordinating tasks, essentially taking on more of a conductor role. Communication and leadership skills will serve you well in that conductor's seat.

Shift Your Mindset: From Consuming to Creating

It's worth noting a mindset shift for juniors in the AI era: you need to move from just *consuming solutions to creating understanding*. In the past, you might have struggled through documentation to eventually write a feature; now an AI can hand you a solution on a platter. If you simply consume it (copy-paste and move on), you haven't grown much.

Instead, use each AI-given solution as a learning case. Dissect it, experiment with it, and consider how you might have arrived at it yourself. By treating AI outputs not as answers to end all questions but as interactive learning material, you ensure that you—the human—are continuously leveling up. This way, rather than replacing your growth, AI accelerates it.

Many experts believe that while AI might reduce the need for large teams of junior "coder-grinders," it also *raises the bar* for what it means to be a junior developer. The role is shifting to someone who can work effectively with AI and quickly climb the value chain. If you adopt the habits discussed in this section, you'll distinguish yourself as a junior developer who doesn't just bring what an AI could bring (any company can get that via a subscription) but who brings insight, reliability, and continuous improvement—traits of a future senior developer.

---

3 For more on this topic, see Mark Richards and Neal Ford, *Fundamentals of Software Architecture*, 2nd edition (O'Reilly, 2025); and Mark Richards, Neal Ford, and Raju Gandhi, *Head First Software Architecture* (O'Reilly, 2024).

Summary and Next Steps

To thrive in an AI-enhanced development world, engineers at all levels should double down on the enduring skills and practices that AI cannot (yet) replicate. These capabilities will remain crucial no matter how advanced our tools become. In particular, focus on these areas:

- Strengthening your system design and architecture expertise
- Practicing systems thinking and maintaining a contextual understanding of the big picture
- Honing your skills in critical thinking, problem solving, and foresight
- Building expertise in specialized domains
- Reviewing code, testing, debugging, and quality assurance
- Improving your communication and collaboration skills
- Adapting to change
- Continuously learning, keeping your fundamentals strong while gaining new skills and updating your knowledge
- Using AI

These skills form the human advantage in software engineering. They are durable because they don't expire with the next framework or tooling change; if anything, AI's rise makes them more pronounced. Simon Willison has argued that (*https://oreil.ly/5F3O7*) AI assistance actually makes strong programming skills *more* valuable, not less, because those with expertise can leverage the tools to far greater effect.

A powerful machine in unskilled hands can be dangerous or wasted, but in capable hands it's transformative. In the AI era, an experienced engineer is like a seasoned pilot with a new advanced copilot: the journey can go faster and farther, but the pilot must still navigate the storms and ensure a safe landing.

Software engineering has always been a field of continuous change—from assembly language to high-level programming, from on-prem servers to the cloud, and now from manual coding to AI-assisted development. Each leap has automated some aspect of programming, yet each time, developers have adapted and found even more to do. In response to a Tim O'Reilly note (*https://oreil.ly/BYrNh*), one HN commenter remarked (*https://oreil.ly/OewGO*) that past innovations "almost always resulted in more work, more growth, more opportunities" for developers. The rise of AI is no different. Rather than making developers irrelevant, it is reshaping the skill set needed to succeed. The mundane 70% of coding is getting easier; the challenging 30% becomes an even larger part of our value.

To maximize that human 30%, focus on the timeless engineering skills: understanding problems deeply, designing clean solutions, scrutinizing code for quality, and considering the users and context. Experienced programmers are gaining more from AI because they know how to guide it and what to do when it falters. Those who combine these skills with AI tools will outperform those who have only one or the other. In fact, the consensus emerging among experts (*https://oreil.ly/5gfvc*) is that AI is a tool for the skilled: that "LLMs are power tools meant for power users." This means the onus is on each of us to become that "power user"—to cultivate the expertise that lets us wield these new tools effectively.

Ultimately, the craft of software engineering is more than writing code that works. It's about writing code that *works well*—in a real-world environment, over time, and under evolving requirements. Today's AI models can assist with writing code but cannot yet ensure the code works well in all those dimensions. That's the developer's job.

By doubling down on the skills just outlined, senior developers can continue to lead and innovate, midlevel developers can deepen their expertise, and junior developers can accelerate their journey to mastery. AI will handle more and more of the routine, but your creativity, intuition, and thoughtful engineering will turn that raw output into something truly valuable. AI is a powerful tool, but it's all about how we use it. Good engineering practices, human judgment, and a willingness to learn will remain essential.

In practical terms, whether you are pair programming with an "eager junior" AI that writes your functions or reviewing a diff full of AI-generated code, never forget to apply your uniquely human lens. Ask, Does this solve the *right* problem? Will others be able to understand and maintain this? What are the risks and edge cases? Those questions are your responsibility. The future of programming will indeed involve less typing every semicolon by hand and more directing and curating—but it will still require developers at the helm who have the wisdom to do it right.

In the end, great software engineering has always been about problem solving, not just code slinging. AI doesn't change that: it simply challenges us to elevate our problem solving to the next level. Embrace that challenge, and you'll thrive in this new chapter of our industry.

CHAPTER 5

Understanding Generated Code: Review, Refine, Own

You've learned how to prompt an AI to generate code, and by this point you've likely produced some code using these techniques. Now comes a critical phase: making sure that code is correct, safe, and maintainable.

As a developer, you can't just take the AI's output and blithely ship it. You need to review it, test it, possibly improve it, and integrate it with the rest of your codebase. This chapter focuses on how to understand what the AI gave you, iteratively edit and debug it, and fully take ownership of the code as part of your project.

This chapter covers:

- Interpreting the AI's code in terms of your original intent
- The "majority solution" phenomenon, or why AI-generated code often looks like a common solution
- Techniques to review code for clarity and potential issues
- Debugging AI-written code when it doesn't work as expected
- Refactoring the code for style or efficiency
- Writing tests to validate the code's behavior

By mastering these skills, you'll be able to integrate AI contributions into your projects with confidence.

From Intent to Implementation: Understanding the AI's Interpretation

When you get the AI's code, your first step should be to compare it to your intent (the prompt you gave). Does the code fulfill the requirements you set out? Sometimes the AI might slightly misinterpret or only partially implement what you asked.

Read through the code carefully. Step through it in your mind or on paper:

- Trace what it does for a typical input.
- If your prompt had multiple parts ("do X and Y"), verify that the AI has done them all.
- Ensure that the AI didn't add functionality you didn't ask for—sometimes it will add an extra feature it "thinks" is useful, like adding logging or a parameter, which could be OK or not.

Just as you would with a colleague's code, if something is unclear, note it. If you look for a good reason for it to be there, you might find one. If you don't, query it or consider removing it.

For example, if you ask for a prime-number checker and the AI code also prints something like "Checking 7…" for each number, that may be an artifact of how you prompted it or a pattern from its training data (some tutorial code prints its progress). If you don't want that, plan to remove it or prompt the AI to remove it.

Also make sure the edge cases are handled as you expect. If you intended it to handle empty input, does it? If the input could be None or negative, did the AI consider that?

If something about your prompt was ambiguous and the AI had to choose an interpretation, identify where that happened. Perhaps you didn't specify an output format, and it chose to print results instead of returning them. Now you have to decide if you want to accept that or modify the code.

This understanding phase is crucial; don't skip it. Even if you're going to test the code, understanding it by reading is important because tests might not cover everything (and reading is faster for some obvious things).

Last, consider the AI's assumptions. AI often goes for the "majority" or most common interpretation (which leads us to the next section).

The "Majority" Problem: Most Common Doesn't Mean Most Appropriate

AI models trained on lots of code will often produce the solution that's most represented in that training data (or the simplest solution that fits). I call this the *majority solution* effect. It's correct in general cases, but it might not be the best for your specific situation.

For example, if you ask for a search algorithm without further context, the AI might output a basic linear search, because that's straightforward and common. Maybe you actually needed a binary search, but the AI didn't know that efficiency was critical, because you didn't say so. Linear search works for many moderate cases but not if performance is key.

Similarly, the AI might use a global variable because many simple examples do, but perhaps in your project, that's not acceptable practice.

Be mindful that the AI's solution might optimize for a generic scenario. As a human developer, you have insight into context that the AI lacks.

To address this:

- Identify assumptions in the code. If it assumes a list is sorted or an input is valid, was that assumption OK? Did you specify it? If not, maybe it should have included a check.
- Consider alternatives: If you know multiple ways to solve the problem (like different algorithms), did the AI pick one? Is it the one you want? If not, you can prompt for the alternative or just change it.

If the AI code works for the "usual" case but not for edge conditions that matter to you, that's something to fix. For instance, maybe it didn't consider integer overflow in some math. In many training examples, that might not have been addressed, but in your context, it could be important.

Understanding that the AI tends toward generic solutions will make you better at reviewing its code. It's not magic or tailor-made; it's a very educated guess at a solution. The tailoring is your job.

Code Readability and Structure: Patterns and Potential Issues

AI-generated code often has some telltale patterns. It might:

- Include more comments than usual or oddly phrased comments (since it learned from tutorial code, which tends to be heavily commented)
- Use certain variable names consistently (like i, j, k for loops)
- Lay out code in a somewhat verbose style (to cover general cases)

Check for these and consider whether they match your project's style. The code might be functionally fine but need a readability pass. In that pass, you may want to:

- Rename variables to be more descriptive or consistent with your codebase.
- Remove or refine comments. If it added a comment like `# check if number is prime` above a self-explanatory `if` statement, you could remove that. But if it has a comment explaining a complex bit of logic, that's good—keep or improve it.
- Ensure consistent formatting by running the code through a linter or formatter (like Black for Python or `gofmt` for Go) to match the spacing and bracket styles you want.

Also look for any unusual structure. Did the AI define multiple classes or functions when you expected one? Sometimes it might break a problem into multiple functions because that's how a training example did it. If that's overkill, you can inline them (or vice versa). Is the code too clever or too naive? AI sometimes produces a very straightforward solution or, occasionally, a fancy one-liner. Does that align with your team's preferences? If not, adjust accordingly.

Other potential issues to watch out for include:

Off-by-one errors
Yes, AI can make those, too. For example, loop boundaries can be tricky. If you have time, mentally test a simple case through the loop.

Unhandled exceptions
Does the code assume that a file opens successfully or that all input is in the correct format? Add error handling if it's needed.

Performance pitfalls
Maybe the AI is using an inner loop on a large dataset for membership checks, even though a better approach exists, like using a set. The AI solution might be correct but not optimal.

Library usage

If the code uses a library, ensure it's one you want to use (and that it's available). Sometimes it might use, say, numpy for a simple sum (because it saw that in examples in its training data). If dragging in that dependency isn't worth it, you can switch to pure Python or the library you intended.

Inconsistencies

Occasionally, the AI code might have minor inconsistencies, like a function docstring saying one thing but the code doing another (if it revised the logic but not the comment, for instance). Fix those.

Minor syntax issues

This is rare with well-tested models but not impossible in languages where it might confuse something.

Using outdated APIs

The AI might use an old version of a library's function that has changed, for instance. If you see a function call you don't recognize, quickly check the library docs to ensure it's correct for the version you use.

Placeholders

If the AI output uses placeholders like "Your code here" (rare, but it can happen in a generic template), fill those in.

In short, treat the AI code as if an intern wrote it and left for the day. You need to review it for quality and integrate it properly.

Debugging Strategies: Finding and Fixing Errors

Let's say you run the code (or write tests for it, which we'll cover soon) and something's not working. Debugging AI-generated code is no different than debugging your own or someone else's code—except you didn't write it, so you might be less familiar. But because you've carefully read it already, you're in good shape (see Figure 5-1).

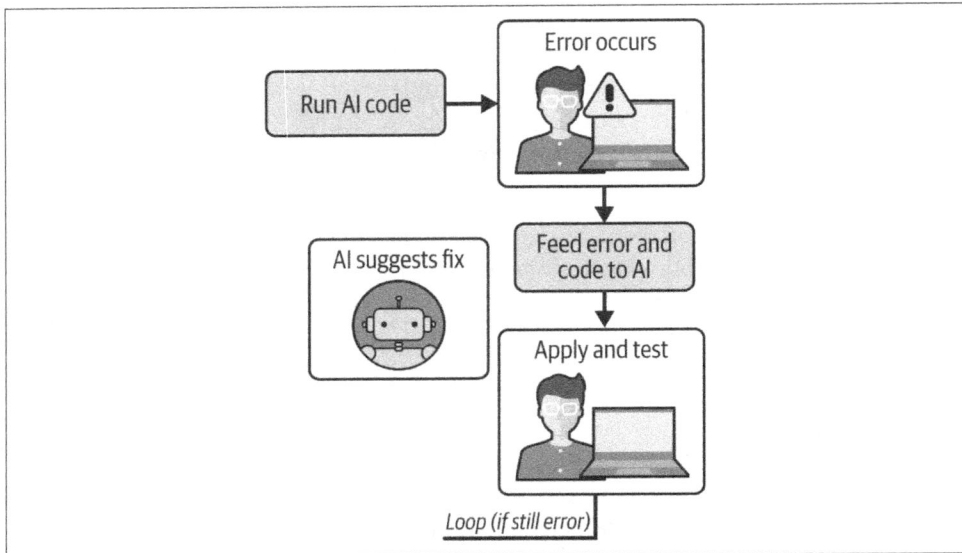

Figure 5-1. The AI code debugging cycle: execute AI-generated code, capture errors, provide error context back to AI for analysis, implement suggested fixes, and iterate until resolution.

Here's a six-step approach to debugging:

1. *Reproduce the issue.*

   Run the function or code with inputs that fail. Observe the output or error.

2. *Locate the source of the issue.*

   Use typical debugging techniques like print statements, or use a debugger to step through. If it's a logical error (wrong output), trace the logic manually or with prints to see where it diverges from your expectations.

3. *Check the prompt against the code.*

   Sometimes the bug is simply that the code didn't fully implement the requirement, like if you asked for something to be sorted but it isn't sorting properly. That might mean the AI's logic is flawed or that an edge case (like an empty list) isn't handled.

4. *Leverage the AI to debug!*

   You can actually feed the problematic code back into the AI and say, "This code is giving the wrong result for X. Can you help find the bug?" Often, it will analyze it (like a code review) and point out issues. For example, maybe it sees that a loop should go to `len(arr)` but goes to `len(arr)-1`. It might catch that quicker. (Be mindful to not fully trust it either—but it's like asking a colleague to help debug.)

5. *Fix the code.*

   Now you have a choice: fix it manually or prompt the AI for a corrected version. If the fix is obvious, just do it. If it's not, you can try something like "The above function fails on input X (expected Y, got Z). Please correct it." The AI might then adjust the code accordingly.

6. *Test again.*

   Ensure the bug is resolved and that no new issues have been introduced.

I recommend using test-driven debugging. If possible, write a few tests for critical functions (more on that in the testing section later in this chapter). Any failing tests will directly show what's wrong. This can be faster than manual checking, for anything but the simplest functions.

Finally, when debugging, be sure you ask *why*, not just *what*. Try to understand why the AI made the mistake. Was the prompt unclear on that point? This can inform how you prompt next time or whether you need to always double-check that aspect in AI outputs. For example, if you notice the AI often doesn't handle empty inputs unless told, you'll start always specifying that in prompts and reviewing for it.

Refactoring for Maintainability: Making AI Code Your Code

Once the code is functionally correct, consider refactoring it to align with your project's standards and to make it easier to work with in the future. The AI's job was to get you code quickly; your job is to polish it.

Here is another six-step process, this time for refactoring:

1. *Align with style guidelines.*

   Run the code through your formatter or linter. Fix any warnings like "Variable name should be lowercase" or "Line too long." This instantly makes the code look like the rest of your codebase. Many AI tools do a decent job at style, but slight adjustments might be needed.

2. *Improve naming and structure.*

   If the AI named functions _helper1 and _helper2 in a class, and you prefer meaningful names, rename them. If it created a bunch of small functions that are only used once, maybe inline them, unless they add clarity.

3. *Remove any unnecessary parts.*

   For example, perhaps the AI included a main block or test code in the output that you didn't ask for. If you don't need that, remove it. Conversely, maybe it wrote everything in one function but you want to split it into smaller pieces for clarity; if so, do that split now.

4. *Add documentation.*

   If this code is intended to be part of a library or a module that others will use, add docstrings or comments where appropriate. The AI might have commented some, but ensure it meets your standards. For example, maybe your project requires a certain docstring format with parameters and returns documented.

5. *Optimize if needed.*

   Now that the code works, is it efficient enough? If this code might be called in a tight loop or on large data, check its complexity. The AI might not have used the most optimal approach (again, the "majority solution" might be a simple loop, not a more optimized approach). If performance is a concern, refactor to a better algorithm. You can again involve the AI:

   > Optimize this code to run faster by using a set instead of a list for lookups.

   But you, as a developer, often know what pattern you want, so you might just implement that change.

6. *Simplify if needed.*

   Sometimes AI code can be overly verbose. For instance, it might use an if-else with returns where a single return with a condition would suffice. While explicit code is not necessarily bad, you might want to simplify it to fewer lines to improve readability without losing clarity.

The goal of refactoring is that if another developer pulls up this code later, it shouldn't be obvious that "an AI wrote this." It should just look like good code. That often means giving it the small human touches that make code clean.

When you refactor, you need to verify you didn't break anything. So let's segue into testing.

The Importance of Testing: Unit, Integration, and End to End

Testing is always important, but it's especially important for AI-generated code for two reasons. First, since you didn't write it from scratch, you want assurance that it will work in all cases. Second, if you prompt the AI for changes later or integrate more AI code, tests help you ensure that any new changes don't break the existing functionality. Let's look quickly at different kinds of tests:

Unit tests

Write tests for each function or module you got from the AI, particularly covering edge cases. For our prime example, you might test with a prime number, a nonprime, 1 (an edge case), 0 or negative (maybe defining the expected behavior), a large prime, and so on. If the code passes all those tests, it's likely correct.

You can even ask the AI to generate these tests:

Write PyTest unit tests for the above function, covering edge cases.

It often does a decent job. Still, review them to ensure they're valid and cover what you think is necessary.

Integration tests

If the AI code interacts with other parts of the codebase, like a function that uses a database, write a test that calls it in context. Does it actually store to the database what it should? If it produces output consumed by another function, chain them in a test.

End-to-end tests

If this code is part of a larger workflow, run a scenario from start to finish. For example, if the AI code was part of a web route, do a test request to that route in a test environment and see if the format, error handling, and everything else holds up.

The level of testing you need to do depends on how critical and complex the code is. But even a quick manual test run or simple assert statements in a script are better than nothing for verification. Remember, testing doesn't just find bugs; it locks down behavior. If you change something later (or an AI does), testing helps you ensure the code's functionality doesn't regress.

Testing is also a good way to assert ownership. Once you've tested for and fixed any issues, you can be confident in the code. At this point, it's fair to say the code is "yours," just like any other code in the codebase. You understand it, you trust it, and you have tests to guard it.

A Note on AI and Testing

Some AI coding tools are starting to integrate testing suggestions. For example, CodeWhisperer will sometimes suggest an assert after a piece of code. Use those suggestions as a starting point, but don't assume they're 100% comprehensive. Think of creative edge cases—that's one place where human intuition is still very valuable.

Summary and Next Steps

We've gone through generating, understanding, debugging, and refactoring the code. This loop might happen in a short span (within minutes, for a small function) or take longer (for a complex module, over hours or days, with intermittent AI assistance).

It's important to acknowledge that *you, the developer, are responsible for the final code.* AI is a tool to accelerate creation, but it won't take the blame if something fails. There's also a licensing or copyright risk: some AI providers (*https://oreil.ly/kYyO_*) say that outputs over a certain length might be statistically likely to contain copied material. It's rare, and the providers mitigated the problem a lot, but just as you scan Stack Overflow answers for any obviously licensed text or attributions, do a quick check—especially if the output is big or too clean. For instance, if you prompt "implement quicksort" and the AI gives you 20 lines of pristine code, that's probably fine and common knowledge. But if you ask for something obscure and get a large chunk of code, try searching a unique string from it online to see if it was pulled verbatim from somewhere. This issue has become more apparent recently, with documented cases (*https://oreil.ly/h_BzA*) of AI systems reproducing text from journal articles and other copyrighted sources. As part of responsible code ownership, developers should verify the provenance of any AI-generated content that appears to go beyond generic patterns or seems unusually specific to particular sources.

Finally, integrate the code into your project: add it to your version control system, perhaps mentioning in your commit message that AI helped. There's no requirement to do this, but some teams like to track it.

Over time, you'll likely modify this AI-generated code as requirements change. Treat it like any other code: don't think, "Oh, that's the AI's code; I'll ask the AI to change it." You can, if you want, but you can also freely modify it by hand. Do whatever is most efficient and maintainable.

Through careful review and testing, AI-generated code becomes just more code in your project. At that point, whether an AI wrote line 10 or you did is irrelevant— what matters is that it meets the project's needs and standards.

By following these practices, you harness the speed of AI coding while ensuring quality. You avoid the pitfalls of unquestioningly trusting AI output and instead integrate it into a professional development workflow.

Next, Chapter 6 examines how AI tools can fundamentally transform the prototyping phase of software development. I will explore practical techniques for leveraging AI assistants to accelerate the journey from initial concept to working prototype, often reducing development time from days to hours. The discussion covers specific AI-powered prototyping tools, including Vercel v0 and screenshot-to-code utilities, along with strategies for iterative refinement under AI guidance.

I will also address the critical transition process from AI-generated prototypes to production-ready code, examining both the opportunities and potential challenges that arise when AI becomes a central part of the development workflow. Through real-world case studies, I will demonstrate how developers are successfully using AI to test ideas rapidly while maintaining code quality—and avoiding common pitfalls that can emerge when moving too quickly from concept to implementation.

CHAPTER 6

AI-Driven Prototyping: Tools and Techniques

This chapter explores how AI-driven vibe coding accelerates the prototyping phase of software development. Prototyping is all about rapidly turning an idea into a working model. With AI assistants, developers can achieve in hours what might normally take days, quickly iterating on concepts. I'll discuss techniques for going from concept to prototype with AI, compare popular AI prototyping tools (including Vercel v0 and screenshot-to-code utilities), and examine how to refine prototypes iteratively under AI guidance. I also address the crucial step of transitioning a rough AI-generated prototype into production-quality code. Throughout the chapter, I'll also look at case studies where AI-driven prototyping led to successful outcomes and demonstrate both the potential and the pitfalls of this approach.

Rapid Prototyping with AI Assistants

Prototyping benefits greatly from the speed of AI-generated code. The goal in prototyping is not polished, production-ready code but a *proof of concept* that you can evaluate and refine. AI coding assistants shine here by producing functioning code quickly from minimal input. For example, instead of manually coding a UI mockup, a developer can describe the desired interface in natural language and let the AI generate the HTML/CSS or React components. This allows for a very fast idea-to-implementation cycle.

One UX engineer (*https://oreil.ly/dP5U3*) describes how using a generative AI tool has completely transformed his workflow: "The speed at which I could generate functional prototypes with Generative AI was amazing. I built prototypes in a few hours [that] would normally take days." The AI handles routine boilerplate and repetitive patterns automatically, freeing him to focus on higher-level design decisions. In prototyping, this means you can try out more ideas in the same amount of time. Another benefit is that AI can fill in the tedious parts of a prototype (basic UI components, form handling, sample data) almost instantly, allowing the human developer to concentrate on the core concept or unique feature being tested.

However, it's important to remember that a prototype's code is often throwaway code. An AI may generate a working solution quickly, but that code might not be structured for maintainability or scale. This is acceptable in prototypes, where speed and experimentation matter more than elegance—as long as you plan to refactor or rewrite critical parts for production (I'll discuss this process later in the chapter). As Chapters 3 and 4 explored, the AI can confidently handle about 70% of the coding for a prototype, while you guide the overall architecture and correct any critical flaws.

Programming with intent, a concept introduced in Chapter 1, is essential here. You provide high-level instructions (the intent of what you want the prototype to do or look like) and let the AI fill in the implementation. To illustrate, let's walk through a very simple prototyping example using an AI assistant. Suppose you have an idea for a sign-up page for a new service. You want to prototype the frontend quickly, so you start with the following developer prompt:

> Create a simple HTML page for a sign-up form with fields for Name, Email, and Password, and a Submit button. Make it look presentable with basic styling.

A modern code assistant like Cline might provide a complete HTML/CSS example:

```
<!DOCTYPE html>
<html lang="en">
<head>
  <meta charset="UTF-8" />
  <meta name="viewport" content="width=device-width, initial-scale=1.0" />
  <title>Sign Up</title>
  <style>
    body { font-family: Arial, sans-serif; max-width: 400px; margin: 2em auto; }
    form { display: flex; flex-direction: column; }
    label { margin-top: 1em; }
    input, button { padding: 0.5em; font-size: 1em; }
    button { margin-top: 1em; background: #4CAF50; color: #fff; border: none; }
  </style>
</head>
<body>
  <h2>Sign Up</h2>
  <form>
    <label>Name: <input type="text" name="name" required></label>
    <label>Email: <input type="email" name="email" required></label>
    <label>Password: <input type="password" name="password" required></label>
    <button type="submit">Create Account</button>
  </form>
</body>
</html>
```

This AI-generated code is a decent starting point for a prototype of the sign-up form. It includes a basic layout and some inline CSS for styling. As a developer, you didn't have to write any HTML/CSS by hand—you simply described the outcome, and the AI provided an implementation. This demonstrates programming by intent: you focus on *what* the UI should do, and the AI figures out *how* to do it.

Of course, this is a trivial example. In practice, prototypes can be more complex and involve multiple files, frameworks, or data. But the principle is the same: You use the AI to create a first draft swiftly. You might then open this prototype in a browser, see how it looks, and refine it further. That leads me to the next topic: using specialized AI prototyping tools that go beyond plain-language prompts.

AI Prototyping Tools

While general-purpose assistants like Gemini, ChatGPT, and Claude can generate prototype code from prompts, the landscape of specialized AI-assisted prototyping tools continues to evolve rapidly. As I write this, the available tools offer different approaches to the fundamental trade-off between fidelity and control in AI-generated prototypes.

The ecosystem has matured to serve distinct prototyping needs. Some tools excel at transforming visual designs into code, allowing designers to upload screenshots or sketches and receive working HTML, CSS, or React components within seconds. This "screenshot-to-code" capability dramatically accelerates the design-to-code process, particularly valuable when you have hand-drawn sketches or Figma designs that need rapid implementation. Tools like Vercel v0 exemplify this approach, offering high fidelity to the original design while trading off some control over code structure.

Other platforms focus on generating complete applications through conversational interfaces. These allow users to describe functionality in natural language and receive full stack implementations. For instance, a designer wanting a quick app without coding might use tools like Lovable or Bolt.new, which offer high-level prompt interfaces that can scaffold entire applications. Some designers report building functional prototypes in hours that would traditionally take days, with the AI automatically handling tedious components and patterns.

A third category integrates AI directly into development environments, functioning as intelligent pair programmers during the prototyping phase. These AI-augmented IDEs like Cursor, Windsurf, and Cline allow developers to maintain more control over the code generation process while still benefiting from AI acceleration. The distinction often lies in workflow philosophy: some prioritize automated application of changes for rapid experimentation, while others require explicit acceptance of modifications for more careful iteration.

The common thread across all these approaches is their ability to compress the journey from concept to working prototype. However, they differ significantly in two key dimensions that shape their utility for different users and use cases.

Fidelity refers to how closely the generated output matches your input or intention. Screenshot-to-code tools typically offer high fidelity to visual designs but may produce code that doesn't align with your architectural preferences. Conversational tools might interpret your requirements more loosely, generating functional but generic implementations that require refinement.

Control encompasses your ability to guide and modify the generation process. Some tools operate as black boxes that produce complete outputs, while others allow iterative refinement through continued dialogue or direct code editing. This dimension becomes crucial when you need specific architectural patterns, performance optimizations, or integration with existing codebases.

Understanding these trade-offs helps in selecting the right tool for your prototyping needs. A designer validating a new interaction pattern might prioritize fidelity and speed, accepting less control over implementation details. A developer exploring technical feasibility might value control and transparency, even if it means more manual intervention in the generation process.

None of these tools produces production-quality code without human oversight. They typically deliver what I call the "80% prototype"—functional enough to test concepts and demonstrate to stakeholders but requiring additional work for production deployment. The remaining 20% often involves security hardening, performance optimization, error handling, and architectural refinement.

Even during rapid prototyping, a quick code review remains essential. While you might not polish every detail in a prototype, scanning for obvious issues like exposed API keys or insecure data handling prevents problems from propagating into later development stages. Most modern tools provide transparency into their generated code, allowing you to inspect and understand what's being created.

As the AI prototyping landscape continues to evolve, the specific tools will undoubtedly change, but these fundamental considerations of fidelity versus control, and the need for human oversight, will remain constant. The key is understanding your prototyping goals and selecting approaches that align with your specific needs, whether that's rapid visual implementation, functional demonstration, or technical exploration.

From Concept to Prototype: Iterative Refinement

One of the strengths of AI-driven prototyping is the *iterative loop*: you can generate an initial version and then refine it by interacting with the AI. Instead of manually editing code, you just tell the AI what you want changed (see Figure 6-1). While I advocate a more responsible approach than pure "seat-of-the-pants" vibe coding, the fast feedback cycle is definitely something to embrace in prototypes.

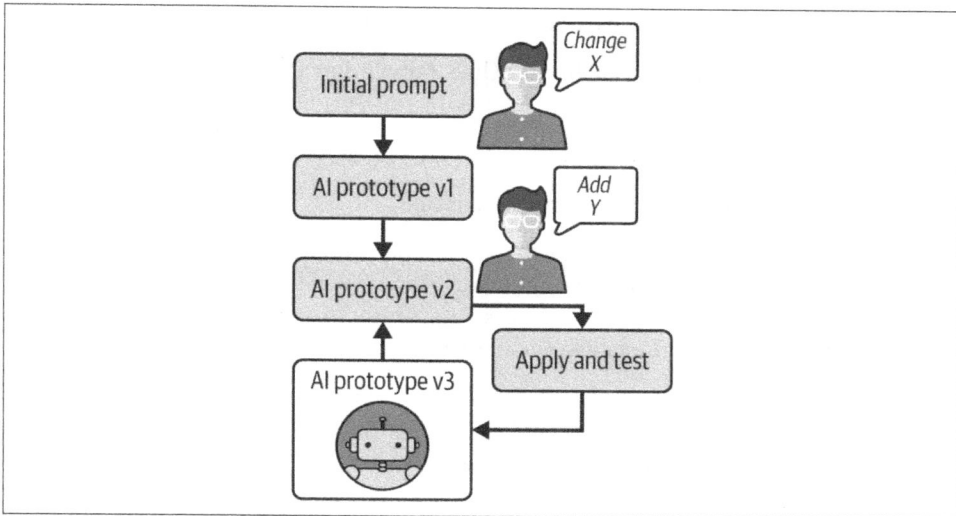

Figure 6-1. Iterative prototype refinement process: initial prompts generate baseline prototypes, and developer feedback drives successive improvements, creating increasingly refined solutions through AI collaboration.

Most AI prototyping tools keep a history or context of your requests, which is extremely useful. It means the AI remembers the *purpose* of your app and previous instructions, so you don't have to re-explain everything each time. This *context persistence* is a hallmark of vibe-coding environments: the conversation with the AI becomes the development log.

Here's how a typical iterative refinement might go:

Step 1: Initial generation

You provide a prompt or input to create the prototype:

> Generate a basic expense-tracker app with a form to add expenses and a table to list them.

Step 2: Review and run the code

You get the generated code and run it. Maybe it works, but you notice some things that could be improved. For example, the UI is functional but plain, or the table doesn't sort the expenses.

Step 3: Refine your prompts

You go back to the AI and provide additional instructions. For instance:

> Make the expense list sortable by amount or date.

The AI might modify the code to include sorting logic or use a library for sortable tables:

Add some color styling, maybe use a modern CSS framework.

The AI could integrate a CSS library (like Tailwind or Bootstrap) or just add custom styles to make it look nicer:

Validate the form so you can't add an expense without a name and amount.

The AI might add simple frontend validation.

Each of these prompts modifies the prototype. Because the AI understands the context (tools like Cursor and ongoing chat tools will keep the code state), it can often apply changes in the right places—for example, inserting validation code in the form or rewriting the table rendering to include sortable columns.

Step 4: Rinse and repeat

After each refinement, you check the result. If the AI introduced a new issue or didn't do exactly what you intended, you clarify or fix it via prompts:

- The sorting is backward—please sort ascending by default.
- The new color scheme is good, but make the header dark blue instead of black.

Each iteration cycle is quite fast—often taking just a few seconds of processing—which means you can go through a dozen iterations within an hour. Compared to manually coding and checking all those changes, the AI approach can be significantly faster. That's especially true for broad changes, like restyling or adding a feature.

Importantly, iterating with AI requires clear communication. This is where your *prompt engineering* skills come into play. The more explicit and clear you are about the change you want, the more likely the AI will do it correctly. For example, saying "Make it look nicer" is vague. A more specific prompt gives the assistant a concrete direction:

Apply a light theme with a blue header and increase the font sizes for readability.

If you're using a tool like Vercel v0 or Lovable, you might even point to a part of the UI using its interface and say, "Change this to X."

Let's look at a short conversational iteration process between a developer and an AI coding assistant:

Generate a React component for a to-do list. It should display a list of tasks and a text input to add a new task.

The AI produces a React component with state for tasks and renders a list, an input, and a button to add tasks:

> Great. Now make each task editable and add a checkbox to mark it complete.

The AI updates the code, rendering each task with a checkbox and an edit function and modifying state accordingly. The developer runs the app and finds that editing works, but there's no delete button:

> Add a delete button for each task.

The AI adds a delete feature in the code:

> The layout is a bit cramped. Add some basic CSS to space out the list items and make the font a bit larger.

The AI outputs CSS styling, possibly as a `<style>` in the component or a separate CSS snippet:

> Looks better!

This kind of back-and-forth could continue until the prototype meets the vision. In the end, the developer gets a working prototype for a to-do list app, with create, edit, complete, and delete functionalities—all built via natural-language requests and quick AI code outputs.

Throughout this process, remember that the developer remains the director of what happens. The AI might propose a way to implement a feature, but *you* decide if that fits your needs. Sometimes the AI's implementation is correct but not what you expected (maybe it uses a different UI approach than what you had in mind). You can either accept it (if it doesn't harm the prototype goals) or instruct the AI to change to your preferred approach.

Evolving a Prototype Toward Production

A prototype is meant to be a proof of concept and a tool for learning what works. Once it has served that purpose—say, you've validated the design with users or proven that a certain feature is feasible—the next step is often to turn it into a production application. This transition is a critical juncture. AI can still help, but human developers must sand down the rough edges of the prototype. This section looks at some key considerations when moving from prototype to production code.

First, review the architecture and code structure carefully. Prototypes can be messy under the hood. Perhaps all your code ended up in one file or you bypassed certain best practices for speed. Now is the time to introduce a proper structure. For example, if the prototype was a single-page script, you might separate it into multiple modules; for a web UI, you might introduce a proper component structure; for a backend, you might set up a formal model–view–controller (MVC) architectural pattern.

While AI wrote much of the prototype, you, as the developer, understand the architecture goals best. You might even start a fresh project and use the prototype as a reference or as scaffolding, perhaps reusing some of the prototype code but generally treating it as throwaway code. Others might incrementally refactor the prototype codebase into shape, with AI suggesting refactorings or generating tests to ensure nothing breaks during cleanup.

Next, add error handling and edge cases. Prototype code often focuses on the sunny-day scenario, but what if the API call fails? What if the input is empty? Go through each feature systematically and consider potential failure modes.

AI can help you brainstorm edge cases, given a prompt like this:

> What are potential error cases for this feature and how to handle them?

The assistant will likely list some scenarios (network errors, bad input, concurrency issues) for which you can implement handling (or ask AI to help implement it). Ensuring your code's robustness is part of making it production-ready.

Your prototype code probably isn't optimized, so check for any parts that are inefficient or could pose security issues. For instance, maybe the AI in the prototype used a naive algorithm that works on small test datasets but would be slow with real data. Identify such spots and optimize them. (I'll cover common AI-generated code flaws in Chapter 8.)

One strategy is to run performance tests or use profilers on the prototype to see bottlenecks, then ask AI to help optimize that function. Definitely review security features like authentication and data handling too—it's not uncommon for AI prototypes to use SQL queries without proper parameterization (risking SQL injection attacks) or to include sensitive information (*https://oreil.ly/gzUjn*). These problems *must* be fixed. A 2021 study (*https://oreil.ly/a72lb*) found that about *40% of AI-generated code had potential vulnerabilities*. So part of productionizing is staying vigilant. Run static analysis and/or security tests on the code manually, or prompt the AI to "scan this code for security issues."

Prototypes often lack documentation, which you'll need to add as you formalize the code: a clear, human-reviewed explanation of each module will help future team members, as well as you, when you revisit the code months later. Once you've cleaned up your code, you might prompt an AI tool to produce a Markdown API document or README based on the code that describes how the system works. Chapter 1 discussed how AI can produce explanations of code; this is a great moment to leverage that.

It's crucial to test your prototype thoroughly, as you learned in Chapter 5. You might write unit tests for core logic, integration tests for major flows, etc. You can accelerate this by asking the AI to generate test cases:

> Write Jest tests for the to-do list component covering adding, editing, completing, deleting tasks.

Then run and adjust the tests it generates. Having a good test suite gives you confidence as you refactor the prototype code.

Sometimes you might decide to replace certain sections of your code entirely—such as if the prototype used some quick-and-dirty library or a hack that isn't suitable in the long term. AI can speed this up as well. Suppose your prototype code uses local arrays for data, but now you need a proper database integration. Your prompt might be something like this:

> Integrate an SQLite database for storing the tasks instead of an in-memory array.

The AI can provide a starting point for this integration, which you should then refine.

In making these changes, it's wise to switch your mindset from "rapid prototyping mode" to a more disciplined engineering approach. The AI is now your assistant in improving code quality—it's no longer just spitting out quick features. The dynamic is a bit different: you might evaluate each AI suggestion more critically now that stability and quality are your top priorities. As I mentioned back in Chapter 4, *senior developers can derive enormous benefit from AI* because they know what to accept and what to fix. At this stage, you'll be exercising that senior mindset heavily: you have a vision of the final system, so you task the AI with specific improvements or implementations.

To ground this discussion, let's consider a brief example. Imagine a solo developer, Jane, who wants to build a small web app that converts data from CSV files into charts. She uses an AI assistant to get a quick prototype done in just one weekend: a basic Node.js script with an API, plus a simple frontend to upload CSVs and render charts using a JavaScript chart library.

She demonstrates this prototype to a few potential users and gets positive feedback, so Jane decides to turn it into a real product (a web service). Here's how she navigates the transition:

Hardening the backend

The prototype's Node.js API had no authentication (anyone could upload data). For production, she needs user accounts and auth. She uses the AI to integrate an authentication system (maybe JWT-based). The AI provides a scaffold, but she carefully reviews it to ensure passwords are hashed properly and tokens are secure. She also adds input validation to the upload endpoint (the AI had not done that), using a combination of AI-suggested code and her own tweaks.

Refactoring the frontend

The initial frontend was a single HTML file with script tags pointing at a CDN for dependencies. Jane decides to refactor into a structured React app for maintainability. She first asks the AI to refactor her project to be more production-ready by using a build system and npm rather than script tags. She then asks the AI to help integrate them as React components. For example, it turns the chart-rendering code from the prototype into a `<Chart>` component. Jane uses the AI to expedite writing these components, but she ensures that the state management and component hierarchy follow best practices (something the prototype didn't consider deeply).

Testing and checking performance

Jane writes unit tests for critical functions (CSV parsing, data transformation). When she's unsure about edge cases, she queries the AI:

> What edge cases should I test for CSV parsing?

It suggests scenarios like empty fields and irregular columns, which she incorporates into her tests. She also notices that the prototype loaded entire CSV files into memory; for large files, this could crash. She modifies the code to stream the processing and uses AI to double-check her stream logic. Now the app can handle bigger files more reliably.

Polishing the UI

The prototype UI was utilitarian. For her product, Jane spends a bit more time on user experience. She asks the AI to recommend a responsive layout and perhaps integrate a CSS framework. The AI adds Bootstrap, which she then uses to improve the look (forms, buttons, layout). She manually fine-tunes some CSS afterward. This polishing stage is less about heavy coding and more about design choices, but AI still helps by providing quick code for standard UI patterns (like a navigation bar and a loading spinner).

After these efforts, the once-rough prototype is a far cleaner, more secure, and more scalable application ready for real users. Jane deploys it, feeling confident because she added tests and reviewed the AI-generated code. This process from prototype to production might have taken her a couple of weeks, whereas writing the entire product from scratch would have taken much longer. The AI accelerated the initial prototype and continued to assist in the transition, but Jane's human oversight and restructuring were indispensable in reaching production quality.

Addressing Challenges in AI Prototyping

While AI-driven prototyping is powerful, it's not without challenges. As a developer, you should be aware of these and know how to mitigate them. Two areas of particular interest are scope creep and integration.

Because it's so easy to add features with AI, you might be tempted to keep going and going, adding "one more thing" to the prototype, a phenomenon known as *scope creep*. This can lead to an ever-growing prototype that tries to be the final product. Remember the purpose of a prototype: to focus on the key question you want to answer or the core experience to demonstrate. If you find yourself implementing login systems, payment processing, etc., ask if that's really needed at the prototype stage. It might be better to stub those out (the AI can generate a fake login flow that isn't real, just to simulate it). Keeping the prototype focused will save you time and make it easier to throw away or rework later.

Stay Focused

Write down the goal of your prototype ("Demonstrate that users can upload a CSV and get a chart to test viability"), and use that as a North Star. Use the AI to get to that goal quickly, and resist the allure of gold-plating the prototype.

Second, there's the question of integration to real systems. Prototypes often use mock data or simplified subsystems. If your AI prototype uses dummy data or a local file, integrating it with real databases or services in production can be nontrivial. Be mindful when prototyping that some shortcuts were taken. For example, maybe the prototype emails weren't actually sent but just logged to console. In production, you'll need a real email service. The AI can help integrate those later, but it's good to keep track: maintain a list of "things to address if we move forward" while prototyping. That way you won't forget which parts were temporary. If working in a team, communicate these clearly. For instance, you might leave a comment in code: `// TODO: integrate real email service here`. Many AI tools actually include such TODO comments themselves when they generate a simplified solution, which is helpful.

By anticipating these challenges, you can use AI prototyping effectively without falling into its traps. When it is used thoughtfully, the result is a robust prototype developed in record time, ready to either be transformed into a final product or set aside after extracting the lessons it offered.

Summary and Next Steps

In this chapter, you saw how AI-assisted vibe coding turbocharges the prototyping process. By letting AI handle the heavy lifting of code generation, developers can move from concept to working model with unprecedented speed. I covered tools like Vercel v0 for UI generation, Lovable for full stack prototypes, and AI-augmented IDEs like Cursor and Windsurf—each enabling different aspects of rapid prototyping. I also emphasized the iterative nature of AI prototyping: generating, testing, and refining in quick cycles, with natural-language prompts guiding the changes.

While AI-driven prototyping can produce a functional demo in hours, we also discussed the critical transition to production. The message is clear: a prototype is not a final product. It's the first draft. Human developers must refactor and harden the code, with AI continuing to assist in that journey (suggesting improvements, generating tests, etc.). Case studies of individuals and teams using these techniques highlight the real productivity gains—prototypes built in days instead of weeks, enabling faster user feedback and business decisions.

By now, you should appreciate how vibe coding makes prototyping feel more like brainstorming with an assistant rather than grinding out boilerplate. It's a fundamentally different vibe: more conversational, more high-level, and a lot faster. However, you've also seen the importance of maintaining code quality awareness even in a quick prototype—and definitely when evolving it beyond the prototype stage.

In Chapter 7, I'll shift focus from rapid prototyping to comprehensive web application development with AI assistance. While prototyping explores possibilities, full-scale development demands systematic approaches to architecture, implementation, and deployment.

Building Web Applications with AI

This chapter shifts the focus from prompting quick prototypes to developing complete web applications using AI assistance. Web apps typically involve a frontend (often written in frameworks like React, Angular, or Vue), a backend (APIs, databases, servers), and glue to connect everything. Vibe coding can accelerate each of these layers.

I'll walk you through an end-to-end workflow for building a web application with an AI pair programmer, including:

- Setting up the project and its scaffolding
- Coding the frontend UI
- Implementing backend logic
- Integrating with a database
- Testing and validating the whole stack

Along the way, I'll highlight AI development patterns for frontends (for example, having AI generate React or Vue components from descriptions) and backends (writing routes, business logic, and database queries through natural-language prompts). I'll also cover how to optimize collaboration between humans and AI in a full stack project, ensuring that each side contributes its strongest work. By the end of this chapter, you should have a clear roadmap for using AI not just for isolated coding tasks but for managing entire web development workflow efficiently and effectively.

Setting Up the Project: Scaffolding with AI

Every web application starts with some *scaffolding*—the initial setup of build tools, file structure, dependencies, etc. AI can automate the creation of a lot of the boilerplate. Modern web frameworks often come with command-line interface (CLI) tools that can generate a base project, but you might still need to configure certain things or integrate additional libraries. An AI assistant can help by either guiding you through these CLI tools or setting up custom project structures on demand.

For example, suppose you want to start a new application project using React for the frontend and Express for the backend. A pre-AI workflow for this task would probably look something like this:

1. Run a CLI tool or Vite to set up the React project.

2. Initialize an Express app (perhaps with `npm init` and installing Express).

3. Set up a proxy for development or configure Cross-Origin Resource Sharing (CORS) (*https://oreil.ly/bgw1V*) so the React frontend can talk to the Express backend.

4. Maybe integrate a database like MongoDB or set up an SQLite file for simple usage.

Using an AI coding environment like Cursor or Cline, you can instead describe your desired setup in one go:

> Set up a new project with a React frontend (using Vite) and an Express backend. The backend should serve a REST API for a to-do list and use an in-memory array to start. Configure the frontend to proxy API requests to the backend in development.

An advanced AI IDE can take this instruction and do the following:

- Create two directories (frontend and backend).

- Run `npm create vite@latest` (if it has shell access) or template out a basic React app.

- Initialize a basic Express server file in the backend, with an endpoint like */api/to-dos* (returning some sample data).

- Include a *package.json* in each directory with relevant scripts (like `start both`).

- Set up communication between frontend and backend by either configuring a proxy in the React development server or providing instructions for implementing CORS headers.

Within a couple of minutes, you'll have the skeleton of a full stack web app. Even if the AI doesn't do everything automatically, it might present you with code and the instructions you need to finalize it (for example, "Add this proxy setting to your React *package.json* file"). This saves a lot of mindless setup time and allows you to focus immediately on features.

If you aren't using an AI IDE, you can still use ChatGPT or another assistant step-by-step as you go; for example:

> I want to create a new React app. What commands should I run?

The AI can guide you through steps or recommend newer alternatives like Vite or Next.js:

> Now set up an Express server with a /api/to-dos route.

It can generate the code for the Express server, which you copy into a file:

> How do I connect my React app to this API during development?

It might suggest either a proxy configuration or tell you how to call the API (including the full URL, if not proxying).

This way, even setting up the basic plumbing becomes a conversation rather than a hunt through documentation. As noted in earlier chapters, *programming by intent* means you tell the AI what outcome you want, and it figures out the steps. Setting up a project is a perfect scenario for that.

At this stage, it's important to assert your architectural decisions. The AI will follow your lead. Humans are essential for architectural and high-level decisions, so decide on the stack and major patterns yourself: Do you want a monorepo or separate repos for front and back? Will you use REST or GraphQL? Which database?

Once you have these in mind, you can instruct the AI accordingly:

> Also set up a basic Prisma schema for the SQLite database.

Or:

> Include a GraphQL server instead of REST.

The AI might not perfectly execute complex setups, but it will get the bulk of the work done, and you can refine from there.

Many experienced developers integrate these steps into project templates or use boilerplate generators, but AI offers a more flexible approach: you can customize on the fly using natural language. This means if your project is slightly unusual (maybe you need three services instead of the usual two tiers, or you want to preconfigure a particular library like Tailwind CSS), just ask the AI to include what you want.

Frontend Development Patterns with AI

Once the scaffolding is ready, developing the frontend of a web app is a major part of the effort. This section explores how you can leverage an AI pair programmer for your frontend code.

Implementing components from descriptions

You can ask the AI to create components by describing their functionality and appearance; for example:

> Create a React component called TodoList that takes a list of to-do items and displays them. Each item should show its title and a checkbox to mark it complete.

The AI should produce the code as a functional component, with props and state as needed:

> Create a Vue component for a login form with inputs for username and password, and emit an event with the form data on submit.

The AI will likely output the `<template>`, `<script>`, and `<style>` sections accordingly. You, as the developer, skip writing boilerplate and directly get the structure you need. It's then easy to tweak if needed. Often the AI will even include basic validation or state handling, if your prompt implies that they're needed.

It's important to ensure consistency at this stage. If you generate multiple components in isolation, you might need to adjust them to work together. For instance, if the Todo List expects items as a certain prop shape, make sure any component that uses Todo List provides that. You can either generate components in one prompt (so the AI is aware of everything) or simply wire them up yourself and ask the AI to fix any mismatches.

Styling and layout

CSS and styling can be tedious. Describe the look you want and let the AI handle the CSS details:

- Style the to-do list component: use a flex column for the list, add some spacing, and change the text color of completed items to gray and crossed out.
- For the login form component, center it on the page and make the input fields larger with rounded borders.

The assistant can output CSS-in-JS, plain CSS, or inline styles, depending on context. If you're using a framework like Tailwind CSS, you could even ask it to output the appropriate classes (though keep in mind that not all models know Tailwind thoroughly).

The point is: you can iterate on design without manually fiddling with CSS values. This keeps your focus at a higher level of abstraction—specifying *what looks good* rather than writing every `margin` and `color`.

Integrating APIs and state management

Web frontends often need to fetch data from backends and manage state with something like Redux, context, or simple component state. AI can help write these integration pieces; for example:

- Add code to fetch the to-do list from /api/to-dos when the `TodoList` component mounts, and store it in state.
- Implement a function in the `TodoList` that, when a checkbox is toggled, sends a `POST` request to *api/to-dos/{id}/complete* and then updates the state accordingly.

The AI can generate the `useEffect` hook in React to do the fetch or the `mounted()` hook in Vue. It can also stub out the HTTP calls (using `fetch` or Axios, etc.). You'll want to confirm that the API endpoints and payloads match what your backend expects (if you've built the backend or have a spec for it).

If you haven't built the backend yet, you might simultaneously be using the AI to create it—we'll get to that soon. But you can work on front and back in parallel with AI assistance, because each can be specified and generated relatively independently, as long as you keep track of the interface between them.

Handling complexity with AI guidance

If your frontend has complex logic, such as dynamic form validation rules, conditional rendering, or intricate user interactions, you can implement these step-by-step with AI. A good practice is to break the problem down:

Add a feature: when the user checks the "complete" box on a to-do, fade out that list item (CSS transition), then remove it from the list after 1 second.

The AI might produce the code to add a CSS class on check and use a timeout to remove the item, including the necessary CSS for fading out:

The form has an optional field for 'notes'. Only show the notes text area if an 'Add notes' checkbox is checked.

The AI can modify the component state and JSX to conditionally render the notes field.

Each of these can be an iterative prompt. Essentially, you describe the UX behavior and AI writes the code. Always test after each addition to ensure it behaves as expected.

Framework-specific tips

Different frameworks have different idioms:

- In React, the AI might use hooks (like `useState`, `useEffect`). Double-check that it's following best practices (for instance, that the dependencies array in `use Effect` is correct).

- In Vue, the AI might output Options API style or Composition API style depending on what it has seen. If you prefer one, you should specify that (for instance, "Use Vue 3 Composition API").

- In Angular, the AI can generate components, but Angular has a steeper learning curve. The AI might be able to produce a template, a TypeScript class, and basic service injection on request, but you'll likely need to do more manual work or use Angular CLI for structure, then ask AI to fill in specific parts (like form validation logic).

Backend/API Development Patterns with AI

Now let's turn to the backend. Using AI to build the server side of a web application follows a similar paradigm: you describe the endpoints, data models, and logic you want, and the AI produces code. Common backend components include route handlers, business logic, database interactions, and validations. AI can help with all of these.

Implementing API endpoints

Suppose you're building a RESTful API for your to-do list app. You might have endpoints like `GET /to-dos`, `POST /to-dos`, `PUT /to-dos/:id`, `DELETE /to-dos/:id`. You can go endpoint by endpoint:

- In the Express app, add a `GET /api/to-dos` route that returns the list of to-dos (just use an array stored in memory for now).

- Add a `POST /api/to-dos` route that accepts a JSON body and adds a new to-do to the list. Return the new to-do with an ID.

The AI will write the Express route handlers accordingly, likely using something like `app.get('/api/to-dos', ...)`. If you've indicated that you're using Express with JSON, it might include the necessary middleware if it's not already present:

```
app.use(express.json())
```

As your backend grows, you can ask the AI to refactor:

> Refactor the Express routes into a separate router module.

It might split the routes out into a separate file, which is a good practice for maintainability.

Database integration

You might use in-memory data for a prototype, but for a more complete application, you'll want a database. Let's say you choose MongoDB or PostgreSQL. You can prompt:

> Integrate MongoDB into the Express app using Mongoose. Create a to-do model with fields: title (string), completed (boolean). Modify the GET/POST routes to use the database instead of an in-memory array.

The AI may output the Mongoose model definition and adjust the route handlers to query the database (like `Todo.find()` for GET and `Todo.create()` for POST). Similarly, for SQL, you could ask it to set up an *object-relational mapping* (ORM) (*https://oreil.ly/AoWDL*) like Prisma or Sequelize. Keep in mind you might need to provide configuration details (like connection strings). The AI might not know your database URI; you'll have to slot that in. But it will handle the generic code.

Business logic and validation

If your backend has specific rules (for example, that users cannot delete a to-do that is marked important or that list titles must be unique), you can encode those via AI:

> Add validation to the `POST /api/to-dos` route: reject if the title is empty or longer than 100 chars, and return 400 status.

The AI will include checks and send proper responses.

> Add logic: when a to-do is marked complete (say via `PUT /api/to-dos/:id`), if all to-dos are complete, log a message 'All done!'

It can insert that logic in the `PUT` handler.

You describe these requirements in plain terms, and the AI modifies the code accordingly. You still need to test that the code does what you expect.

Using frameworks or boilerplates

Many web backends use frameworks beyond raw Express (like NestJS for Node or Django for Python). AI can work with those, too, though you may have to break down more involved tasks:

- For Django (Python), you might prompt:

  > Create a Django model for to-do with fields X, and corresponding views for list and create.

- The AI might output model code and a generic view or DRF (Django REST Framework) serializer/viewset if it knows that context.

- For Ruby on Rails, you can get help generating models and controllers. (At that point, you might just use Rails scaffolding, but the AI could supplement by adding validations or adjusting routes).

AI models demonstrate varying levels of proficiency across different programming languages and technology stacks, largely determined by the prevalence of those technologies in their training data. While models can work with any language they've encountered during training, their effectiveness varies significantly. Popular languages like JavaScript, Python, and Java typically receive stronger support due to their abundant representation in open source repositories, documentation, and educational materials that form part of the training corpus.

Determining a model's proficiency with your chosen stack requires practical evaluation. Start by testing the model with basic tasks in your target language, then progressively increase complexity to gauge its capabilities. Pay attention to whether the model generates idiomatic code that follows language-specific conventions, recognizes common frameworks and libraries without extensive explanation, and suggests appropriate design patterns for that ecosystem. Strong proficiency manifests as contextually appropriate suggestions, while weaker support often results in generic or outdated code patterns.

Many AI providers publish documentation about their models' capabilities, though these rarely include detailed language-specific benchmarks. The most reliable approach involves running small experiments with your actual technology stack. For instance, if you're working with Ruby on Rails, test whether the model understands Rails conventions like ActiveRecord patterns or can generate proper RSpec tests. Similarly, for newer frameworks or less common languages, expect more variable results, and be prepared to provide additional context in your prompts to compensate for potential gaps in the model's training.

Orchestrating multistep operations

Some endpoints might involve multiple steps, like creating an entry in one table and then another, or calling an external API. You can outline the sequence and let the AI draft it:

> When a new user signs up (POST /api/users), create a user record and also send a welcome email via SendGrid API.

The AI can write code to save the user (maybe using an object-relational mapper, or ORM) and then an HTTP request to SendGrid's API with appropriate payload. You'd fill in actual API keys or tweak content, but most of the boilerplate is done:

Implement a transaction: when transferring money (POST /api/transfer), deduct from account A and add to account B, ensure it's atomic (all-or-nothing).

If you're using an ORM or database that supports transactions, the AI might use those features (like an SQL transaction block or an ORM's transaction method). Review such code cautiously for correctness—transaction logic, especially, can be tricky. But the AI might know common pitfalls and include checks. For instance, when prompted to handle a money transfer endpoint, an AI generated the following code structure:

```
async function transferMoney(fromAccountId, toAccountId, amount) {
  const session = await db.startSession();

  try {
    await session.startTransaction();

    // Deduct from source account
    const sourceAccount = await Account.findByIdAndUpdate(
      fromAccountId,
      { $inc: { balance: -amount } },
      { session, new: true }
    );

    if (sourceAccount.balance < 0) {
      throw new Error('Insufficient funds');
    }

    // Add to destination account
    await Account.findByIdAndUpdate(
      toAccountId,
      { $inc: { balance: amount } },
      { session }
    );

    await session.commitTransaction();
    return { success: true };
  } catch (error) {
    await session.abortTransaction();
    throw error;
  } finally {
    session.endSession();
  }
}
```

The AI correctly wrapped both database operations in a transaction, included validation for insufficient funds, and properly handled rollback on any error. While you'd still need to review edge cases and add appropriate logging, the fundamental transaction structure demonstrates understanding of atomic operations.

API documentation and testing

When building APIs, you can also have the AI produce documentation. For instance, *"Write a brief documentation for the /api/to-dos endpoints."* It may generate something like this:

```
GET /api/to-dos - returns list of to-dos.
POST /api/to-dos - create a new to-do. Expects JSON: {title: string}. Returns
the created to-do.
...
```

This is handy for quick reference and also to share with frontend developers (if you're working in a team). Additionally, you can use AI to write tests for your API endpoints, using a testing framework like Jest or Mocha for Node, or PyTest for a Python API. With a prompt like "Generate tests for the to-dos API (one test for listing, one for creating, one for validation error)," the AI will output test code that you can run and verify.

Database Design and Integration

Human knowledge of the business domain is crucial in designing a database schema, but AI can assist in translating that design into code (like migration scripts or ORM models). Also, if you're unsure about your schema, you can brainstorm with the AI.

For example, say your app is expanding beyond to-do lists to become a full project-management tool. You need to design several tables: Projects, Tasks, Users, and so on. You could ask, "What data models would I need for a simple project management app with users, projects, and tasks? Include relationships." The AI might respond with something like this:

- User (id, name, email, etc.)
- Project (id, name, owner_id referencing User)
- Task (id, description, project_id, assigned_to (User), status, etc.)

It might not be exactly what you want, but it gives you a starting point. You confirm or tweak these design ideas, then implement them.

Using an ORM

If you use an ORM like Prisma, Entity Framework, or SQLAlchemy, you can have the AI generate model classes or schema definitions:

> Using Sequelize (for Node), define models for User, Project, Task with associations: One User has many Projects, Project belongs to User; Project has many Tasks, Task belongs to Project; Task can be assigned to a User (many-to-one).

The AI would then write JS/TS code to define those Sequelize models and associations, which you can then integrate into your codebase. It might also suggest foreign keys or cascade rules if it's familiar with them.

If you aren't using an ORM and you're writing raw SQL migrations, you could even have the AI draft migration scripts:

> Write an SQL script to create tables for users, projects, tasks with appropriate foreign keys.

It will output an SQL DDL script, which you can review for correctness and run.

Database Queries

When integrating the database in your code, you might need queries more complex than simple CRUD. Suppose you want to get all projects, along with their tasks and the user assigned to each task—that's a join across Project, Task, User. You could prompt:

> Write an SQL query to retrieve projects with their tasks and each task's assigned user name.

The AI could produce an SQL join query for you.

Or if you're using an ORM:

> Using Sequelize, fetch all projects with associated tasks and the user for each task.

You could expect the code to come with something to load related data, like:

```
include: [Task, { model: User, as: 'assignedUser' }]
```

Checking AI-Generated Queries

Database operations require careful verification to ensure the AI-generated code aligns with your actual schema and maintains data integrity. The AI cannot automatically know your specific table names, field names, or relationships unless you provide this information explicitly in your prompt. Even when models have conversation memory, you should include schema details in each complex database-related prompt to ensure accuracy. This explicit approach prevents the common issue of AI-generated queries that reference generic field names like user_id when your schema actually uses userId or customer_ref.

Performance considerations often require human oversight. While AI models understand basic database concepts like primary keys and joins, they may not automatically suggest performance optimizations such as adding indexes on frequently queried fields or considering query execution plans. Review generated queries for efficiency, particularly for operations that will run frequently or against large datasets.

Data consistency rules represent another critical area requiring explicit specification. When implementing delete operations, clearly define the cascading behavior you expect. For example, when deleting a `Project` record, you must decide whether the database should automatically delete associated `Task` records through cascading deletes or whether your application logic should handle this cleanup. Communicate these business rules clearly to the AI:

> When a project is deleted, configure the database to cascade delete all related tasks.

Or alternatively:

> When deleting a project, first check for existing tasks and prevent deletion if any exist.

The AI can implement either approach effectively when given clear direction. For cascade deletes, it might generate foreign key constraints with `ON DELETE CASCADE`. For application-level handling, it could produce code that queries for related records before permitting deletion. The key lies in explicitly stating your data-integrity requirements rather than assuming the AI will infer the appropriate behavior for your specific domain.

Full Stack Integration: Marrying Frontend and Backend

Now that you've built both your frontend and backend with AI help, the next challenge is integrating them into a seamless web application. This involves making sure that the API endpoints are called correctly from the frontend, the data flows properly, and the overall system is coherent.

Aligning Frontend and Backend Contracts

This is crucial: the frontend expects to receive data in a certain shape, so what the backend sends should match that expectation. If you let AI work on each end in isolation, small mismatches can occur (maybe the backend returns { `success: true,` `data: [...]` }, but the frontend expects to receive the array directly). To avoid this, you can explicitly instruct the AI on the response format to use when coding both sides. Alternately, once both are done, test an end-to-end call: for instance, open the web app and see if the list loads. If it doesn't, check the browser console against the server logs.

I often use the AI to adjust one side to match the other:

- If the backend returns slightly different JSON key names than what the frontend expects and you notice a bug, you can say to the AI (on either side):

> Modify the code to use 'tasks' (plural) instead of 'taskList' (singular) in the JSON.

- If the frontend is sending form data as form-encoded but the backend expects JSON, you can ask the AI to convert that, maybe by using `JSON.stringify` on the frontend or adding `body-parser` on the backend.

Real-Time Collaboration with AI

AI-augmented IDEs that hold the context of the whole project, like Cline or Cursor, can be especially helpful during this integration phase. You could open the frontend and backend files side by side in your IDE-based tool and prompt:

> Ensure that the frontend fetch from /api/to-dos matches the Express route's expected request/response. Fix any discrepancies.

The AI might then harmonize the content (like adding await response.json() in the frontend if it was missing or adjusting the JSON structure).

State management and sync

In a full stack app, consider implementing things like loading states and error handling on the frontend for failed API calls for a professional result. You might use prompts like:

> Add loading indicators: when the React component is fetching tasks, show a 'Loading...' text until data is loaded.

Or:

> Handle errors: if the API call fails (non-200 response), show an error message on the UI.

It will add the `isLoading` state and conditional rendering or implement a try/catch around `fetch` to catch errors and display a message. This kind of polish makes your app *feel* robust.

WebSockets and advanced integrations

If your app requires real-time updates (like using WebSockets or SSE), you might prompt something like this:

> Set up a WebSocket using Socket.io. When a new task is created on the server, broadcast it to all connected clients. Modify the frontend to listen for new tasks and add them to the list in real time.

This is complex, but an AI might generate the server-side Socket.io setup (like adding `io.on('connection', ...)` and emitting an event upon creation of a new task), as well as client-side code to connect and listen for that event. You would need to integrate this carefully, but it's quite astonishing that these descriptions can lead to working real-time code. If it doesn't work perfectly off the bat, iterative prompting and testing can get it there.

Example: full stack flow with AI

To illustrate, let's imagine you're building a simple contact-manager web app:

- You scaffold a React frontend and a Node/Express backend, as you did earlier in the chapter.
- First, for the frontend, prompt for a `ContactList` and a `ContactForm` component. Then prompt to add API calls:

    In ContactList, fetch contacts from */api/contacts* on mount.

    In ContactForm, on submit, send a `POST` to */api/contacts* with the form data, then update the list of contacts on success.

- For the backend, you may want to use an in-memory array or integrate a database first. Then prompt for Express routes `GET /api/contacts` (to return a list) and `POST /api/contacts` (to add a contact to the database or memory).
- Try adding a contact via the UI. If it shows up in the list, great. If not, debug. Maybe the `POST` route didn't return the new contact properly or the form code didn't refresh the list. Identify the gap and prompt the AI to fix it:

    After adding a contact, the backend should return the new contact object in the response, and the frontend should append it to the list without requiring a full reload.

    This might lead the AI to adjust the backend response and frontend state logic to push the new contact (maybe using React state update).

- Implement edit and delete functions similarly, each time letting AI handle the routine parts and focusing your input on *what the feature should do.*

Doing all this manually could easily amount to a week or two of work for a junior dev but could be done in a day or two with an AI codeveloper, given that a lot of template code and wiring is automated.

Optimizing AI-human collaboration in full stack development

When working through an entire stack, it's useful to establish a productive rhythm with your AI assistant. Here are some strategies to optimize your collaboration:

Use the AI for boilerplate; write any custom logic yourself
Identify which parts of the code are mundane and which are the unique core logic. Let the AI generate a CRUD API or a standard component—but if there's a particularly tricky piece of logic, maybe a proprietary algorithm or a specific business rule that is easier to implement directly, do that part manually, then ask the AI to review or test it. Think of it as delegating repetitive tasks to the AI, while you handle the novel ones.

Use AI to tackle your to-do list one item at a time

As you develop, keep track of tasks (like features to add and bugs to fix). Then explain each task to the AI, one by one, and let it propose a solution. For example, let's say you have a note that reads "Implement password hashing on user registration." Try a prompt like this:

> Add password hashing using bcrypt in the `POST /api/register` route before saving the user.

This targeted, systematic approach helps ensure you don't forget anything.

Prompt AI to improve code quality as you go

After achieving functionality, you might prompt, "Refactor this code for better readability" or "Optimize this function." The AI can often make the code cleaner or suggest performance improvements, like an assistant doing a second pass for polish under your supervision. Be sure to verify that any changes still pass your tests.

Use AI for cross-checking

If you're uncertain about your design approach, ask the AI:

> Is using an array to store contacts in memory fine or should I use a database? What are the pros and cons?

While you likely know the answer (use a database for persistence), it's like bouncing ideas off a colleague. Sometimes the AI might mention a consideration you hadn't thought of:

> If there are multiple server instances, an in-memory store won't sync across them.

Use AI to coordinate with your team

If you're working in a team, not everyone may be using the AI directly. In that case, make sure to ask the AI to document what you did. Also, it's good to communicate your approach to the team: "I used an AI to generate these controllers quickly. I've checked them, but keep an eye out for any unconventional patterns." Encourage a code-review culture in which everyone reviews AI-written code just like they would any other code to catch any quirks.

Real-world teams that adopt AI (like those at Snyk (*https://oreil.ly/8Dmn7*)) report that it can boost productivity, but they also stress keeping a human in the loop for validation. In one 2024 survey by GitHub (*https://oreil.ly/oivAx*), 97% of developers reported using AI coding tools at work in some capacity.

Testing and Validation for AI-Generated Web Applications

After building your web app with AI help, test thoroughly to ensure everything works as intended and to catch issues that you or the AI might have introduced. Here's how you can approach testing in this AI-assisted context:

Unit tests

> For backend logic, write unit tests for critical functions (like a function that calculates something or validates input). If the AI wrote the function, writing a test for it can reveal any hidden bugs. You can even have the AI generate these tests, as mentioned. Be cautious, though: AI-generated tests are sometimes trivial or assume an implementation, so you may need to guide it to test edge cases:

>> Write tests for the password strength function, including edge cases like empty password, very long password, password with special chars, etc.

Integration tests

> Test the API endpoints with something like Supertest (for Node) or direct HTTP calls. Check that each endpoint returns the expected results. AI can help you scaffold these:

>> Write integration tests for the /api/to-dos endpoints using Jest and Supertest.

> It might produce tests that start the app, hit the endpoints, and assert on responses.

Frontend tests

> Web UI testing can be done with tools like Jest (for component logic) and Cypress or Playwright for end-to-end UI tests. You can certainly ask AI to generate a Cypress test scenario:

>> Write a Cypress test that loads the app, adds a new to-do via the form, and checks that it appears in the list.

> You'll get a test script, which you can run. This is quite powerful—you quickly get end-to-end test coverage by leveraging the AI to script user interactions.

Manual tests

> Whatever automated tests you run, always do some manual exploratory testing, too. Click around the web app yourself (or have QA do it, if you're working in a team). The AI might not anticipate every real-world scenario: for example, maybe using the browser Back button breaks some state, or a particular sequence of actions causes a glitch. As you find bugs, fix them or ask the AI to help fix them. Manual testing is also important for UI/UX judgment—does the app feel good to use? Are there any awkward flows? The AI won't know how to judge these subjective UX issues, so human feedback is key.

Code review

If you're working with others, have them review the AI-generated code. Fresh eyes can catch things you might have glossed over—they might spot a security oversight or simply suggest a more idiomatic way to write something. Teams using AI often maintain normal code-review processes, just with more focus (*https://oreil.ly/O5Dbj*) on reviewing for subtle bugs or security issues that an AI might inadvertently introduce.

Security audit

Chapter 8 will dive into security, but even at development time, it's worth scanning your code for known vulnerability patterns. There are automated tools you can run, like linters and Static Application Security Testing (*https://oreil.ly/T531z*) (SAST) tools, or you can prompt the AI:

> Review the Express app code and list any potential security vulnerabilities or best practice violations.

The AI might flag some surprising things, like "You are not sanitizing user input here" or "You should set up CORS properly." Use that as a checklist for hardening the app.

One interesting effect of using AI is that you may write tests you wouldn't have otherwise, because the AI makes it so easy to create them. This can actually lead to *more* robust code in the end. If you adopt a practice of generating tests immediately after generating features (essentially AI-assisted test-driven development, or at least post hoc tests), you ensure that the rapid development doesn't compromise quality. Think of it like this: since the AI saved you time writing code, invest some of that saved time into writing and running tests.

AI can suggest insecure code if the user isn't careful. For example, earlier AI versions might generate SQL queries that are vulnerable to injection attacks if not specifically prompted to avoid that. By testing and reviewing, you catch these issues. One study (*https://oreil.ly/U3b8H*) found that developers using AI assistance tended to be overconfident in their code's security, even when it was worse than it would've been if written manually.

Never skip validation just because an AI wrote the code. Assume it can have bugs, just like any human-written code.

Examples of Successful AI-Built Web Projects

Let's highlight a couple of examples (composites drawn from various reports) where AI assistance played a significant role in delivering real web applications.

Ecommerce site by a solo developer

A solo developer wanted to create a small ecommerce web app to sell custom T-shirts but had limited time. He used GPT, through an IDE extension, to build the entire stack. He prompted the AI to generate a React frontend with product listings, a cart, and checkout pages, as well as a Node.js backend with endpoints for products and orders. He used Stripe for payments, integrating it by asking the AI to help with Stripe's API. After working on it in the evenings for two weeks, he had a functioning site.

This developer reported that AI had done probably 70% of the coding, especially the repetitive UI parts and form handling, while he focused on configuring Stripe correctly and fine-tuning the UI for branding. In the end, customers could browse products, add them to the cart, and purchase them—all in a system built largely via vibe coding. It also highlights that external service integration (like Stripe) is feasible with AI guidance, as long as documentation is available for the model to draw from or you provide it.

Internal company dashboard

A product manager with some coding skills used an AI pair programmer to create an internal analytics dashboard for her team. Normally, she would have had to wait for engineering resources, but using a tool like Replit's Ghostwriter or GitHub Copilot in a web project, she managed to build a basic web app herself. The AI helped with setting up a simple Flask backend to query their database (with safe read-only credentials) and a Vue.js frontend to display graphs (using a charting library). She described what each chart should show ("total sign-ups over time," "active users by region"), and the AI wrote the SQL queries and chart code.

The whole process took a couple of weeks of tinkering and testing, but eventually she delivered a working dashboard. The code quality wasn't enterprise grade, but since it was internal, it was fine. More importantly, she empowered her team with a tool in a fraction of the time. This example illustrates how AI tools can enable nonspecialist programmers to produce useful web apps, unblocking tasks that might otherwise sit in a backlog. It's an example of the "unbundling of the programmer" that I'll discuss in Chapter 10, which is all about how individuals can create personal or team-specific software more easily now.

Startup minimum viable product (MVP)

A small startup (just two cofounders: one business, one technical) needed an MVP web application to show to investors. The technical cofounder used vibe coding extensively to build an MVP in record time. Using an AI assistant, he scaffolded a modern web app using Next.js for the SSR React frontend and a simple Node API. He leveraged AI to implement features like social login (the AI wrote the OAuth flows), image uploads (the AI integrated with a cloud-storage API), and an AI-based feature within the product itself. They even used the AI to help integrate an NLP model from an API. In a few months, one developer achieved what might normally take a small team four to six months. The result was a somewhat hacky but functioning product that they could demo, and they could even onboard beta users onto the platform.

When the cofounders later hired more devs to polish the product, the new devs found the AI-written code to be mostly understandable, though they did refactor significant portions for scalability. This underlines that AI can get you to the first stage quickly, but you might need to invest in quality as you move to the next stages.

These stories, while anecdotal, align with emerging patterns in the industry. In web development specifically, which often involves wiring many components together, the productivity boost is very tangible. Microsoft (*https://oreil.ly/QLunu*) and others (*https://oreil.ly/BNVrB*) reported studies finding that developers with AI could complete tasks significantly faster than those without.

However, there have also been cautionary tales. For instance, a developer might deploy an AI-generated web app with a security flaw because they don't fully understand the code. This risk reinforces why testing and review are crucial.

In conclusion, building web applications with AI assistance is becoming a mainstream approach. It doesn't remove the need for skilled developers; rather, it augments them. The developers still plan the architecture, ensure correctness, and handle the complex or novel aspects of the code, while the AI handles the repetitive boilerplate code that glues everything together. The end-to-end workflow we walked through—from scaffolding to frontend to backend to testing—demonstrates that practically every step of web development can be accelerated with AI, as long as you apply your human judgment and expertise along the way.

Summary and Next Steps

In this chapter, you've seen how vibe coding extends to full-scale web application development. By treating the AI as an always available pair programmer, you can tackle frontend and backend tasks in parallel, generate components and APIs from natural descriptions, and iteratively refine a prototype application to production quality. The keys to success include clearly communicating your intent (so the AI knows what you want at each step), carefully verifying (to catch issues in the AI output), and leveraging the AI not just to generate code but for things like brainstorming schema designs and writing tests.

This chapter also explored how a developer can effectively be a full stack engineer, augmented by AI bridging gaps in their knowledge by suggesting code in areas they are less familiar with. This greatly reduces development time for common features and democratizes development in some ways, enabling people to create custom web solutions without large teams (a theme I'll revisit in Chapter 10).

AI doesn't replace understanding the requirements or ensuring quality; it accelerates execution.

Now that your web application is up and running, the next concern is making sure it is secure, reliable, and maintainable. Chapter 8 dives into the challenges of security and reliability in AI-generated codebases, identifying common vulnerabilities that might slip in, how to audit for and fix them, and best practices (like the ones we've started applying here with tests and reviews) to ensure that moving fast with AI doesn't break things. Essentially, we'll shift from building to hardening—making sure your vibe-coded software stands up to real-world conditions and threats.

PART III

Trust and Autonomy

Security, Maintainability, and Reliability

This chapter confronts a critical aspect of vibe coding and AI-assisted engineering—ensuring that the code you produce with AI assistance is secure, reliable, and maintainable. Speed and productivity mean little if the resulting software is riddled with vulnerabilities or prone to crashing.

First, I'll examine common security pitfalls that arise in AI-generated code, from injection vulnerabilities to secrets leakage. You'll learn techniques for auditing and reviewing AI-written code for such issues, effectively acting as the security safety net for your AI pair programmer.

Next, I'll discuss building effective testing and QA frameworks around AI-generated code to catch bugs and reliability issues early. Performance considerations will also be covered. AI might write correct code, but it's not always the most efficient code, so I'll outline how to identify and optimize performance bottlenecks. I'll also explore strategies to ensure maintainability, such as enforcing consistent styles or refactoring AI code, since AI suggestions can sometimes be inconsistent or overly verbose.

I'll show you how to adapt your code-review practices to an AI-assisted workflow, highlighting what human reviewers should focus on when reviewing code that was partially or wholly machine-generated. Finally, I'll round up best practices for deploying AI-assisted projects with confidence, from continuous integration pipelines to monitoring in production. By the end of this chapter, you'll have a toolkit of approaches to keep your AI-accelerated development safe and robust.

Common Security Vulnerabilities in AI-Generated Code

AI coding assistants, while powerful, can inadvertently introduce security issues if not guided properly. They learn from lots of public code—which includes both good and bad practices—and may regurgitate insecure patterns if the prompt or context doesn't steer them away. It's vital for you to know these common pitfalls so you can spot and fix them. This can include using both manual and automated means to detect potential security issues (see Figure 8-1).

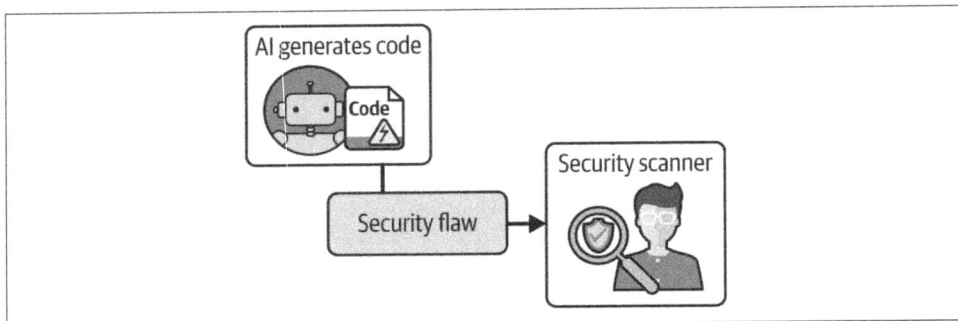

Figure 8-1. AI-introduced security vulnerabilities: AI-generated code may contain subtle security flaws that require careful review and automated security scanning to identify and remediate.

Some typical security issues observed in AI-generated code include:

Hard-coded secrets or credentials
Sometimes AI outputs API keys, passwords, or tokens in code, especially if similar examples were in its training data. For instance, if you ask it to integrate with AWS, it might put a dummy AWS secret key directly in the code. This is dangerous if left in—it could leak sensitive info if the code is shared. Always ensure that secrets are properly managed via environment variables or config files. If an AI suggests something like `api_key = "ABC123SECRET"`, treat it as a flag—real keys should not be in source code.

SQL injection vulnerabilities
If you have your AI model generate SQL queries or ORM usage, check that it's not constructing queries by concatenating user input directly. For example, an insecure pattern would be:

```
sql = "SELECT * FROM users WHERE name = '" + username + "'";
```

This is susceptible to injection attacks. An AI might produce this if you don't specifically tell it to parameterize queries. Always use prepared statements or parameter binding. Many AI assistants will do so if they recall best practices (like using ? or placeholders for user inputs in SQL), but it's not guaranteed. It's on you to verify and ask the AI to fix it if needed:

```
Modify this query to use parameters to prevent SQL injection.
```

Cross-site scripting (XSS) in web apps

When generating web code, AI tools don't always automatically escape user input in outputs. For example, your AI might produce a templating snippet that directly inserts {{comment.text}} into HTML without escaping, which could allow a malicious script placed in a comment to run. If using frameworks, AIs often escape by default, but if they're handling raw HTML construction, be careful. Implement output encoding or sanitization routines. You can prompt the AI:

```
Add sanitization for user inputs to prevent XSS.
```

Many modern frameworks have built-in mechanisms, so ensure that the AI uses them, like `innerText` versus `innerHTML` in Document Object Model (DOM) manipulation (*https://oreil.ly/5o_2x*).

Improper authentication and authorization

AIs can write authentication flows, but subtle mistakes might creep in: for instance, generating a JSON Web Token (JWT) (*https://oreil.ly/rf7JL*) without a sufficiently strong secret or not checking a password hash correctly.

The same is true for authorization: an AI might not automatically enforce that an action (like deleting a resource) is limited to the user who owns that resource. These logic issues are hard to catch automatically—they require thinking through the security model. When writing such code, specify clearly:

```
Ensure that only the owner of the resource can delete it. Add checks for
user ID.
```

Then test those conditions. It's easy for an AI to omit a check because it doesn't truly "understand" the context unless told.

Insecure defaults or configurations

AI might choose convenience over security unless prompted to do otherwise. Examples include:

- Using HTTP instead of HTTPS for API calls (if TLS is not specified)
- Not validating SSL certificates (some code examples on the internet use `verify=false` in requests, which AI might copy)
- Widely enabling CORS for all origins and methods without restriction (potentially opening the app to any cross-origin requests)
- Choosing outdated cryptography (like MD5 or SHA1 for hashes, which are weak, instead of SHA-256/Bcrypt/Argon2 for passwords)

These issues are often subtle, which is one reason it's good to audit your configuration files and initialization code. If the AI sets up something like `app.Use Cors(allowAll)` or chooses an old cipher, you should spot that and correct it.

Error handling revealing sensitive info

AI-generated error handling might print or return stack traces. For example, a Node.js API might catch an error and do `res.send(err.toString())`, which could leak internal details. Ensure that error messages to users are sanitized and logs are properly handled. Adjust as needed to avoid giving attackers clues like full error messages or file paths.

Dependency management and updates

If the AI adds dependencies (such as libraries) to your project, ensure that they're up to date and from reputable sources. An AI might pick a library that was popular in its training data, but that is no longer maintained or has known vulnerabilities. For instance, if it suggests using an older version of a package, you should bump it to the latest stable. Running `npm audit` or equivalent after generation is wise too. Or ask the AI:

> Is this library still maintained and secure?

It might not fully know, but it could tell you if there's a known deprecation.

A 2023 large-scale analysis of GitHub Copilot in real-world projects revealed that as much as 25%–33% of generated code—depending on language—contained potential security weaknesses, including high-severity CWEs such as command injection, code injection, and cross-site scripting (*https://arxiv.org/abs/2310.02059*). These findings underscore that Copilot reflects insecure patterns present in its training data, as opposed to intentionally producing flawed code. The consistent recommendation? Developers must stay alert: manually review AI-generated code, use security-aware tooling, and maintain strict code hygiene. Especially during "vibe coding," the speed and scope of AI-generated content demand even more vigilance. More code in less time means more surface area to audit.

Let's look at a short example.

Improper Authentication and Authorization

Imagine you ask an AI to create a login route in an Express app. It might produce something like this:

```
// Insecure example
app.post('/login', async (req, res) => {
  const { username, password } = req.body;
  const user = await Users.findOne({ username: username });
  if (!user) return res.status(401).send("No such user");
  if (user.password === password) { // plain text password comparison
    res.send("Login successful!");
  } else {
    res.status(401).send("Incorrect password");
  }
});
```

What are the issues here?

- It compares passwords directly, implying that the password is stored in plain text in the database—a big no-no.
- It sends very generic responses, which may be appropriate for security but could also inadvertently expose sensitive information.

Consider authentication error messages as a critical example. A properly secure system should return a generic message like "Invalid credentials" when login fails, regardless of whether the username or password was incorrect. However, AI-generated code might produce more specific errors such as "Username not found" or "Incorrect password for this user."

These specific messages create a security vulnerability by confirming to potential attackers which piece of information they have correct. If an attacker receives "Incorrect password" as an error, they now know they have discovered a valid username in your system. This enables them to build a list of legitimate usernames through repeated attempts, then focus their efforts on cracking passwords for those confirmed accounts. This technique, known as *user enumeration*, transforms a guessing game into a more targeted attack. The AI's tendency toward helpful, specific error messages inadvertently aids malicious actors unless you explicitly instruct it to maintain appropriately vague responses for security-sensitive operations.

While it isn't shown in the code, no rate limiting or other protections are included here.

A secure implementation would incorporate several critical safeguards:

- First and foremost, passwords should never be stored in plain text. Instead, the system should store cryptographically hashed passwords and use a secure comparison function to verify login attempts.
- This comparison process must employ constant-time algorithms to prevent timing attacks, where attackers analyze response times to deduce information about password correctness. Many security-focused libraries provide these constant-time comparison functions specifically to address this vulnerability.
- Additionally, the authentication system should implement rate limiting or throttling mechanisms to prevent brute-force attacks. Failed login attempts should be logged for security monitoring, allowing administrators to detect and respond to suspicious patterns. These measures work together to create a defense-in-depth approach that protects user credentials even if one security layer is compromised.

You can ask AI to help fix this:

> Improve the login route to use bcrypt to hash and compare passwords, and ensure the password in the database is hashed.

It might then output:

```
const bcrypt = require('bcrypt');

app.post('/login', async (req, res) => {
  const { username, password } = req.body;
  const user = await Users.findOne({ username });
  if (!user) {
    return res.status(401).send("Invalid credentials");
  }
  const match = await bcrypt.compare(password, user.passwordHash);
  if (!match) {
    return res.status(401).send("Invalid credentials");
  }
  res.send("Login successful!");
});
```

This is better: it uses `bcrypt` to compare against a hashed password (assuming the variable `user.passwordHash` stores that). When creating users, you'd also want to make sure to use `bcrypt.hash` to hash their passwords.

With a bit of guidance, the AI can do the right thing, but its initial naive output might well be insecure. This underscores the pattern: *review and refine*.

Package Management Issues

Another common vulnerability category is package management. AI sometimes invents a library or misremembers a name, a problem known as *package hallucination*. Such a package might not exist, but an attacker could, theoretically, publish packages under commonly hallucinated names that contain malicious code. If you install such a package without confirming that it both exists and is the correct package, you could be introducing serious risk. If you're not sure about a particular package, try a quick web search or check npm/PyPI directly.

Additionally, the AI might inadvertently produce code that is identical to a licensed snippet from training data. This is more an intellectual property concern than a security issue, but it warrants careful attention. GitHub Copilot, for instance, includes a duplicate detection feature that can flag when generated code closely matches public repositories, helping developers avoid potential licensing conflicts. Similar tools are emerging to address this specific challenge of AI-generated code provenance. Chapter 9 will delve into licensing and intellectual property considerations in more detail, providing comprehensive guidance on navigating these complex issues.

In summary, the main message remains—and yes, I realize I've emphasized this point throughout the book to the point where you could probably recite it in your sleep—that *AI output requires the same careful review you would apply to a junior developer's code*. The repetition is intentional, because this principle underpins virtually every aspect of safe and effective AI-assisted development. Whether you're prototyping, building backends, or implementing security features, this mental model provides the right balance of trust and verification to make AI a powerful ally rather than a risky shortcut. It can write a lot of code fast, but you need to instill security best practices into it and double-check for vulnerabilities. Novelist Frank Herbert put it this way in an often-quoted (*https://oreil.ly/yr2B_*) line from *God Emperor of Dune* (Putnam, 1981): "They increase the number of things we can do without thinking. Things we do without thinking—there's the real danger."

Using AI can lull you into doing less thinking about routine code, and you should be consciously thinking about how to apply a security-review mindset. It's crucial for catching those "things we can do without thinking."

Security Audits

Given the types of vulnerabilities outlined, how can you effectively audit and secure our AI-generated code? This section looks at several techniques and tools you can employ.

Leverage Automated Security Scanners

Static analysis tools (SASTs) can scan your code for known vulnerability patterns; for example:

- ESLint + security plug-ins (*https://oreil.ly/55ppH*) can detect insecure functions or unsanitized input in JavaScript and Node code.
- Bandit (*https://bandit.readthedocs.io*) for Python can flag uses of assert in production, weak cryptography, hard-coded secrets, and more.
- GitHub CodeQL (*https://github.com/github/codeql*) lets you run queries across your codebase to find SQL injection, XSS, and other common patterns.
- Semgrep (*https://semgrep.dev*) has rules for many languages, including community-maintained ones for JavaScript, Python, Java, Go, and more, and can spot top issues out of the box.

You can integrate these tools into your CI/CD or dev pipelines. Run them on your AI-generated code—it won't catch everything, but it will probably flag the obvious mistakes (e.g., plain-text password checks, unsanitized SQL, insecure crypto). It's a solid safety net.

Use a Separate AI as a Reviewer

Two distinct approaches can leverage AI for security review of generated code, each with unique advantages. The first involves using the same AI model that generated the code, asking it to switch perspectives and audit its own output. After generating code, you can prompt the model with something like this:

> Review this code for security vulnerabilities and explain any issues you find.

This approach often yields surprisingly effective results, as the model can identify common security problems such as plain-text password storage, missing input validation, or potential SQL injection vulnerabilities.

The second approach employs a different AI model as an independent reviewer. For instance, if you generated code using ChatGPT, you might paste that code into Claude or Gemini for security analysis. This cross-model review can surface different perspectives and catch issues the original model might have overlooked, much like how different security tools or human reviewers bring varying expertise and focus areas. Different models may have been trained with different emphases or datasets, potentially catching distinct categories of vulnerabilities.

Both techniques serve as valuable additional layers of security review, complementing but never replacing proper security testing and human expertise. While AI reviewers may occasionally flag false positives or miss subtle vulnerabilities, they excel at catching common security antipatterns quickly. Think of this process as automated pair programming focused specifically on security considerations. The key lies in treating these AI-generated security reviews as another input to your security assessment process rather than as definitive security clearance.

Perform a Human Code Review with a Security Checklist

If you're in a team, have a checklist for reviewing code with an eye to security. AI often produces code that "works" for the expected case but isn't hardened to deal with malicious cases. For AI-generated code, be sure to consider:

- ☐ Authentication flows: Are they solid?
- ☐ Any place data enters the system: Are we validating inputs?
- ☐ Any place data leaves the system: Are we sanitizing outputs? Are we protecting sensitive data?
- ☐ Use of external APIs: Are we handling failures? Are we exposing keys?
- ☐ Database access: Are we using ORMs safely? Are we using parameterized queries?
- ☐ Memory management in low-level code: If AI is writing C/C++ or Rust, are there overflows? Is there any misuse?

Penetration Testing and Fuzzing

Use dynamic approaches. For fuzz testing, feed random or specially crafted inputs into your functions or endpoints to see if they break or do weird things. AI can help generate fuzz cases, or you can use existing fuzz tools (*https://oreil.ly/OoFzT*), such as OSS Fuzz by Google (*https://oreil.ly/FvKSU*).

Running penetration-testing tools like OWASP's ZAP against your AI-made web app can automate scanning for things like XSS and SQL injection vulnerabilities. For example, ZAP might attempt to inject a script and get it reflected, and detect that a certain input isn't sanitized.

If you're building an API, tools like Postman or custom scripts can try sending ill-formed data to see how the system behaves: does it throw a 500 error or handle errors gracefully?

Add Security-Focused Unit Tests

For critical pieces of code, write tests that assert security properties. For instance, you might test that your login rate limiter triggers after X bad attempts, or that certain inputs (like `"<script>alert(1)</script>"`) come out escaped in the response. To test that unauthorized users cannot access a protected resource, simulate both authorized and unauthorized calls and ensure the app behaves correctly.

You can ask the AI to help generate these tests:

> Write tests to ensure an unauthorized user gets 403 on the /deleteUser endpoint.

And then run the tests.

Provide Updates to Compensate for Training Cutoffs

AI models possess a fundamental limitation that directly impacts security: their knowledge freezes at a specific point in time. When a model completes training, it cannot learn about vulnerabilities discovered afterward, security patches released subsequently, or new best practices that emerge. This knowledge cutoff creates a critical gap between what the AI knows and current security standards.

Consider a model trained in 2023 generating code in 2025. During those intervening years, numerous security vulnerabilities have been discovered, patched, and documented. New attack vectors have emerged, frameworks have added security features, and best practices have evolved. The AI, however, remains unaware of these developments unless you explicitly provide updated information within your prompts.

This limitation becomes particularly acute with rapidly evolving security standards and vulnerability databases. The OWASP Top 10 (*https://oreil.ly/US-uh*), for instance, undergoes periodic updates to reflect the changing threat landscape. If you prompt an

AI to "write a secure file upload function," it might implement reasonable protections based on its training data—perhaps including file type validation, size limits, and storage outside the web root. However, it could miss recently discovered attack vectors or fail to implement newly recommended mitigations.

The solution involves actively supplementing the AI's knowledge with current security information. When requesting security-sensitive code, include references to current best practices in your prompts. For example, rather than simply asking for secure code, you might prompt:

> Write a file upload function that addresses the security concerns in the 2025 OWASP Top 10, particularly focusing on injection attacks and server-side request forgery.

This approach grounds the AI's response in current security standards rather than potentially outdated training data.

Similarly, framework-specific security features often emerge after an AI's training cutoff. Express.js applications, for instance, benefit significantly from the Helmet middleware (*https://oreil.ly/WSPar*) for setting security headers. An AI trained before Helmet became standard practice might generate Express applications without this crucial security layer. By explicitly mentioning current security tools and practices in your prompts, you help the AI generate code that aligns with contemporary security standards rather than historical ones.

Optimize Your Logging Practices

Ensure that the code (AI and human) has good logging, especially around critical operations or potential failure points. This helps in debugging issues in production. If an AI wrote a section with minimal logs, consider adding more. For example, if there's an AI-generated catch block that just swallows an error, change it to log the error (and maybe some context) for visibility. Also, sanitize the logs so they contain no sensitive info.

Use Updated Models or Tools with a Security Focus

Some AI coding tools aim to blend code generation with built-in security scanning. Snyk is a prime example: it uses a hybrid approach (*https://oreil.ly/0ZGFv*) combining LLM-generated suggestions with rule-based taint analysis. According to Snyk, when you request code (even from LLM libraries like OpenAI, Anthropic, or Hugging Face), Snyk Code tracks potentially unsafe data flows and flags untrusted inputs before they reach sensitive sinks. In practice, that means if an AI suggests a database query, Snyk ensures it's parameterized, preventing SQL injection—even if you forget to do so yourself. This kind of tool is particularly useful because it works to avoid introducing insecure code through AI-generated suggestions.

Pay Attention to Warnings in Context

If you're using an IDE, often you'll see warnings or squiggly lines to highlight suspicious code. Modern IDEs with IntelliSense can sometimes catch, for instance, a string concatenation of SQL that looks suspicious. Don't ignore those warnings and flags just because the AI writes them—address the issue. The AI doesn't have the benefit of those real-time warnings when generating the code.

Slow Down

After using AI to generate a lot of code quickly, shift gears and *slow down* when it's time for auditing. When you can produce features fast, it's tempting to chase the next one, but schedule time for a thorough review. Think of it as "AI-accelerated development, human-accelerated security." Snyk's best practices (*https://oreil.ly/uUExW*) recommend scanning AI code right in the IDE, and caution against letting AI's speed outpace your security checks. In other words, integrate security scanning into your dev loop, so you can catch vulnerabilities as soon as the code is written.

In summary, when you audit AI-generated code, you'll use many of the same tools you use in traditional development—static analysis, dynamic testing, code review—but you might apply them more frequently, because code is produced more quickly. *Treat every AI output as needing inspection.*

Building Effective Testing Frameworks for AI-Generated Systems

While security forms one pillar of reliability, the broader concept encompasses the fundamental dependability of your software system. *Reliability*, in software architecture terms, addresses critical questions about system failure and its consequences. Does your system need to be fail-safe? Is it mission critical in ways that could affect human lives or safety? If the system fails, will it result in significant financial losses for your organization? These considerations determine the rigor required in your development and testing practices.

When you're building with AI assistance, these reliability stakes remain unchanged. A banking application generated with AI assistance carries the same requirements for transaction accuracy and data integrity as one written entirely by humans. A healthcare system must meet identical standards for patient safety regardless of how its code originated. The AI's involvement in code generation does not diminish these fundamental reliability requirements.

This reality underscores why comprehensive testing becomes even more critical in AI-assisted development. A strong testing framework ensures that your code performs its intended functions correctly and maintains that correctness as the project evolves. While testing AI-generated code follows the same fundamental principles as testing human-written code, certain nuances and opportunities emerge from the AI development process that warrant specific attention.

The following sections explore how to leverage AI not just in generating code but in creating robust test suites that validate reliability, maintain system stability, and provide confidence that your software will perform correctly when the stakes are highest.

First, embrace automated testing early and often. It's easy to skip writing tests when development is slow because you want to push features. Ironically, when development is *fast* (with AI), it's *also* easy to skip tests, because new features keep coming at you. But when code is churned out rapidly, that's precisely when you most need tests to catch regression or integration issues. So after implementing a feature with AI help, get into the habit of immediately writing tests for it (or even using AI to write those tests). This verifies the feature and also guards it as you change things later.

A 2022 study (*https://oreil.ly/Vc8Gd*) found that developers who were using an AI assistant were *more confident* in the security of the code they wrote even when it was objectively less secure than code written by those without AI assistance. You need to counteract that overconfidence with actual tests.

As I noted in Chapter 4, you can use the AI not just to generate the code but also to produce a suite of tests. This way, AI helps double-check itself. It's like having it do both the implementation and an initial pass at validation. For example, after writing a new module, you could ask:

> Write unit tests for this module, covering edge cases.

If they pass, great. If they fail, either there's a bug or the tests expected something else. Investigate and fix either code or test as appropriate.

Be cautious that the AI may assume some output or behavior incorrectly; treat its tests, like its code, as suggestions, not the ground truth. You might need to adjust the test's expectations to match the intended behavior—but even that process is valuable, because it forces you to define the intended behavior clearly.

Incorporate your test suite into a CI pipeline that runs on every commit. This way, whenever AI-generated code is added or changed, all tests run automatically. If something breaks, you'll catch it early. Sometimes AI might introduce subtle breaking changes (like changing a function signature or output format slightly), and a robust test suite will detect that. Include security scans in the CI too (like `npm audit` or static analysis) so that any new introduction of a risky pattern is flagged. Types of tests to try include:

Property-based testing and fuzzing
  Property-based testing (with tools like Hypothesis for Python (*https://oreil.ly/JcYBf*) or fast-check for JavaScript (*https://fast-check.dev*)) is another valuable

technique. Instead of writing individual test cases with specific inputs and expected outputs, you define high-level properties that your code should always satisfy. The framework then generates a wide range of inputs to check whether those properties hold.

Take sorting as an example. Rather than asserting that `sort([3, 1, 2]) === [1, 2, 3]`, you can define properties:

- The output should be in order
- It should contain the same elements as the input

The tool then generates dozens or hundreds of input arrays to test those conditions—and finds edge cases you might not think of manually.

This can be especially useful for AI-generated code. If your AI writes a function to normalize email addresses (such as by lowercasing the domain), a property test might check that the output is *idempotent*—meaning running the function twice gives the same result as running it once. If an edge case violates that invariant, the test framework will generate a counterexample to help you diagnose the bug.

Load and performance testing

AI might write code that's not optimized. It's a good idea to test your system under load. This is reliability in terms of performance. Use tools like JMeter, Locust, or k6 to simulate many requests or heavy data and see if the system holds up. If not, identify the bottlenecks.

For instance, maybe the AI writes a naive $O(n^2)$ algorithm that works fine on 100 items but will tank at 10,000. Without performance tests, you might not notice that until it's in production. So incorporate some performance scenarios, if applicable. Time some critical operations with increasing input sizes, or use profiling tools to see where CPU time or memory goes for heavy tasks.

Error handling

Intentionally cause errors to ensure the system responds gracefully, such as:

- For an API, shut down the database and see if the API returns a friendly error or crashes. If it crashes, add code (or ask AI to add code) to handle DB connection errors.

- For the frontend, simulate the backend returning 500 errors and ensure the UI shows an error message, not a blank page or infinite spinner.

AI might not think of these failure modes on its own when writing code, so you have to test them and then refine. Testing these scenarios will improve reliability by prompting you to add proper fallback logic, retries, or user feedback.

Monitoring and logging

Incorporate logging and perhaps use the logs in tests for verification. For instance, if a certain action should trigger an audit log entry, test for that. AI can generate log lines; verify they print out as expected.

Also, think about setting up monitoring (like an in-memory simulation of how your service will be monitored in production). For example, you might track if any uncaught exceptions are logged during test runs. If yes, treat it as a test failure; that means there's some case not properly handled.

Maintainability

Maintainability testing, like ensuring code style and standards, is important. Use linters and formatters to keep code consistent, since AI can produce slightly different styles from different prompts. A formatting tool like Prettier (*https://prettier.io*) or Black (for Python) (*https://pypi.org/project/black*) can unify style. For more logical consistency and to catch overly complex AI-generated code that might need refactoring, consider adding linting rules that enforce things like function complexity limits. (See "Ensuring Maintainability in AI-Accelerated Codebases" on page 160 for more.)

Once your tests are in place, you can refactor AI code more confidently. Perhaps the AI produces a working but clunky solution; you can improve it and rely on tests to ensure you haven't broken its behavior. You might even ask AI to refactor its own code:

> Refactor this function for clarity while keeping it passing the current tests.

If your tests are good, you can check that the refactoring didn't break anything.

Understanding nondeterminism in AI systems requires distinguishing between two fundamentally different scenarios. When AI operates at runtime in production systems, such as a chatbot responding to customer queries or a recommendation engine personalizing content, the outputs can vary even with identical inputs. This variability stems from factors like model temperature settings, random seeds, or evolving model states. Testing such systems requires specialized approaches that account for acceptable variation ranges rather than expecting exact matches.

However, AI-assisted code generation presents a different paradigm entirely. Once an AI generates code and that code is committed to your repository, it becomes as deterministic as any human-written code. The function that calculates tax rates will produce the same output for the same input every time, regardless of whether a human or AI originally wrote it. This determinism is crucial for system reliability and makes traditional testing approaches entirely applicable to AI-generated code.

The more subtle challenge emerges when integrating multiple AI-generated components, each potentially created in isolation with different implicit assumptions. Consider a concrete example from an ecommerce system. You might prompt an AI to generate an order processing module, instructing it to handle international orders. Separately, you ask the AI to create a shipping calculation service for the same system. The order processing module, following American conventions, formats dates as "12/25/2024" for December 25. Meanwhile, the shipping service, perhaps influenced by European examples in its generation, expects dates formatted as "25/12/2024." Both components function perfectly in isolation, passing their individual unit tests.

The mismatch only surfaces during integration testing when the order processor passes a date to the shipping calculator. The shipping service interprets "12/01/2024" as January 12 rather than December 1, potentially calculating shipping times based on the wrong month entirely. This type of assumption mismatch is particularly common with AI-generated components because the AI might draw from different examples or conventions when generating each piece independently. Comprehensive integration testing that exercises the actual data flow between components becomes essential for catching these subtle incompatibilities before they cause production failures.

The QA process for AI-assisted projects might require a bit more creativity, since AI can introduce unusual edge cases. For instance, an AI might output a feature you didn't explicitly consider—if so, test that as well. If it added a hidden behavior, either remove it or properly test it.

Finally, if possible, test your application in an environment similar to production, with a realistic data load. Sometimes performance issues only appear with larger data volumes or higher concurrency. Use those test results to pinpoint inefficiencies.

Performance Optimization

While the AI often writes correct code, it may not always write *optimal* code. LLMs don't inherently do performance analysis; they typically reproduce what is common in their training data. Therefore, be vigilant about potential performance issues, especially in critical paths or for large-scale use.

You can even chat with the AI for hints about performance optimization:

- What is the complexity of this code? Can it be improved?
- This function is slow—any ideas on how to make it faster?

It might not always be right, but it can sometimes give useful suggestions or at least confirm your thinking.

That said, don't overoptimize, and don't optimize prematurely or where it's not needed. Sometimes the AI solution is perfectly fine, if the data sizes are small or the operation infrequent. Use your profiling data to focus on real bottlenecks and optimize the parts that really need it. The advantage of vibe coding is that you haven't spent a ton of time handcrafting code from scratch, so you can afford to let some noncritical parts be simple and not superoptimized, as long as they don't impact user experience or cost. This approach aligns with agile practices: make it work, then make it fast (if needed).

Here are some areas to cover as you ensure your AI-augmented project runs efficiently:

Complexity analysis

When the AI generates an algorithm, take a moment to consider its complexity. Sometimes it will use a brute-force solution where a more efficient algorithm exists. For example, it might double-sort a list because it didn't recall a single-step method, resulting in $O(n \log n \times 2)$ where $O(n \log n)$ could do (the capital O stands for memory usage). Or it might use nested loops that make an operation $O(n^2)$ when there's a known $O(n)$ approach. If you spot something like that, ask for improvements:

> Can we optimize this to avoid nested loops? Perhaps use a set for lookups.

The AI often will oblige and give a better solution if you hint at the approach. If not, you might have to implement that part manually.

To identify slow functions, run a profiler or measure execution time of key code paths with representative or worst-case data. If something is too slow, you can attempt to optimize manually or with AI assistance:

> Optimize this function, which is currently a bottleneck; try to reduce its complexity.

The AI might restructure the code for performance. Use tests to make sure it still works.

For critical algorithms, write a small benchmark harness. If AI gives you a piece of code to, say, compute something, test it against another approach, or at least measure how it scales with input size. You might decide to rewrite in a more efficient way if needed.

Memory usage, leaks, and retention

AI-generated solutions might use more memory than necessary: reading entire files into memory instead of streaming, for example, and thus holding large data structures. If your use case involves big data, check your system's memory usage and optimize by streaming or chunking if needed. For instance, if you need to process millions of records, you'd want to refactor your AI-generated function `loadAllRecords()` to process them in batches or stream from the database.

Also check that the AI-generated code is releasing resources. In languages like Java or C#, maybe it opens a file or DB connection and doesn't close it. In a front-end single-page app, maybe event listeners aren't removed, leading to leaks. Tools can help (like Chrome dev tools' Memory Inspector for frontends or Valgrind for C++ leaks), but often just reading the code helps. Identify these and fix them. If you see an open file handle not closed, add a close in a `finally` block.

Concurrency and parallelism

If you're using languages that support threads or async, look for places where the AI code might be single-threaded when it could be parallel. AI might not automatically use async/await where appropriate, and may not know to offload a heavy CPU task to a worker thread. Identify such opportunities. For example, for I/O-bound tasks in Node or Python, ensure asynchronous usage so that the system doesn't block. For CPU-bound tasks, maybe the AI can't help much in code, but you might decide to implement in a more performant language or offload to a background job.

Caching

A common performance optimization that AI doesn't always automatically add is to cache results of expensive operations. Look at your code: is it recalculating something repeatedly? If so, implement caching (either in-memory or using an external cache like Redis). You can prompt AI:

> Add caching to this function to avoid redundant calculations.

It may implement a simple memorization or suggest using a caching library.

Database query optimization

If your application uses a database, examine the queries the AI creates. Are they using indexes properly? Perhaps the AI wrote `SELECT *` where only a few columns are needed. Or it's fetching extensive data to filter in code, creating performance bottlenecks like the N + 1 query problem. These inefficiencies require optimization by pushing more work to the database or leveraging proper indexing.

For instance, if the generated code calls `findOne` repeatedly within a loop, resulting in multiple database round trips, you can refactor this into a single batch query using `WHERE id IN (...)`. Similarly, if the AI omitted index creation in a migration for frequently queried fields, adding those indexes becomes essential for maintaining acceptable performance. The AI often generates functionally correct but suboptimal database interactions that require human expertise to identify and resolve.

To illustrate, let's take an example. Suppose AI writes you a function that merges two sorted arrays by simply concatenating and sorting the result: (O(n log n))—even though there's a known linear algorithm it could be using to merge two sorted lists (like merge step or merge sort, O(n)). In code review, you realize this could be a bottleneck for large arrays, so you prompt AI to implement the linear merge:

> Optimize the mergeSortedArrays function to perform the merge in linear time without using built-in sort.

The AI recognizes this as the classic merge algorithm and writes it. The solution passes your tests, so congratulations: you gained performance without sacrificing correctness.

AI-assisted development doesn't remove the need for performance tuning; it just shifts *when* you do that tuning. You'll often get a correct solution first (which is extremely valuable), then turn your attention to measuring and optimizing targeted parts. When you do need to optimize something, the AI can help, as long as you guide it on what you need.

Ensuring Maintainability in AI-Accelerated Codebases

A codebase's *maintainability* describes how easy it is to modify, extend, and comprehend over time. Some worry that AI-generated code could be messy or inconsistent, especially if multiple suggestions have varying styles or patterns. This section covers several practices you can use to address these concerns and keep your vibe-coded project clean and maintainable.

While Prompting

As you prepare your prompts, a few things to keep in mind:

Use consistent coding standards
Use linters and formatters to enforce a consistent style. As mentioned, AI might sometimes use different naming conventions or formatting in different outputs. Running a formatter (like Prettier for JS, Black for Python, gofmt for Go, etc.) on all code after generation ensures it conforms to a unified style. This makes reading code much easier (no cognitive load switching styles). Additionally, define naming conventions for your project and stick to them. If the AI outputs get_user_data in one place and fetchUserData in another, decide which convention you prefer (snake_case versus camelCase, etc.) and refactor to one style.

Use architectural patterns to encourage modularity and avoid sprawl
Encourage the AI to write modular code by prompting it to separate concerns. For example, instead of asking it to write one huge file implementing everything, break the work into tasks:

- Create a UserService class for user logic.
- Create a separate module for sending emails.

This leads to a codebase that's logically divided. It's easier to maintain when each module has a clear responsibility. You can guide the architecture:

> Put database access code in a separate file or class from the API routing code.

Because it's so very easy to add features when using AI, it's crucial to guard against feature creep and code sprawl. Without disciplined architectural thinking, you risk your codebase devolving into what software architects call a *big ball of mud*: an antipattern where code lacks clear structure or boundaries. This risk intensifies with AI assistance, as the friction traditionally associated with adding features disappears, potentially accelerating architectural decay.

To combat this, ground your AI-assisted development in proven architectural patterns and principles. When instructing AI, explicitly reference the patterns your project follows:

- Add this new feature following the repository/service pattern used in the project.
- Implement this using the hexagonal architecture established in our domain layer.

This specificity helps maintain consistency even as features accumulate rapidly.

For developers seeking deeper architectural grounding, several foundational texts provide essential guidance:

- *Design Patterns: Elements of Reusable Object-Oriented Software* (Addison-Wesley, 1994) by Erich Gamma, Richard Helm, Ralph Johnson, and John Vlissides (the "Gang of Four") remains the definitive catalog of reusable design solutions.
- *Fundamentals of Software Architecture: An Engineering Approach* by Mark Richards and Neal Ford offers comprehensive coverage of architectural patterns and principles across technology stacks.
- *Domain-Driven Design: Tackling Complexity in the Heart of Software* by Eric Evans (Addison-Wesley, 2003) provides crucial techniques for aligning software design with business domains—particularly valuable when AI generates code that must reflect complex business logic.

These resources equip you to guide AI tools effectively, ensuring generated code adheres to sound architectural principles rather than contributing to technical debt. Remember: AI excels at implementing patterns but cannot determine which patterns are appropriate for your specific context. That architectural judgment remains fundamentally human.

Working with Code Output

Once the AI responds with generated code, maintainability techniques to use include the following:

Refactor continuously
Don't hesitate to refactor AI-generated code when needed. Sometimes the first pass is correct but not ideally structured: for example, the AI might write a very long function or duplicate its logic in two places. A common challenge is unintentionally duplicated code: the AI might not realize two functions do similar things and create both. If you notice similar blocks, refactor to one. Tools like code linters can detect duplicates (there are linters for too-similar code). Running those could highlight places to "DRY out" (don't repeat yourself).

To ask the AI to help refactor, you could prompt:

> Refactor this code to remove duplication and improve clarity.

It might create helper functions or simplify some logic. Always test after refactoring.

Test
This chapter has already covered testing, so I'll just note that a good test suite makes maintenance easier. When you or others modify code in the future (possibly with AI again), your tests will catch if the changes break anything, so you can refactor or change implementations with peace of mind. Testing decouples "what it does" from "how it does it," giving you flexibility to maintain or improve "how" without altering "what."

Avoid excessive complexity or overrelying on AI-specific constructs
Sometimes the AI might use a clever trick or less common function that other developers might not know. While that's not inherently bad, consider maintainability: if an average developer would scratch their head at the code, maybe simplify it. For instance, if AI uses a bit of regex magic or list comprehension that's too terse, rewrite it in a more explicit loop for clarity (or at least comment it).

Similarly, an AI trying to be helpful might overengineer a solution, like adding layers that aren't needed. For instance, maybe a direct approach was fine, but the AI introduced an abstraction that isn't pulling its weight. Remove it to keep things straightforward. Simpler code is usually easier to maintain.

Build in resilience and fallbacks
Think about fallback strategies in case of failures. For example, if an AI-coded component calls an external API and that API is down or returns unexpected data, do we have a fallback (like using cached data or a default response)? Implementing such resilience patterns (circuit breakers, retries with backoff, etc.) can

make the system more robust. The AI likely won't do this on its own unless asked. Ensure the system can handle partial failures gracefully. One microservice going down shouldn't take the whole app down, if possible. Use timeouts and fallback logic.

Follow-Up

Once you're satisfied with the code, a few more practices help to keep it maintainable:

Provide thorough documentation and comments
Make sure the code is properly documented. AI often writes minimal comments unless prompted. You can request docstrings or comments with prompts:

- Add comments to explain the purpose of each section in this code.
- Write a docstring for this function.

These can save future readers time. The AI can usually generate fairly good explanations but sometimes misexplains subtle points, so review for accuracy.

Also consider maintaining a high-level documentation (like a README or design doc) for the project, describing its architecture, main components, and so on. You can largely write this yourself, but AI can help by summarizing the codebase if needed.

If you encounter some quirk like "The AI always names this parameter weirdly," mention it in your dev notes for others. It's part of the new collaborative environment. If it's just you using the AI-generated code, a few quirks are fine—but if others join the project, they might wonder, "Why is this thing named like that?" Perhaps just standardize those names.

There's also an aspect of maintainability in terms of knowing which pieces of code were AI-generated and which were human-written. It's not strictly necessary to label, but some teams might comment, "Generated with the help of GPT-4 on 2025-05-01" for traceability. Ideally, flag anything you're unsure about in your PR description: "Used ChatGPT to help with this function; it seems to work, but please check the error-handling logic carefully."

This isn't a widespread practice. It can be helpful during code review, but you might not need it if a human has already reviewed the code and it's now just code. If you do keep any transcripts or prompts, you could link them in comments for complicated code: "This algorithm derived via GPT-4, based on prompt X; see docs for derivation." A reviewer doesn't need to treat it differently in terms of scrutiny (you should scrutinize all code), but it can help to understand the context. For example, if code has a certain style mismatch or an odd idiom, knowing it came from AI might clue the reviewer in that this isn't a deliberate authorial choice but an AI artifact.

Code reviews and team norms

If you're working in a team, have all team members review code—even if one person and AI cowrote it. They might spot awkward patterns or things that break team norms. Over time, you'll develop a sense of how to prompt the AI to match your team's style (maybe including specifics in system prompts or initial guidelines). If multiple developers use AI, make sure everyone knows the desired style patterns so they can prompt accordingly (like "Write this in functional style" or "Use async/await, not callbacks"). See the next section for some tips on code review with AI code.

Track technical debt

If, during development, you accept an AI solution that you know isn't ideal, track it as technical debt in your comments or the project to-dos: "TODO: The solution works but is $O(n^2)$; if data grows, optimize this," or "TODO: This uses a global variable for simplicity; refine this later." The AI can even insert TODO comments itself if you ask:

> If there are any areas that need future improvement, add to-do comments.

Just address those to-dos eventually.

Learn from AI patterns

If AI introduces a design pattern or library you're not familiar with, take time to learn more about it rather than ignoring it. Understanding a particular caching approach or a library it uses will help you maintain or modify that part confidently in the future. If it's too arcane, you might decide to remove it in favor of something you know—but sometimes AI can pleasantly surprise you with a useful library or pattern you didn't know. If it's a well-known solution that you and the team can learn, this can even improve maintainability.

In practice, maintainability comes down to applying the same good software-engineering principles as always—just applying them to code that was partially written by AI. Fortunately, because AI reduces the grunt work, you may have more time to focus on cleaning up the code and writing docs, which *improves* maintainability.

Some companies report (*https://oreil.ly/2lrTW*) that after an initial burst of generating code with AI, they invest time in a "hardening sprint" to refactor and document it all. Consider alternating between generation-heavy sprints and cleanup sprints as a potential strategy.

Code Review Strategies

As discussed in Chapter 4, code review is a critical process in traditional development and remains so in AI-assisted development. This section discusses some nuances to consider when a chunk of the code under review is machine-suggested. Because AI can produce code so quickly, it's reasonable to worry that code review will become a bottleneck—but don't let that worry hamper the review process. It's crucial to allocate proper time for reviews. Don't skimp on the assumption that "we wrote it fast, let's merge fast." If anything, commit smaller changes more frequently to make reviews easier (generally a good practice anyway). Frequent, smaller pull requests (PRs) are easier to review thoroughly than one giant PR. The AI can help break tasks into smaller PRs as well, if you plan accordingly.

Don't assume code is correct just because "the AI wrote it and the tests pass." Think critically and try to reason through the logic. If possible, test it mentally or with additional cases outside the provided tests, because tests might not cover everything. You can also run the code and even experiment by running a snippet with a tricky input to see if it behaves.

Code reviews can also be important learning moments. If the AI introduces a novel solution that is actually good, the reviewer might learn something new while verifying its correctness. Similarly, if the AI/human combination does something suboptimal, the reviewer can explain a better approach. Over time, this feedback loop can improve how the team uses AI (like helping everyone understand which things to avoid or ask differently). In a sense, code review helps to close the human learning loop, since the human author should learn and understand anything the AI wrote that is new to them.

When you review code, your first priority should be making sure it meets the requirements and intended design. Does this code do what the feature/bugfix is supposed to? Does it cover any edge cases mentioned in the specifications? If the prompt is off, AI might solve a slightly different problem: maybe it handles a case that wasn't needed or misses a case. This is normal, but watch that the developer didn't just accept AI output that only partially addresses the issue. For example, an AI might produce code to format a date but assume a certain time zone, which might or might not align with requirements.

If something in the code isn't obvious, ask the author to explain how it works or why it's done that way. If they struggle to explain or reach for "the AI did it and I assume it's right," that's a red flag. The team should understand everything in the codebase. Encourage the author to double-check with the AI or documentation and provide a proper explanation, possibly as a comment in code.

Pay attention to the security and performance vulnerabilities discussed earlier in this chapter, too, and if any known best practice is violated, call it out—like if output isn't escaped (in web dev) or if you find credentials in the code.

Request changes or refactoring if you see code that works but could be simpler or more in line with team style:

> The AI created 3 separate functions for different user roles that mostly duplicate each other. Can we merge these into one function with a parameter for role?

The code's author can then do so (maybe with AI's help). If the AI suggestion didn't use the team's consistent style or standard libraries, mention that too:

> We usually use the requests library for HTTP calls, but this code is using http.client. Let's stick to requests for consistency.

The author can then prompt the AI to rewrite using the preferred library.

If the AI has written something really complex, like a tricky algorithm, consider discussing it with another reviewer or the team for a deeper review.

You may want to try some of the emerging tools that use AI to assist in code review—like GitHub's Copilot for Pull Requests, which can generate summaries and flag potential bugs and other issues. Such a tool might highlight something like "This code snippet is similar to one in module X with slight differences" (pointing out possible duplication). These hints can complement the human review but should not replace it.

Finally, be respectful and constructive in your reviewing, even when the code has flaws due to AI. Avoid blaming the developer for what could be an AI artifact: while they are still responsible for their code, recognize the context. AI is a tool, and both author and reviewer are working with it. The goal is to improve the code and share knowledge, not point fingers. For example: "This part seems to have a security issue—likely an oversight from the AI suggestion; let's fix it."

Ultimately, code review in vibe coding is how we fully exercise the *human intelligence* side of the human/AI partnership. It's where oversight and expertise come in to catch what the AI might miss and to keep the quality bar high. It's also a knowledge-sharing moment for the team, since discussing code in reviews spreads understanding of both the domain and how to best use AI.

Code review also formalizes the concept of "developers as editors" introduced by Grant Gross in *CIO* (*https://oreil.ly/INPFV*): the reviewer is an editor, making sure the code is polished and fit for production. This aligns perfectly with vibe coding as a concept, where the vibes (AI suggestions) are there but human judgment refines them.

Best Practices for Reliable Deployment

Once you know your code is secure, tested, and maintainable, you need to deploy it and keep it running reliably in production.

While AI-assisted development doesn't alter the core principles of software deployment, it does introduce considerations around deployment velocity and operational complexity. For those seeking comprehensive coverage of deployment fundamentals, *The DevOps Handbook* (IT Revolution Press, 2016), by Gene Kim, Jez Humble, Patrick Debois, John Willis, and Nicole Forsgren, provides the definitive guide, covering everything from continuous integration and deployment pipelines to monitoring, security, and organizational transformation. This foundational knowledge becomes even more critical when AI accelerates your ability to generate deployable code, as the principles ensure your deployment practices can scale with your increased development velocity.

Before and During Deployment

As you ramp up to deployment, consider the following best practices:

Automate your CI/CD pipeline
> Given the fast pace of AI development, a robust continuous integration/continuous deployment (CI/CD) pipeline is valuable. Every commit (with or without AI-generated code) should be built, tested, and potentially deployed through an automated pipeline. This reduces human error and confirms that all deployment steps (tests, lint, security scans) are consistently run. If AI code introduces something that breaks the build or fails the tests, the CI will catch it immediately. Also, an automated CI/CD pipeline allows for quick iteration, so you can patch any AI-introduced issues and deploy fixes rapidly.

Infrastructure as code
> Use infrastructure as code (Terraform, CloudFormation, etc.) to define your deployment environment. While not directly related to AI coding, it's part of reliable deployments. You could even use AI to help write Terraform scripts, but treat those with the same caution and testing as other AI code, including perhaps testing them in a sandbox before applying them to production. A valuable starting point is the book *Terraform: Up & Running* (O'Reilly, 2022), by Yevgeniy Brikman, which provides a comprehensive introduction to the principles and practices of IaC with Terraform.

Use staged rollouts—and have a rollback plan
> Use staged rollout strategies like deploying to a staging environment or a canary release before full production rollout. This way, you can catch anything you've overlooked before it affects all users. For example, you might deploy a new

AI-coded feature to 5% of users and monitor (with metrics and logs) for any errors or performance issues. If all is good, roll it out to 100% of users.

Always have a rollback plan. Despite all tests and reviews, sometimes things slip through. If a new release goes wrong, be ready to revert to the last stable version. If you're using a containerization strategy like Kubernetes, maintain previous deployments for quick switchback. If it's a serverless function, keep the previous version alive until you're confident in the new one.

Set up observability

Set up comprehensive monitoring in production, of both system metrics and application logs:

- Use tools like Sentry to track errors and capture exceptions. If the AI code throws an unexpected error in production (perhaps an edge case wasn't covered), you'll get an alert so you can fix it.

- Use performance-monitoring tools like application performance monitoring (APM) to track response times, throughput, and memory usage. This will show you if any code in the new deployment has introduced a slowdown or memory leak.

- Monitor availability: for instance, ping the service endpoints to confirm they're up. If something crashes (maybe due to some untested scenario), an alert should fire, so you can react quickly.

Stay vigilant about security

Make sure that secrets like API keys are handled properly in deployment. For example, if your AI wrote code that expects a secret in an environment variable, set up that secret in the CI/CD or cloud config, so it's not accidentally logged or exposed. Use secret management tools like HashiCorp Vault (*https://oreil.ly/NqQ-T*) (HashiCorp Vault offers secrets management, key management, and more with many integrations) or AWS Secrets Manager (*https://oreil.ly/LlYX-*) (AWS Secrets Manager allows you to securely store and rotate secrets like database credentials, API keys, and tokens, and can integrate with CI/CD tools like GitHub). Also, if you're using container images, scan them for vulnerabilities.

Test using techniques like blue-green deployments or shadow testing

For major changes, consider a blue-green deploy. This involves setting up two identical production environments: "blue" (the current live version) and "green" (the new version). Traffic is initially directed to the blue environment. Once the green environment is ready and tested, traffic is switched over to it. If any issues arise with the green environment, traffic can be quickly rerouted back to the blue environment, minimizing downtime and risk. This method tests the new version in a full production setting before making it the sole live version.

Alternatively, if a specific AI-coded algorithm change is risky or you want to validate its behavior with real-world data without impacting users, you could shadow test it. This involves deploying the new version alongside the current live version. Real production inputs are fed to both versions in parallel. However, only the current version's outputs are shown to users. The outputs from the new (shadow) version are collected and compared against the current version's results to evaluate its performance, accuracy, and stability. If the shadow version's results are satisfactory and performance is good, you can then confidently switch it to be the active version.

Ongoing Best Practices

After deployment, these strategies can help keep everything running reliably:

Create operational runbooks

Provide runbooks for the ops team that describe any special aspects of the AI-generated parts of the code: "This service uses an AI model for X; if the model output seems erroneous, try restarting service or check the model's version." Or "Feature Y heavily uses caching to perform well; if performance issues arise, check the cache hit rate." Essentially, document any operational considerations that might not be obvious. If AI has introduced a dependency (like using a temp file), note that, so ops will know to monitor disk space and the like.

Test in production

In addition to testing during development and as part of the rollout, some companies do testing in production (TiP) in safe ways, like running continuous small experiments. For instance, you might use feature flags to turn on an AI-generated feature for a small subset of users and see if any error rates change. This overlaps with canary releases, but you can make it more granular using feature toggles.

Audit regularly

Schedule periodic security and performance audits of the codebase, especially as more AI contributions accumulate. This is similar to managing tech debt: it helps you catch things that were fine at first but that could turn problematic as the scale or context changes. Watch for "drift," too—if AI code is generating SQL queries, make sure that your migrations and code stay in sync and that the deployment runs migrations properly before new code takes traffic.

Keep humans in the loop

The theme continues—humans should monitor the automations. AI might help you write code, but it won't fix a production incident at 2 a.m. Have someone on call who understands the system. Over time, you might enlist AI for troubleshooting help like analyzing logs (a feature of some emerging tools), but at the end of the day, a human should make decisions about fixes.

Learn from failures

No process is 100% perfect. If an error gets through your defenses and causes an incident, do a postmortem. Identify if the problem was related to AI usage (like "We trusted the AI code here and it failed under scenario X"), and update your processes and tests to prevent that class of issue. Doing this kind of analysis every time continuously improves reliability.

Reliability isn't just about code, of course; it also involves the infrastructure and operations *around* the code. AI helps mostly on the code side. Robust operational practices (which can be partially assisted by AI) keep the overall system reliable.

In essence, treat an AI-heavy project the same as any high-quality software project when it comes to deployment: employ thorough testing, roll out gradually, monitor heavily, and make sure you can roll back quickly. Because AI can create changes faster, you may end up deploying more frequently (which is fine, if your CI/CD pipeline is good). Frequent small deployments (*https://oreil.ly/ATjYo*) are actually known to reduce risk (*https://oreil.ly/Y5uDn*) compared to infrequent big ones. The reason is that each individual change is smaller, making it easier to identify and fix any issues that arise. If a problem occurs, rolling back a small change is also simpler and faster. This approach contrasts with large, infrequent releases where numerous changes are bundled together, making it difficult to pinpoint the cause of any problems and increasing the potential impact of a failed deployment.

By following these best practices, you can be confident that even though a lot of its code was machine-generated, your system as a whole will behave reliably for users. The combination of automated testing, careful deployment, and monitoring closes the loop to catch anything that slipped through earlier stages. As a result, you can reap the speed and productivity benefits of AI development without sacrificing your ability to trust your software in production.

Summary and Next Steps

In summary, vibe coding does not remove the need for engineering rigor—it amplifies the productivity of the engineers who apply that rigor. Your mantra should be the old Russian proverb: Trust but verify. Trust the AI to handle the grunt work, but verify everything with your tools and expertise.

Security and reliability are one dimension of responsible development; ethics is another. AI-assisted coding raises important questions about intellectual property, bias, the impact on developer jobs, and more. Chapter 9 will delve into those broader implications. How can you use AI coding tools responsibly and fairly? How do you deal with licensing of AI-generated code and ensure your models and prompts are used ethically?

The Ethical Implications of Vibe Coding

As AI-assisted development becomes increasingly commonplace, it's critical to address the ethical and societal implications of this new paradigm. This chapter steps back from the technical details to examine vibe coding through an ethical lens: these new development methods can be effective, but they also need to be implemented responsibly and to benefit individuals and society at large.

I begin with questions of intellectual property (IP). Who owns the code that AI generates, and is it permissible to use AI outputs that may be derived from open source code without attribution? From there, I consider bias and fairness. Transparency is another focus: should developers disclose which parts of a codebase were AI-generated, and how can teams ensure accountability for code quality and bugs?

I outline responsible development practices in AI usage, from establishing transparency and accountability to avoiding sensitive data in prompts to ensuring accessibility and inclusivity. The chapter finishes with a set of guidelines for using AI tools responsibly.

Legal Disclaimer

The following section touches on complex legal topics, particularly concerning copyright and intellectual property law, from a primarily US perspective. Legal systems and interpretations are evolving worldwide, especially concerning artificial intelligence. This information is for educational purposes only and does not constitute legal advice. You should consult with a qualified intellectual property lawyer before making any decisions based on this information, especially if you have concerns about the ownership or licensing of code you or an AI tool generates.

Intellectual Property Considerations

Who owns AI-generated code? And does using it respect the licenses and copyrights of the source material on which the AI was trained? AI models like GPT have been trained on huge swaths of code from the internet, including open source repositories with various licenses (MIT, GPL, Apache, etc.). If the AI generates a snippet that is very similar (*https://oreil.ly/I3HxT*) (or identical) to something from a GPL-licensed project, using that snippet in a proprietary codebase could inadvertently violate the GPL, which generally requires sharing derivative code (*https://oreil.ly/8inJc*).

According to open source norms and general copyright principles, small snippets of a few lines *might not* be copyrightable if they lack sufficient originality to be considered an independent creative work, or their use *could potentially* be considered de minimis (too trivial to warrant legal concern). However, anything substantial or expressing a unique creative choice is more likely to be protected by copyright. It's crucial to understand that "open source" does not mean "public domain." By default, creative work, including code, is under exclusive copyright by its author. Open source licenses explicitly grant permissions that would otherwise be restricted by copyright law.

If you want to know more about open source norms, good places to start include the following:

The Open Source Initiative
> The OSI (*https://oreil.ly/hmJVN*) defines and promotes open source software, maintains the Open Source Definition, and approves licenses that meet its criteria.

The Free Software Foundation (FSF)
> The FSF (*https://fsf.org*) advocates for "free software" (which has a strong overlap with open source principles) and is the steward of licenses like the GNU General Public License (GPL).

Project-specific documentation
> Individual open source projects typically include *LICENSE* files, *README* files, and *CONTRIBUTING* guidelines that detail the terms of use and contribution for that specific project.

Community and legal resources
> Websites like GitHub offer extensive documentation and discussions on open source practices. Organizations like the Linux Foundation and legal information sites also provide valuable resources on open source compliance and legal aspects.

The question of whether using small code snippets overlaps with the fair use doctrine (*https://oreil.ly/d0ZK8*) (in the US; "fair dealing" in many other jurisdictions) is complex and highly fact-dependent. Fair use (*https://oreil.ly/EwrJ2*) permits limited use of copyrighted material without permission for purposes such as criticism, comment, news reporting, teaching, scholarship, or research. US courts typically consider four factors to determine fair use:

- The purpose (*https://oreil.ly/1TE5B*) and character of the use (commercial versus nonprofit, transformative versus duplicative)
- The nature of the copyrighted work (highly creative versus factual)
- The amount and substantiality of the portion used in relation to the copyrighted work as a whole
- The effect of the use upon the potential market for or value of the copyrighted work

While some might argue that copying very small, functional code snippets for interoperability or to access uncopyrightable ideas could fall under fair use, especially if the use is transformative, this is not a clearly settled area of law for code, and there's no universally agreed-upon number of lines that is definitively "fair use" or de minimis. The safest course is often to get permission or to understand the underlying idea and rewrite the code in your own way. The U.S. Supreme Court case *Google LLC v. Oracle America, Inc.* addressed fair use in the context of software APIs, finding Google's reimplementation of Java API declaring code to be fair use, but this was a specific and complex ruling focused on API declarations, not all code. It's generally understood that copyright protects the specific expression of an idea, not the idea, procedure, or method of operation itself.

Typically, the developer *using* the AI is considered the "author" in the sense that the AI is a tool, similar to a compiler or a word processor. Thus, if code is generated in a work context, the developer's company would likely own the code produced by the developer using the tool, subject to the AI tool's terms of service and underlying IP issues. However, the terms of service (ToS) of AI tools are critical. Most ToS grant the user rights to the output they generate. OpenAI's ToS, for instance, states, "You own the outputs you create with GPT-4, including code."

This "ownership," however, needs careful consideration. It generally means that the AI provider isn't claiming ownership of what *you* create *with their tool*. But this assumes you have the rights to the *inputs* you provide, and it doesn't automatically mean the output is itself eligible for copyright protection or that it's free from third-party intellectual property claims. If you input your own original code to the tool for modification or extension, the output is most likely yours (or your employer's), again, subject to how the AI processes it and what it incorporates from its training data. But if you input someone else's copyrighted code to fix or transform, the output *might* be considered a derivative work of that third-party code (*https://oreil.ly/mBPyq*).

In the US and many other jurisdictions, whether AI-generated output that is substantially similar to training data, or output based on copyrighted input, constitutes a derivative work is a subject of ongoing legal debate and lacks full clarity. Don't feed large chunks of copyrighted code that isn't yours (or licensed appropriately) into an AI tool, because the output could be deemed a derivative work (*https://oreil.ly/O4ktq*) and thus fall under the license of that original copyrighted code.

Given these uncertainties, to be safe, treat AI-generated code as if it's under an ambiguous license, and only use it if you are comfortable that it doesn't infringe on existing copyrights and that you can comply with any potential open source license obligations. Regarding the copyright status of the AI output itself, the US Copyright Office has stated (*https://oreil.ly/Y0PYG*) that works generated solely by AI without sufficient human authorship are not copyrightable. If a human significantly modifies or arranges AI-generated material in a creative way, that human contribution might be copyrightable (*https://oreil.ly/NV3Gl*) but not the AI-generated elements standing alone. Thus, it's often wise to assume that purely AI-generated outputs might not be copyrightable by anyone or that copyright would extend only to the human's creative contributions.

This is not a hypothetical worry. In fact, there's ongoing legal debate. A prominent class-action lawsuit, *Doe v. GitHub, Inc.* (*https://githubcopilotlitigation.com*), was filed against GitHub, Microsoft, and OpenAI, claiming that GitHub Copilot produces code that is too similar to licensed open source code without proper attribution or adherence to license terms. While some claims in this case have been dismissed or are under appeal (as of mid-2025, the case involves ongoing proceedings, including an appeal to the Ninth Circuit regarding DMCA claims and remaining breach of contract claims), it highlights a genuine concern: AI can and sometimes does regurgitate or closely paraphrase copyrighted code from its training data.[1]

An older (but still relevant and later substantiated) study by GitHub itself (*https://oreil.ly/fFUUd*) noted that, in some cases, Copilot's output included suggestions that matched training data, including rare instances of longer verbatim snippets. While most AI tools are designed to avoid direct, extensive copying of identifiable code unless specifically prompted or dealing with very standard algorithms, the risk exists. Furthermore, it's not just open source code that's a concern; numerous lawsuits have been filed by authors, artists, and media companies alleging that their fully copyrighted, privately owned intellectual property was used without permission or compensation to train large language models and other generative AI systems. The challenge with proprietary code is that, unlike open source, it's often not publicly visible,

---

1 Case information can often be found on court dockets (*https://oreil.ly/BdDiV*), like those for the US District Court for the Northern District of California and the Ninth Circuit Court of Appeals, or through legal news outlets and case trackers (*https://oreil.ly/AZrc-*).

making it harder for an end user to confirm if an AI's output is inadvertently similar to such private code.

Nevertheless, the ethical and prudent practice is to *act as if any code you accept from an AI tool is your responsibility*. Thoroughly review, test, and understand any AI-generated code before incorporating it into your projects, and ensure its use complies with all applicable licenses and copyright laws.

What to Do If You Get Suspicious Output

If an AI output seems like a verbatim or near-verbatim copy of known code (especially if it includes distinctive comments or author names), treat it carefully. Consider running a similarity check using a plagiarism detector tool, or do a web search for unique strings to see if you find any matches that could indicate copying.

Another principle to follow is *When in doubt, leave it out*. Either avoid using the output or make sure it's under a compatible license and give attribution if required. For example, if Copilot spits out a well-known algorithm implementation that you recognize from Stack Overflow or an open source project, cite the source or rewrite it in your own way, using the AI's answer as a guide but not quoting it verbatim.

If you suspect the output matches an existing library solution, consider including the library itself instead (with proper license). You can also prompt the AI:

> Please provide an original implementation rather than one copied from a library.

It might then synthesize a more unique solution. (There's no guarantee it won't be influenced by its training code, but at least it will try to not copy outright).

The ethics here also touch on not using AI to willfully strip attribution. For example, it would be unethical to copy code from Stack Overflow via AI without attribution to circumvent a policy that you should credit the answer. That erodes trust in the open knowledge ecosystem. It's better to incorporate the material with proper credit. Depending on the circumstances, that might mean the following:

- If an AI writes a code comment from some source that has an author's name (like copying a snippet with "John Doe 2018" in a comment), you should keep that or move it to a proper attribution section with a full citation rather than deleting it. That respects the original author's credit.

- If an AI provided a solution that you know comes from a known algorithm or code snippet, cite that source as you normally would if you had looked it up yourself.

- If an AI tool creates something arguably creative (like a unique approach or text for documentation), acknowledge its contribution. Though it doesn't have rights, it's about transparency (and maybe a nod to the tech).

Some open source licenses (like MIT) are permissive enough that including copied code with attribution would satisfy the license. Others, like GPL or AGPL, would "infect" your whole codebase if you include that code, which is undesirable for closed projects.

In short: if you suspect the AI has given you something that might cause IP issues, either avoid using it or transform it sufficiently to ensure you're complying with any possible license.

Gray Areas

Even as I write this, AI tools continue to raise new questions about IP, copyright, and ethics. For instance:

- If your vibe coding includes using AI to generate noncode assets like documentation text, config files, or images, similar IP questions arise. For instance, if you generate an icon image via an AI tool that was trained on copyrighted images, who owns that new image?
- If an AI writes a significant part of a software product, should the original authors of the code on which the AI was trained get credit?
- Could someone claim that your AI-generated code infringes on their copyright because it looks similar to theirs? If sections of nontrivial lengths are possibly identical, this is where similarity checking comes in.

There's an emerging notion that AI companies might need to implement license-respecting filters or allow teams to opt out of their code being included in AI training data. It's evolving, but developers on the ground should act conservatively to not violate rights.

It will take time for courts to settle all of the legal issues, but in the meantime, intellectual honesty and respect should guide us. If AI uses a known algorithm from a published paper, cite the paper in a comment. If it uses a common open source helper code, credit the project. It's about respect for authorship. If you recognize where something came from, err on the side of giving credit. It's a good practice that fosters transparency.

Remember that under the hood, the AI's knowledge comes from thousands of developers who shared their code publicly. Ethically, the software industry owes that community the respect of upholding open source licenses and norms. Give credit where it's due and don't abuse others' work under the guise of "the AI wrote it, not me."

Transparency and Attribution

Transparency refers to being open about the use of AI in your development process and outputs, and *attribution* refers to giving proper credit when AI-derived code comes from identifiable sources.

Transparency is important for the sake of accountability. For example, if AI-generated code introduces a bug or security flaw, being transparent that "this code was AI-suggested" might help you analyze the root cause—perhaps an ambiguous prompt should be rewritten. In code comments or a project's README or documentation, you might mention generally that "this project was built with assistance from AI tools like ChatGPT." Or get more specific: "Added a function to parse CSV (generated with ChatGPT's help, then modified)." It's a bit like acknowledging your use of frameworks or libraries.

Transparency is also key to trust: stakeholders (your team, clients, end users, or industry regulators) might want to know how your software was developed and validated. If an AI was involved in code generation, some stakeholders might wrongly trust it too much or too little. Transparency allows a conversation about reliability: "Yes, we used AI, but we tested it thoroughly" or "This part was tricky—we had AI generate the initial code, but we've since verified it."

Attributions are also expected or required in many academic venues. Some open source projects restrict or even forbid AI contributions due to IP concerns, so check the contributor guidelines before using AI. Being transparent with maintainers if a patch was AI-generated helps them evaluate it, especially if licensing is a worry.

In fact, some highly regulated industries require software vendors to disclose any AI use for auditing purposes. The EU's AI Act (*https://oreil.ly/wDNKs*) mandates transparency for automated decision making that affects individuals (such as credit-scoring algorithms). If vibe coding leads to such systems, it becomes a legal/ethical necessity to inform users that "recommendations are generated automatically and may reflect patterns in data."

Similarly, if your product feeds user data or proprietary data like user-provided code examples into an AI model to fine-tune it and help program its analysis, you might need to say in the privacy policy that user data may be used with permission to improve AI models (as always, do consult a lawyer for legal matters). Transparency intersects with privacy here.

It's also just generally ethical to acknowledge the tools and sources you use. If 30% of your code was generated by Copilot, it's fair to mention that in your documentation or internal communication—not to diminish your own role but to be honest about the process.

Some developers might fear admitting that AI helped, worried that it could undermine their perceived contribution or skill or be seen as "cheating." As vibe coding becomes more normalized, this stigma should decrease; eventually, you might be seen as behind the times if you're *not* using the AI available to you. We need to normalize AI as a tool—it's no more "cheating" than using Stack Overflow or an IDE.

On the flip side, providing too many disclaimers could cause undue worry. If you tell a client, "We used AI to code this product," they might question its safety (even if that's due to misconceptions). It's important how you phrase it. Emphasize quality measures in the same breath: "We utilized advanced coding assistants to speed up development, and all AI-generated code was rigorously reviewed and tested to meet our quality standards."

In sum, transparency and attribution foster trust and community values. They ensure that credit flows to human creators and that we remain honest about how our software is built. It's akin to an artist listing their tools or inspirations; it doesn't diminish the art; it contextualizes it. If, like me, you want vibe coding to be accepted widely, being open about using AI and how you mitigate its risks is important.

Bias and Fairness

As you know well by this point in the book, AI models' output reflects the data they're trained on. If that data contains biases or exclusionary patterns, the models can produce outputs that are biased or unfair.

You might ask: "How can code be biased? It's not like an LLM is making hiring decisions or something." But bias can creep into your coding in subtle ways:

- Code often reflects assumptions on its creators' part. User-facing text or content the AI generates might reflect cultural biases or insensitive language present in its training data. For instance, Microsoft's Tay (*https://oreil.ly/d8wxO*), an early chatbot in 2016, infamously learned to parrot racist and misogynistic slurs from Twitter interactions within hours of launch.

- Assumptions can also be geared toward specific cultural norms, like a middle-class North American lifestyle (such as assuming car ownership or universal access to certain technologies). A notable example of unexamined assumptions leading to exclusionary products was the initial 2014 release of Apple's Health app (*https://oreil.ly/67sZG*), which lacked a period tracker—a significant oversight likely stemming from a lack of diversity and perspective on the design team. Even in example code, comments, or synthetic data, the model might always use *he/him* pronouns, reinforcing gender bias.

- It is well known that code repositories and the broader software development landscape predominantly reflect Western perspectives and English speakers. As a result, an AI trained on these repositories might overlook crucial internationalization aspects, such as proper support for Unicode and multibyte characters (essential for languages like Chinese, Japanese, Korean, Arabic, Hindi, and many others using non-Latin or syllabary scripts), or it might default to English-centric examples for things like type names. Developers must bring awareness and design and code for internationalization, even if the AI doesn't spontaneously do so.

- If writing algorithms, be wary of certain variables like race, gender, age, etc. The AI might not spontaneously include them unless asked, but if it hallucinates some criteria or if you're using an AI like Code Assistant on a dataset, apply fairness constraints; the AI won't inherently know the moral or legal context.

Beyond just coding, models can mirror *data bias* in their content domain: the historical biases present in their training data. For example, consider an AI tasked with writing code for a credit-scoring algorithm for loan approvals. In the United States, credit scoring systems have a documented history of reflecting and perpetuating racial biases. These biases stem from historical practices like redlining and other forms of systemic discrimination that have had lasting financial repercussions, particularly for Black communities and other marginalized groups. (See Richard Rothstein's *The Color of Law* [Economic Policy Institute, 2017] for a comprehensive history of how government policies segregated America.)

If the training data reflects these historical biases, the AI might incorporate discriminatory variables, such as using zip codes (which can be a proxy for racial demographics due to segregated housing patterns) or other seemingly neutral data points that correlate with protected characteristics. If not properly guided, the AI might produce code that leads banks to make unfair lending decisions, thus perpetuating historical inequalities and affecting real people's lives. Similar issues arise in areas like predictive policing algorithms, where historical arrest data (itself potentially biased) can lead to AI systems that disproportionately target certain communities (*https://oreil.ly/H4rmr*).

Similarly, if you're using specialized models (like an AI code assistant fine-tuned for, say, medical software), ensure the model isn't locked into biases from that domain's data. For example, historically, some medical guidelines were biased by research studies that predominantly used male subjects, leading to misdiagnoses or less effective treatments for other genders. If AI is recommending code or solutions for medical diagnostics, you need to double-check that it doesn't inadvertently encode those biases.

There are tools emerging to detect bias in AI outputs, though these are more common in GPT models used to generate content, and AI providers themselves attempt to filter overtly biased or toxic outputs. Code-oriented AIs rarely produce hate speech spontaneously, but it's good that they have content filters for it. Building in ethical constraints means, in many AI tools, that if a user tries to get the AI to create malware or discriminatory algorithms, it will refuse. Don't try to break those filters to get unethical outputs.

There are lots of other ways to recognize and mitigate bias at different stages of the development process, though. These include:

Testing with diverse examples

If your AI generates user-facing components or logic that deals with human-related data, test it with diverse inputs. For example, if an AI-generated form validation expects "First Name" and "Last Name," does it allow single names, which are common in some cultures? If not, that's a bias in assumption. If it generates sample usernames, are they all like "JohnDoe"? If so, consider incorporating more diversity in the examples.

Prompting for inclusivity

You can explicitly instruct the AI to be neutral or inclusive: "Generate examples using a variety of names from different cultures." If it always refers to the user as "he," you might prompt:

> Avoid gendered language in this code comment; use neutral phrasing or they/them pronouns.

Also, be cautious about jokes or examples the AI might produce that could be culturally insensitive; you can prompt it to use a professional tone to avoid that. The AI will usually comply. It doesn't have an agenda; it just outputs what seems normal to it, unless told otherwise. We shape that "normal."

Hiring diverse teams

Having a diverse team review outputs can catch issues. For example, someone might say, "Hey, our AI always picks variable names like foo/bar, which is fine, but in documentation, all of its personas are male-typed." Then you can correct that systematically. If all developers are from similar backgrounds, they might not catch a subtle bias. If possible, involve people from underrepresented groups—or at least consider their perspectives—when reviewing AI usage guidelines.

In summary, bias and fairness are about using vibe-coding tools to produce code that is fair to users of all backgrounds and that doesn't reflect—or, worse, perpetuate—historical discrimination. The way we use these tools in teams should also be fair to developers and other colleagues of varying levels and backgrounds. See Chapter 4 for a discussion of the ethical implications of how AI tools are changing workplaces, especially for junior developers.

Golden Rules for Responsible AI Use

Bringing together a lot of what we've covered, it's worth articulating a set of responsible practices for vibe coding:

1. *Always keep a human in the loop.*

   Again: never let the AI work unsupervised. Responsible AI-assisted dev means you, the developer, are reviewing every line and making decisions, not deploying raw AI output without human validation.

2. *Take responsibility for your code.*

   If something goes wrong, it's not the AI's fault—it's the development team's responsibility. Keeping that mindset avoids complacency. Be prepared to justify your code, whether you wrote it from scratch or accepted AI code. If someone asks you, "Why does the code do this?" don't say, "I don't know; Copilot did that." That's why one of Chapter 3's golden rules is "Never commit code you don't fully understand." That's responsible engineering.

3. *Protect users' privacy and ask for their consent.*

   Ethically, you owe it to users and your company to keep their secret data secret. When using AI tools, especially cloud-based ones, be careful not to expose sensitive data in your prompts or conversations. For instance, if you're debugging an issue with a user database, don't feed actual user records to ChatGPT. Use sanitized or synthetic data instead.

   Many tools now allow users (or at least business users) to opt out of having their input data used for training. If you're an enterprise user, use those settings or use on-prem solutions for sensitive code. If you do feed any user data to a model, or if any AI functionality directly touches users (like a chatbot in your app that uses an LLM), get users' consent and allow them to opt out if appropriate. A warning like "This feature uses an AI service; your input will be sent to it for processing" is transparent and lets privacy-conscious users decide for themselves.

4. *Comply with laws and regulations.*

   Keep an eye on legal requirements around AI, which are constantly evolving. For instance, data protection laws like the EU's General Data Protection Regulation (GDPR) and AI Act consider some AI outputs as personal data if they include any personal data. Training a model on users' data might require those users' consent. Regulatory bodies may classify code generation as "general AI" and impose transparency or risk management obligations. Stay informed and work closely with your legal and compliance professionals to avoid breaking any regulations.

While this should go without saying, do not use AI to generate malware, exploit code without ethical justification, or automate unethical or illegal practices.[2] While an AI could probably write a very effective phishing email or code injection attack, using it for that purpose violates ethics, the laws of most countries, and likely the AI's terms of service. Focus on constructive use.

5. *Foster a responsible AI culture in your organization.*

   If your team adopts vibe coding, encourage discussions about ethics and provide relevant ethics training. Consider having developers and code reviewers use a brief checklist like the one in Figure 9-1.

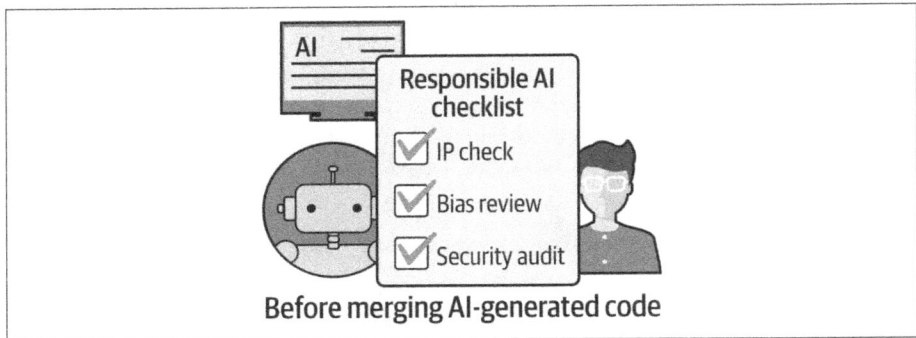

Figure 9-1. Responsible AI development checklist: essential validation steps including intellectual property review, bias assessment, and security audits before integrating AI-generated code into production systems.

Everyone should feel responsible for ethical AI use; it's a collective effort, not just the burden of the individual using the tool at any given moment. To formalize this, consider designating an "ethics champion" or a small ethics committee within your team or organization. This individual or group wouldn't be the sole owner of ethics (as that responsibility remains shared), but they would take the lead on:

- Staying abreast of the latest developments in AI ethics, emerging best practices, and new regulatory landscapes

- Facilitating discussions about ethical considerations in specific projects

- Championing the integration of ethical principles into the development lifecycle

---

2 There are some ethically justified exceptions. Penetration testers and security researchers can ethically use AI to find vulnerabilities that should be fixed, as long as they work under responsible disclosure protocols.

- Helping to curate and disseminate relevant resources and training materials to the broader team
- Acting as a point of contact for team members who have ethical questions or concerns

Since this field is moving incredibly fast, it's crucial to work as a team to stay updated on new versions of AI tools and their capabilities, limitations, and evolving best practices for responsible use.

Since this field is moving fast, work as a team to stay updated on new versions of AI tools and best practices. One important concept to integrate into your workflows is the use of model cards. *Model cards* are essentially standardized documents that provide transparency about a machine learning model. Think of them as nutrition labels for AI models. They typically include details about:

- What the model is, its version, and when it was developed
- The specific use cases the model was designed and tested for
- Scenarios where the model should not be used, due to limitations or potential for harm
- How well the model performs on various benchmarks, including evaluations for fairness and bias across different demographic groups
- Information about the datasets used to train the model, including any known limitations or biases in the data
- Potential risks and societal implications and any mitigation strategies employed

Whenever you are using a pretrained model or evaluating a model for use, look for its model card. If you are fine-tuning or developing models, creating your own model cards is a best practice.

6. *Create guardrails and safety nets.*

   Practicing responsible design means that your AI-generated systems should have safety nets. For example, if AI suggests an out-of-bounds index fix that might mask an underlying issue, it's better for the system to fail safely than to cause silent errors. If an AI-generated recommendation system might be wrong, providing ways for users to correct or override it shows respect for their human agency. Strive to build systems that degrade gracefully if AI components misbehave.

7. *Document AI usage decisions within your team.*

   Keep an internal log of why you used certain AI suggestions (or didn't): "We tried AI for module X, but it tended to produce too much duplicate code, so we wrote that part manually." This can help you refine your processes, provide context to new team members about AI's role in the codebase's history, and augment your team's collective memory. It can also be useful during audits.

8. *Proactively work to avoid bias, discrimination, and unfairness.*

   Be vigilant for signs that your AI usage could lead to discrimination, and work to avoid such situations before they happen. For example, if your app is global, is your AI multilingual or does it favor those who speak English? Do all of your team members have equal access to AI tools and training?

Responsible AI Checklist

1. Prompting and code generation (developers)
   - ☐ Confirm that your prompts contain no confidential or sensitive data such as client info, PII, or secrets.
   - ☐ Check licensing for all output and confirm it includes no proprietary or GPL code, unless allowed. Use tools like FOSSA for scanner checks.
   - ☐ Test output for bias to ensure code and comments don't reinforce stereotypes or discrimination.
   - ☐ Confirm security hygiene by prompting for safe defaults. Confirm the code avoids insecure patterns (eval, unsanitized input).
   - ☐ Specify any constraints in prompts, including style, framework, performance needs, and compatibility guidelines.

2. Code review checks (developers and code reviewers)
   - ☐ Verify that no embedded copyrighted material is used in the code unless licensed.
   - ☐ Confirm that attribution and credit are given when due.
   - ☐ Audit the logic, language, and naming for bias and fairness—especially in user/UI-facing layers.
   - ☐ Ensure that the code doesn't facilitate harm, misuse, manipulation, or discrimination.
   - ☐ Validate your input sanitization, data handling, and logging, and check for secret leaks.
   - ☐ Confirm the code's functionality and correctness via unit tests, edge cases, error handling, and test coverage.
   - ☐ Check for inefficient or power-hungry patterns.
   - ☐ Check dependencies to ensure they include no unvetted libraries or hidden license risks.

- ☐ Check for readability and maintainability: the code should follow style guides and use clear naming conventions.
- ☐ Check that any unused code has been removed.
- ☐ Confirm that code comments explain the code's intent, especially for AI-generated logic.
- ☐ Confirm that your code-review feedback is respectful, specific, and empathetic.

3. Governance and process (organization)

- ☐ Confirm that integrated license scanners, audit logs, and provenance tracking are in place.
- ☐ Provide training in ethics and AI-assisted coding, and share updates regularly.
- ☐ Maintain a vetted list of AI tools; prohibit unapproved or high-risk ones.
- ☐ Put an incident process in place, with escalation channels and whistleblower options for anyone who discovers unethical code.
- ☐ Monitor responsible AI metrics, such as bias incidents, security findings, and license violations. Maintain a checklist of these metrics and revise it periodically.
- ☐ Solicit and listen to community feedback. Include diverse perspectives via retrospective meetings or external audits.

How to Use This Checklist

- Customize this list to include questions specific to your organization and business domain, as well as your team's tech, risk tolerance, and values.
- Start small: begin with key questions like "Did we avoid sensitive data?" and "Did we scan for licenses?"
- Integrate checks and checklists into your workflow via PR templates, CI pipelines, and code-review tools.
- Schedule reviews of this checklist every quarter or after major incidents. Use these reviews to iterate on the list, adding new items or deleting unneeded ones.
- Treat this checklist not as a rigid rulebook but as a conversation starter, just as pilots and surgeons do with their checklists.

As the AI landscape continues changing and growing, the software industry is likely to introduce AI standards or certifications. It's early, but your company could even help shape those guidelines by engaging in standardization efforts, like IEEE or ISO working groups on AI software engineering. Ethically, it's better for the dev community to help set the rules than to leave it solely to regulators or the courts.

Summary and Next Steps

Responsible vibe coding means integrating AI into the software development lifecycle in a way that respects all stakeholders: original creators (by respecting their IP), colleagues (through transparency and fairness), users (through privacy, security, and fairness in outcomes), and society (by not letting misuse cause harm). It's about leveraging AI's strengths while diligently guarding against its weaknesses.

I've often said that vibe coding is not an excuse for low-quality work. It's not an excuse for ethical shortcuts either. As the humans in charge, developers must ensure that speed doesn't compromise values.

Next, Chapter 10 looks at a new technology that's changing the way we work with AI models: autonomous coding agents.

Autonomous Background Coding Agents

Autonomous background coding agents are rapidly emerging as the next evolution of AI coding tools. Unlike familiar "copilot" assistants that suggest code while you type, these agents operate more like background junior developers you can dispatch to handle entire tasks asynchronously. Code is generated in an isolated environment spun up for the agent, tests can be run, and the result often comes back as a fully formed pull request for you to review.

In this section, I'll explore what background coding agents are, how they work, the current landscape of tools (OpenAI Codex, Google Jules, Cursor, Devin, and more), and how they compare to traditional in-IDE assistants. I'll also examine their capabilities, limitations, and the pragmatic changes they signal for the future of software engineering.

From Copilots to Autonomous Agents: What Are Background Coding Agents?

Traditional AI coding assistants (like Cursor, GitHub Copilot, or VSCode extensions like Cline) are *supervised coding agents*—interactive helpers that respond to a developer's prompts or inline context. They're essentially autocomplete on steroids, generating suggestions in a chat or as you write, but the human developer is in the driver's seat guiding every step.

In contrast, autonomous background coding agents operate with much greater independence. You give them a high-level task or goal, then "send them off" to work through the problem on their own, without constant supervision. These agents will read and modify your codebase, formulate a plan, execute code (even running tests or commands), and produce a result (often a commit or pull request)—all in an asynchronous workflow.

Think of the difference between a copilot and an autopilot: your copilot (much like GitHub Copilot) is always in the cockpit beside you, awaiting your input; the autopilot (background agent) can fly the plane on its own for a while. This autonomy means that background agents can tackle multistep coding tasks while you focus elsewhere. Using async agents like Codex and Jules is like expanding your cognitive bandwidth: you can fire off a task to the AI and forget about it until it's done. Instead of a single-threaded back-and-forth with an AI, you suddenly have a multithreaded workflow: the agent works in parallel with you, much like a competent junior dev working in the background.

Crucially, background agents operate in isolated development environments (often cloud VMs or containers) rather than directly in your editor. They typically clone your repository into a sandbox, install dependencies, and have the tools needed to build and test the project. For security, these sandboxes are restricted (with rules like "No internet access unless explicitly allowed") and ephemeral. The agent can run compilers, tests, linters, and the like without any risk to your local machine. When the task is complete, the agent outputs the code changes (diffs) and a summary of what it did. Usually this comes through as a pull request (with code diffs, commit message, and sometimes an explanation), which you can then review and merge.

To sum up, a background coding agent is an AI-powered autonomous coder that understands your intent, works through an entire task in a sandbox environment by reading and writing code and testing it, and then delivers the results for you to review. It's not just suggesting a line or two—it can handle larger-scope tasks:

- Write a new feature X across the codebase.
- Refactor module Y for efficiency.
- Upgrade this project's dependencies.

This is a significant shift in how we might incorporate AI into development workflows, moving from assistive suggestions to delegating *actual implementation work*.

How Do Autonomous Coding Agents Work?

Under the hood, most background agents follow a similar pattern of operation: *plan, execute, verify,* and *report*. Let's walk through these steps and their capabilities.

Plan

When you give an agent a task (typically via a prompt or command describing what you want), the agent first parses the request and formulates a plan of attack. Some agents explicitly show you this plan before proceeding. For example, Google's Jules (*https://oreil.ly/jxDhZ*) presents an execution plan that you can review and tweak before it starts coding, which "prevents the anxiety of wondering whether the agent understood your request correctly." A good agent will break the task into substeps:

> Step 1: search the codebase for relevant sections; Step 2: make changes in files A, B, C; Step 3: run tests; Step 4: commit changes.

This planning stage is key to effective autonomy: it's the AI's way of reasoning about *how* to accomplish your goal before diving in.

The agent launches a dedicated development environment for the task. Jules, for instance, "clones your codebase into a secure Google Cloud VM" and works asynchronously there. OpenAI's Codex similarly runs each task in its own cloud sandbox, preloaded with your repository. Tools like Cursor's background agents use a remote Ubuntu-based machine that has internet access to install packages and can be customized via Docker or snapshots. Ensuring the environment has all needed dependencies (like the correct language runtimes and build tools) is both critical and nontrivial. As I noted in a previous analysis, "Figuring out a smooth experience to spin up just the right environment for an agent is key…and the user experience to configure it is as frustrating, if not more, than it can be for CI pipelines." Nonetheless, agents are tackling this by allowing configuration files to specify setup steps. The goal is to create a *dev environment in the cloud* that mirrors what a human developer would need to successfully run the project's code and tests.

Notably, many agents disable internet access to their code after setup, so they can sandbox the run without unauthorized data exfiltration or unrestricted internet calls. Some allow controlled internet use for specific needs: for example, OpenAI recently enabled optional internet access for Codex tasks like fetching package updates or documentation.

Execute

Next comes the main show: the agent starts writing and modifying code according to the plan. Armed with a large language model (or a mix of models) fine-tuned for coding, it can read multiple files, generate new code, and even create new files if needed. This is where the agent essentially acts like a programmer: locating where changes should be made, editing code, and inserting new logic.

One interesting observation from early runs is that agents often use brute-force text search (like the Unix `grep` command) to find relevant parts of the codebase. For example, an agent might search for a function name or a keyword to figure out where in the repository to make changes. This seems surprisingly simplistic—shouldn't they use fancy semantic code search or AST-based analysis? Yet, it's effective and reliable. As Birgitta Böckeler notes (*https://oreil.ly/wDSkr*), many coding agents default to straightforward full-text search, perhaps finding it the most broadly effective method despite more advanced techniques existing.

As the agent edits code, some systems provide real-time logs or status updates so you can follow along if you want. OpenAI Codex exposes a log of the agent's "thoughts" and commands (summarized) as it works through a task. Cursor allows you to "view their status and enter the machine the agent is running in" to observe or even intervene midtask. In practice, though, the idea is you don't need to babysit—you can let the agent run on autopilot.

Verify

A defining capability of these agents is that they don't stop at writing code—they often compile the code and *run tests to verify* their changes. For instance, OpenAI's Codex is designed to iteratively run tests until it receives a passing result. If an agent can run the project's test suite (or at least a relevant subset of tests), it can catch mistakes and automatically correct them in subsequent iterations. This is huge: it moves the AI from just *generating* code to also *debugging* and *validating* its code.

In theory, an agent with a robust test harness can attempt a fix, see a test fail, adjust the code, and loop until tests pass—without a human in the loop. In practice, environment issues sometimes thwart this. In one case I studied, Codex wasn't able to run the full test suite due to environment mismatches (certain tools were missing), resulting in a pull request that still had two failing tests. Had the environment been fully aligned, the agent could have fixed those trivial issues before making the PR.

This underscores why environment setup is so important for autonomous agents: if they can run everything a developer would (linters, tests, builds), they can self-correct many errors automatically. Agents like Devin emphasize this loop—Devin "writes code, finds bugs in the code, corrects the code, and runs its own end-to-end tests to verify it works" as a normal part of its operation. In fact, Devin will even spin up a live preview deployment of a frontend app it built so you can manually verify a feature in the browser, which is a clever extension of the verification step.

Report

Once the agent has a candidate solution (all tests have passed, or it deems the code ready), it prepares the results for you. Depending on the platform, this might come as a PR on GitHub, a diff and explanation in chat, or files ready to merge.

At this point, you—the human—do a review. Here we come back to "Trust but verify": you trust the agent to produce something useful, but you verify the changes through code review and additional testing. Many agent systems explicitly integrate with the PR review process because it's a familiar workflow for developers. Jules, for example, plugs into your GitHub and will open a branch and PR with its changes. OpenAI's Codex presents the diff inside ChatGPT for you to approve or ask follow-up questions. If you find issues or have change requests, you can often feed that back to the agent for another iteration.

Some agents handle this via chat (Devin can take feedback from a linked Slack thread: if you point out a problem or ask for tweaks, it will "start working on a reply" to address it). Others might require a new run with an adjusted prompt or use a review comment interface. Impressively, Devin even responded to a GitHub PR comment asking *why* it made certain changes—it reacted with an "eyes" emoji to signal it saw the comment, then posted a detailed explanation of its reasoning. (The explanation turned out to be not entirely correct in that case, but the fact that it can discuss PRs says something about how interactive these agents can become.)

If all looks good, you merge the agent's PR or integrate the changes. If not, you might discard it or have the agent try again. One pragmatic question teams face is what to do if an agent's output is *almost* good but not quite. Do you spend time fixing up the last 10%–20% of an agent-generated patch, even if it was a low-priority task you offloaded to the AI? This is what I call the "sunk cost" dilemma for AI contributions. Birgitta Böckeler (*https://oreil.ly/IdJ9d*) muses that if an agent PR only partly succeeds, teams will have to decide "in which situations would [they] discard the pull request, and in which situations would they invest the time to get it the last 20% there" for a task that originally wasn't worth much dev time. There's no one answer—it depends on the context and value of the change—but it's a new kind of trade-off introduced by autonomous agents.

In summary, background coding agents handle the end-to-end cycle of coding tasks: *understand → plan → code → test → deliver*. They essentially simulate what a diligent, methodical developer might do when assigned a task, albeit within the current limits of AI (see Figure 10-1).

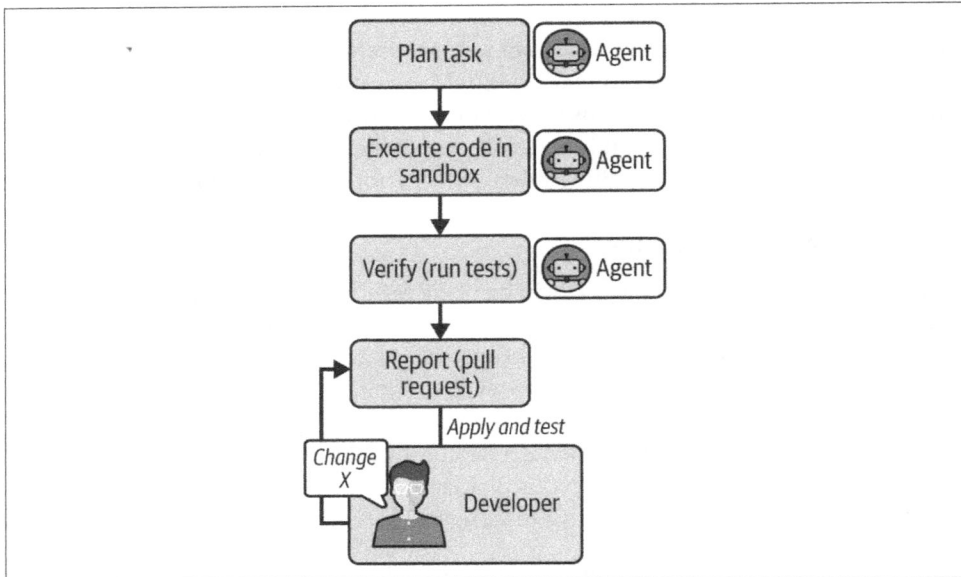

Figure 10-1. Autonomous AI agent workflow: self-directed agents plan tasks, execute solutions, verify results, and report outcomes with minimal human intervention.

How Do Background Agents Compare to In-IDE AI Assistants?

It's worth drawing a clear line between the coding AI tools we've had for a couple years (GitHub Copilot, ChatGPT coding mode, etc.) and this new generation of autonomous agents. Both are useful, but they play different roles and have different strengths/weaknesses.

The most obvious difference is their *level of autonomy*. In-IDE assistants like Copilot or VSCode's AI extensions work *synchronously* with you—they generate suggestions or answer questions when invoked, and their scope is usually limited to the immediate context (like the file or function you're editing or a specific prompt you gave). *You* decide when to accept a suggestion, ask for another, or apply a change.

With background agents, once you hit "go" on a task, the agent will autonomously perform potentially hundreds of actions (file edits, runs, searches) without further confirmation. It's operating *asynchronously*. This requires a higher degree of trust (you're letting it change things on its own) but also frees you from micromanaging. I often describe it as the difference between having an AI *pair programmer* versus an AI *assistant developer* on the team. The pair programmer (Copilot) is with you keystroke by keystroke; the assistant dev (Codex/Jules/etc.) works in parallel on another issue.

The copilot style of AI tools means they excel at microtasks—writing a function, completing a line, generating a small snippet, answering a question about how to use an API. They don't maintain a long narrative or project-wide understanding, beyond what's in your editor's open files or a limited window.

Autonomous agents operate at the *project level*. They load your entire repository (or at least index it) and can make coordinated changes across multiple modules. They keep track of a multistep plan. For example, GitHub Copilot might help you write a unit test if you prompt it, but a background agent could, on its own, decide to add the corresponding implementation in one file, the test in another, and a modified a config in a third—all as part of one unified task. This makes agents far better suited for things like refactoring a cross-cutting concern (logging, error handling), performing upgrades (which often involve many files), or implementing a feature that touches backend and frontend. IDE assistants couldn't easily handle those because they lack long-term task memory and whole-repo visibility.

Copilot-style assistants are *reactive*—they respond to your code or queries. They don't initiate actions. Background agents are *proactive* in the sense that once activated, they will take initiative to reach the goal. A Jules or Devin agent might decide, "I need to create a new file here" or "Let me run the tests now," without being explicitly told at each step. They also can *notify you of things proactively*, like:

> I found another place to apply this change, so I'll include that too.

They behave more like an employee, who might say, "I noticed X while I was in the code, so I fixed that as well." That said, autonomy also means they might do something you didn't expect or necessarily want. The supervised nature of this style of tool means it will only do exactly what you accept (except maybe for subtle missuggestions you didn't notice). So with great power (proactivity) comes the need for greater oversight.

A major difference is that background agents can *execute code and commands*, whereas traditional IDE assistants usually cannot (unless you count things like ChatGPT's Code Interpreter mode, but that's more for data analysis, not integrated with your project's build).

Agents will run your test suite, start your dev server, compile the app, maybe even deploy it. They operate in a sandbox, but it's effectively like having an automated developer who can use the terminal. This is a game changer—it closes the loop of verify/fix. An IDE helper might generate code that looks plausible, but if it didn't actually run it, there could be runtime issues or failing tests.

With an agent that runs the code, you have a higher chance the output is actually functional. It also offloads the debugging step; if something fails, the agent can try to fix it immediately. The flip side is this requires the agent's environment to be correct (as discussed earlier), and it opens the door to potential side effects. Imagine an agent running a database migration or modifying data—usually they're in sandbox mode, so this doesn't affect production, but be careful.

GitHub Copilot and tools like it live in the editor, which is great for in-the-flow coding. Agents often integrate with project management and DevOps tools, too. For example, you might create a GitHub issue and have an agent pick it up and generate a PR, or trigger an agent run from a CI pipeline for certain tasks (like autofixing lint errors on PRs). In fact, CodeGen advertises its agents' ability to attach to issue trackers so that when an issue moves to "In Progress," the AI agent works on it. This kind of integration is beyond what IDE tools do. It hints that AI agents could become part of the CI/CD loop—for instance, automatically attempting to fix build failures or automatically creating follow-up PRs for minor issues. That's a different mode of collaboration: not just helping a dev write code but acting as a bot user in the team's toolchain.

Using copilot-type assistants often still feels like programming, just faster—you type, they suggest, you accept, you test. Using a background agent feels more like delegation followed by review. The human effort shifts from writing code to writing a good task description and then reviewing the code produced. I call this "generator versus reviewer asymmetry"—generating a solution (or code) from scratch is hard, but reviewing and refining it is easier. Async agents capitalize on this: they handle the bulk generation, leaving you with the (typically faster) job of vetting and tweaking. This can be a productivity boon, but it also means as an engineer you need to sharpen your code review and verification skills.

Code review has always been important, but now it's not just for other human colleagues' code—it's for AI-generated code as well, which might have different patterns of mistakes. My mantra is that you should treat agent-produced code as if it were written by a slightly overeager junior developer: assume good intentions and decent competence, but verify everything and don't hesitate to request changes or reject if it's not up to standards.

In practice, I find that I use copilot-style tools and background agents *together*. For instance, I might use Copilot or Cursor's inline suggestions while I'm actively coding a complex piece of logic, because I want tight control over that logic. Meanwhile, I might delegate a peripheral but time-consuming task (like updating all our API client libraries for new endpoints) to a background agent to handle in parallel. They fill different niches. One doesn't necessarily replace the other. In fact, I foresee IDEs offering a unified experience: a palette of options from "Complete this line" to "Generate a function" to "Hey, AI, please implement this entire ticket for me." You'd choose the tool depending on the scope.

Combining Multiple AI Models to Maximize Strengths

So far, I've often referred to "the AI" as if it's one monolithic assistant. In reality, there are many AI models, each with different strengths. Some are great at natural language understanding, others excel at generating code, and some might be specialized in certain domains (like a math problem solver or a UI generator). An advanced practitioner of vibe coding can orchestrate multiple AIs together, using each for what it's best at. This is like having a team of specialists rather than a single generalist.

Consider a future workflow where you have:

- A CodeGen AI highly trained on programming that can produce code and fix code efficiently
- A TestGen AI, specialized in generating test cases and finding edge cases
- A Doc AI that writes clear documentation and explanations
- A Design AI that's skilled at generating UI layouts or graphics
- An Optimization AI focused on performance tuning and perhaps even aware of low-level details

You can pipe your task through several of these AIs. For example, you ask CodeGen AI to write an implementation. Immediately, you feed that output to TestGen AI to generate tests for it (or to critique it). Then feed both code and tests to Doc AI to produce documentation or a usage guide. If the code involves user interface, maybe Design AI is used earlier to propose the layout structure that CodeGen AI then implements. By chaining them, you leverage each model's domain expertise. This is analogous to a software pipeline or assembly line, but instead of different human roles, it's different AI roles.

Even among similar models, combining them can improve reliability. If you have two code-generation models from different providers or of different architectures, you can have them both attempt the solution and then compare or test both outputs. If one model's output passes all tests and the other doesn't, you pick the passing one. If both pass but have different approaches, you might manually choose the more readable one. If one fails, you can even show the failing one the successful code as a hint to learn from. This kind of AI cross-talk can reduce errors since it's less likely that two different models will make the exact same mistake. It's like getting a second opinion. You can already find research and tools that use one AI to check another's reasoning—for instance, one generates an answer and another judges it.

Differentiate Models by Task Type

Use the right tool for the job. Large language models (LLMs) are good generalists, but sometimes smaller, specialized models or tools do better. For example, for arithmetic or certain algorithms, a deterministic tool (or an AI that's more constrained) might be better. Some advanced dev setups use symbolic solvers or older rule-based AI for specific subtasks and LLMs for others. As an advanced vibe coder, you might maintain a toolbox: when you need regex, you call a regex-specific generator; when you need a commit message, maybe a model fine-tuned for summarization is used. The beauty is these can be integrated via simple scripts or prompt wrappers. For instance, you could have a local script like `ai_regex_generator` that internally prompts an AI but with some pre- and postprocessing to ensure the output is a valid regex, and maybe tests it on provided examples.

Use an Orchestration System

If you find yourself frequently combining models, you might use or build an orchestration system, an emerging category of frameworks often referred to as *AI orchestration* or *agents*. These systems allow you to define a flow; for example:

Step 1: Use Model A to interpret user request.

Step 2: If request is about data analysis, use Model B to generate SQL; if about text, use Model C...

Step 3: Feed the result to Model D to explain it.

This is more relevant if you're building an app or service powered by multiple AI steps. But even in personal dev, you can script a multistep approach. For example, one custom CLI tool, `ai_dev_assist`, takes a prompt and behind the scenes uses an AI to classify the prompt into categories like `code`, `design`, `test`, and `optimize`. Based on the category, it forwards the prompt to the appropriate specialist AI. When it receives the result, it can optionally pipe the result into another AI for review or improvement.

This kind of meta-AI coordinating other AIs sounds complex, but an advanced user can set it up with current technology. It will likely get easier as we begin to see dedicated support in IDEs or cloud platforms.

Human-AI Hybrid Teams

While on the subject of multiple intelligences, let's not forget *human* collaborators. An advanced vibe coder also knows when to involve fellow human developers in the loop. For example, you might use AI to generate two or three different design prototypes for a feature, then bring those to your team's UX designer for feedback. Which one aligns with our brand? Which feels intuitive? If an AI writes a complex piece of code, you might do a code review session with a colleague focusing on that piece, acknowledging that "an AI helped write this, so I want another pair of human eyes on it too." In a sense, the "multiple model" approach can include humans as just highly advanced models—each entity (human or AI) has unique strengths. The future of development might often be human + AI pair programming or even team programming where some "team members" are AI.

Imagine building a small web application through vibe coding. Your workflow might look like this:

1. You use a UI Layout AI to generate the HTML/CSS for your page given a description (specialized in frontend).

2. You use a Content AI to generate some placeholder text or images needed (like marketing text, maybe using a model geared for copywriting).

3. You then use your main Code AI to generate the interactive functionality in Java-Script, feeding it the HTML so it knows which element IDs to hook into.

4. You then ask a Testing AI to generate Selenium or Playwright tests for the interface interactions.

5. Finally, you use a Security AI to scan the code for common vulnerabilities. This could be a model or simply a static-analysis tool augmented with AI.

This multimodel approach covers frontend, backend (if there is one), content, testing, and security in one integrated process. Each AI handled its portion and you, as the orchestrator, ensured they all align.

While today you might have to manually copy outputs from one tool to another or use some glue scripts, tomorrow's IDEs might let you configure this pipeline so it feels seamless. The key takeaway is: *don't rely on just one AI model if you have access to several.* Use the best one for each job and make them work together. It leads to better outcomes and also reduces single-point failure—if one model isn't good at something, another might cover that weakness.

Combining AI models is an advanced move, but it's a logical extension of specialization, a principle well known in software engineering (think microservices, each service doing one thing well). Here, each AI service does one thing well. As a vibe coder, your role expands to AI conductor, not just AI prompter. It requires a bit more setup and thought, but the payoff is a symphony of AI collaborators each contributing to a high-quality end product.

Now that you know how they work, let's meet some of the leading examples and see how they stack up.

Major Players in Autonomous Coding Agents

As I write this in 2025, the autonomous coding agent landscape has rapidly evolved over the past year, with distinct approaches emerging across different platforms. These tools represent a shift from passively completing code to acting as active development partners that can execute complex tasks independently.

Cloud-based command-line agents: OpenAI Codex
OpenAI's Codex (*https://oreil.ly/Ml-NU*) exemplifies the cloud-based agent approach, operating through ChatGPT's interface or an open source CLI. It spins up isolated sandboxes to execute coding tasks in parallel, handling everything from React upgrades to unit test creation. What distinguishes Codex is its reinforcement-learning training on real coding tasks, enabling it to follow best practices, like running tests iteratively until they pass. While results can vary between runs, Codex typically converges on working solutions for well-bounded tasks. Its strength lies in actual code execution within CI-like environments, representing the first wave of agents that truly "pair" with development pipelines.

Workflow-integrated agents: Google Jules
Google Jules (*https://jules.google*) takes a different approach by deeply integrating with GitHub workflows. Running on Google Cloud VMs with full repository clones, Jules emphasizes visible, structured planning—presenting its reasoning and allowing plan modifications before execution. This "plan, then execute" philosophy, combined with real-time feedback capabilities, positions Jules as a supervised assistant rather than a black-box automation. Its GitHub-native design means it operates directly where teams work, creating branches and PRs without context switching. The agent even experiments with novel features like audio changelogs, pointing toward more accessible code review processes.

IDE-integrated agents: Cursor
Cursor's background agents (*https://oreil.ly/V-Pci*) represent the IDE-centric approach, launched directly from the editor but executing on remote machines. This hybrid model lets developers orchestrate multiple AI workers from their command center while maintaining local control. Cursor provisions Ubuntu instances with customizable environments (via *environment.json* or Dockerfiles), giving agents full internet access and package installation capabilities. The key innovation is seamless IDE integration: developers can monitor agent progress, intervene when needed, and immediately access changes locally when complete. This approach blurs the line between local AI assistance and cloud execution power.

Team-integrated agents: Devin
Devin (*https://devin.ai*) positions itself as an "AI teammate" rather than just a tool, integrating with Slack, GitHub, and issue trackers like Jira. Built by

---

Cognition Labs, it uses custom AI models tuned for long-term reasoning and multistep execution. Devin excels at parallel execution of small maintenance tasks like bugfixes, test additions, and linter cleanups that often get deprioritized. Its collaborative design includes status updates, clarification requests, and even automatic preview deployments. While it handles straightforward tasks well, complex issues can still require significant human intervention, highlighting the current boundaries of autonomous coding.

The field is expanding rapidly, with both established players and startups racing to define the category. Microsoft has hinted at "Copilot++," moving beyond inline suggestions to agent capabilities. Enterprises are being courted by startups like CodeGen (which uses Anthropic's Claude) promising "SWEs that never sleep." Meanwhile, open source projects and academic research continue pushing boundaries, exploring how to make code generation more reliable and contextual.

This proliferation suggests that we're witnessing the birth of a new development paradigm where individual developers orchestrate multiple AI agents, each specialized for different aspects of the software lifecycle. The key differentiators emerging are:

- Execution environment (local versus cloud)
- Integration depth (IDE versus workflow tools)
- Autonomy level (supervised versus independent)
- Target use cases (maintenance versus feature development)

Challenges and Limitations

While autonomous coding agents inherit the foundational challenges of AI-assisted development, as discussed throughout this book—particularly the 70% problem, explored in Chapter 3—their autonomous nature introduces distinct complications that warrant separate examination:

The compounding effect of sequential decisions
Unlike interactive AI assistance where humans intervene at each step, autonomous agents make chains of decisions that can compound errors in unique ways. When an agent misinterprets the initial requirements, it doesn't just generate one flawed function: it builds an *entire implementation architecture* on that misunderstanding. Each subsequent decision reinforces the original error, creating what I call "coherent incorrectness": code that's internally consistent but fundamentally misaligned with actual needs.

This sequential decision making particularly challenges agents that tackle multi-file changes. An agent implementing a new feature might correctly modify the backend API but then propagate incorrect assumptions through the frontend, database schema, and test suites. By the time you review the complete pull request, untangling these interconnected mistakes tends to require more effort than the interactive, incremental corrections that are possible with traditional AI assistance.

Environmental brittleness at scale

While Chapter 8 discusses general environment configuration challenges, autonomous agents face unique complications from their sandbox execution model. Each agent run requires spinning up an isolated environment that *precisely* mirrors your development setup—a challenge that scales poorly. When you're running multiple agents concurrently, even slight variations in the environment can lead to dramatically different outcomes.

Consider a scenario where five agents work on different features simultaneously. Agent A might have a slightly older Node version in its container, Agent B might lack a specific system library, and Agent C might have different time zone settings. These variations, invisible during execution, surface as subtle bugs that only appear when you begin integrating their work. This "environmental drift" between agent sandboxes represents a new class of integration challenge that is absent from single-developer workflows.

The async coordination paradox

Autonomous agents promise parallel development, but this introduces coordination challenges that are quite distinct from human team dynamics. When multiple agents modify overlapping code sections, they lack the implicit communication channels humans use—there's no quick Slack message asking, "Are you touching the auth module?" or informal awareness of what colleagues are working on.

This creates what I term the *async coordination paradox*: the more agents you run in parallel to increase productivity, the more complex integrating them becomes. Unlike human developers, who naturally coordinate through standups and informal communication, agents operate in isolation. You might discover that Agent A has refactored a utility function, while Agent B was busy adding new calls to the old version, creating conflicts that wouldn't occur if agents had human developers' natural awareness of each other's work.

The review bottleneck—amplified

While code review remains essential for all AI-generated code (as discussed in previous chapters), autonomous agents amplify this challenge through sheer volume and timing. Unlike interactive AI assistance, where code arrives incrementally as you work, agent-generated PRs appear as complete implementations—often as multiple PRs arriving simultaneously after overnight runs.

This creates a kind of cognitive overload that's distinct from the kind you get when reviewing human PRs. With human contributions, you can often rely on commit messages and PR descriptions to reflect a coder's actual thought processes. Agent PRs, however, require you to reverse-engineer the agent's "reasoning" from the code itself. When five agents each deliver PRs of 500 lines or more on Monday morning, the review burden shifts from being a collaborative quality check to something more like an archaeological expedition.

Delegating to agents requires trust

Perhaps most significantly, autonomous agents challenge our trust models in ways interactive AI tools don't. When you delegate a task to an agent and walk away, you're making an implicit bet about acceptable risk. This differs fundamentally from supervised AI assistance, where you maintain moment-by-moment control.

Consider agentic technologies' security implications. Autonomous agents with repository write access and execution capabilities present unique attack surfaces. A compromised or misdirected agent doesn't just *suggest* bad code—it actively *commits* it and potentially even *deploys* it. Our sandboxing and access controls for agents must be correspondingly more sophisticated than for suggestion-based tools (covered in Chapter 8).

Emerging organizational challenges

As teams scale up their agent usage, new organizational patterns are emerging that don't exist with traditional AI assistance. Who "owns" agent-generated code when the requesting developer is out sick? How do you track agent resource usage across teams? What happens when an agent's monthlong refactoring project conflicts with urgent feature development?

These aren't technical limitations but organizational challenges, and they're unique to autonomous systems. They require new roles (agent coordinators?), new processes (agent impact assessments?), and new tools (agent fleet management?) that extend beyond the individual developer considerations this book has addressed in earlier chapters.

The autonomous nature of these agents—their ability to work independently, make sequential decisions, and operate at scale—transforms them from productivity tools into something approaching team members. This shift demands not just the technical practices discussed throughout this book but entirely new frameworks for coordination, trust, and integration that we're only beginning to understand.

Best Practices for Using AI Coding Agents Effectively

While many general AI development practices apply to autonomous coding agents, certain aspects of agent-based development require specific consideration. Based on collective experience with tools like Codex, Jules, Devin, and Cursor's background agents, these practices address the unique challenges of delegating entire development tasks to AI systems operating independently.

Strategically Select the Tasks Autonomous Agents Are Going to Implement

The fundamental difference between AI assistants and autonomous agents lies in their scope and independence. Agents excel at well-defined, encapsulated tasks with clear success criteria—particularly those involving parallel execution of many small tasks. Ideal agent assignments include comprehensive test coverage improvements, systematic dependency updates, bulk refactoring operations, and standardized feature implementations across multiple components.

Consider the difference between asking an AI assistant to help write a single test versus tasking an agent to achieve 80% test coverage across an entire module. The agent can methodically work through each untested function, generate appropriate test cases, run them to verify correctness, and iterate until the coverage target is met. This type of systematic, measurable work is the sweet spot for autonomous agents.

Conversely, tasks that require making significant architectural decisions, interpreting complex stakeholder requirements, or designing novel algorithms remain better suited to human-led development with AI assistance. The key lies in recognizing which aspects of a larger task can be effectively delegated to agents and which require human judgment and creativity.

Leverage Agent-Specific Planning and Oversight Features

Modern autonomous agents distinguish themselves through sophisticated planning and execution transparency features that demand active engagement. When Jules presents its execution plan before beginning work or when Cursor displays real-time logs of agent activity, these represent critical intervention points that are unique to agent-based development.

The *planning phase* serves as your primary quality gate. Review proposed plans not just for correctness but for efficiency and alignment with your codebase conventions. If Jules plans to update a Next.js application but omits critical webpack configuration changes, catching this during planning prevents extensive rework later on. This proactive review differs fundamentally from reactive code review and represents a new skill in the developer toolkit.

Runtime monitoring provides another layer of agent-specific oversight. While you need not watch every operation, periodic checks can prevent agents from pursuing inefficient solutions or making unnecessarily broad changes. Cursor's ability to "enter" the agent's environment midtask exemplifies how modern tools support intervention without completely abandoning the autonomous workflow. To maximize efficiency, you'll need to learn when to intervene and when to let the agent self-correct.

Manage Concurrent Agent Operations

Unlike traditional development, where a single developer works on one task at a time, agents enable true parallel development. This capability requires new coordination strategies. When running multiple agents simultaneously—perhaps one updating dependencies while another adds logging infrastructure—you must consider the potential conflicts and dependencies between their work.

Establish clear boundaries for each agent's scope to minimize merge conflicts. Assign agents to different modules or layers of the application when possible. Consider the order of integration: an agent that is adding new features might need to wait for another agent's infrastructure improvements to complete. This orchestration resembles managing a distributed team more than it does traditional solo development.

Evolve Your Team Practices to Integrate Agents

The introduction of autonomous agents fundamentally alters team dynamics and review processes. Unlike reviewing a colleague's carefully crafted PR, agent-generated PRs may contain technically correct but stylistically inconsistent code. Teams must develop new review practices that account for this difference.

Consider establishing agent-specific review checklists that emphasize not just correctness but also alignment with team conventions and architectural patterns. Document common quirks you spot as you work with the agent: perhaps your chosen agent consistently uses certain antipatterns or misses specific optimization opportunities. This institutional knowledge helps reviewers quickly identify and address recurring issues.

Build Feedback Loops with Autonomous Systems

Perhaps most importantly, autonomous agents enable a new form of iterative development in which the feedback loop extends beyond mere code review. When an agent's pull request needs refinement, you can often send it back and ask for another iteration with specific guidance. This differs from traditional development, where sending work back to a human colleague carries social and time costs.

Work to develop prompting patterns that work well with your chosen agents. When you find successful prompt formulations that consistently yield high-quality results, document them. Create templates for common task types that include all necessary context and constraints. This is a kind of prompt engineering specifically for agents that considers their planning, execution, and revision cycles, and it represents a distinct skill from general AI interaction.

The goal remains unchanged: delivering high-quality software efficiently. Autonomous agents simply provide a new tool for achieving this goal, one you should integrate into your existing practices thoughtfully rather than replacing established methods wholesale. By understanding these agents and leveraging their unique capabilities while maintaining rigorous quality standards, teams can realize significant productivity gains without sacrificing code quality or architectural integrity.

Summary and Next Steps

To wrap up, I'll echo a sentiment from Chapter 4: AI won't replace developers, but developers who can use AI effectively may well replace those who can't. The advent of autonomous coding agents is a leap in that direction—those who learn to harness these "headless colleagues" will be able to do more in less time. It's an exciting time to be a software engineer, as long as we adapt and continue to hold our work to high standards. The tools may be changing, but the goals remain: build reliable, efficient, and innovative software. With AI agents at our side (or in the background), we have new ways to reach those goals—and perhaps get a good night's sleep while the bots burn the midnight oil.

Next, the final chapter of this book takes a broader look at the future of AI in coding, including the future of agentic AI.

CHAPTER 11

Beyond Code Generation: The Future of AI-Augmented Development

Vibe coding may have started with AI generating code from our prompts, but its implications reach far beyond just writing code. As AI technologies advance, they are poised to transform *every* aspect of the software development lifecycle. In this chapter, I take a speculative yet informed look at how AI's role in software might expand in the future. I will explore AI-driven testing, debugging, and maintenance; how AI could influence software design and user experience personalization; the evolution of project management with AI assistance; and even the future of programming languages themselves. The aim is to imagine a future where AI isn't just a code generator but a holistic participant in software engineering—all while grounding the discussion in fundamental principles, so it remains relevant even as specific technologies come and go.

AI in Testing, Debugging, and Maintenance

Imagine a future development environment where as soon as you write a function (whether by hand or via vibe coding), an AI tool immediately writes a suite of unit tests for it, finds potential bugs, and maybe even fixes them—all in a matter of seconds. This scenario is quickly becoming plausible. Let's break down AI's potential (and already emerging) contributions in quality assurance and maintenance.

Automated Test Generation

Writing thorough tests is time-consuming and often neglected due to deadlines. As you saw in Chapter 7, current AI assistants can alleviate this by generating tests automatically. For example, given a piece of code, an AI can suggest a set of unit tests covering typical cases, edge cases, and error conditions.

In the future, this could go further: the AI could examine your entire codebase, identify functions or modules with insufficient test coverage, and generate additional tests. It might even simulate inputs that a human tester wouldn't think of (like fuzz testing), potentially catching corner-case bugs. The benefit is a more robust codebase with minimal manual test writing.

The caveat is that tests are only as good as the AI's understanding of the specification. Thus, a human should review AI-generated tests to ensure they align with the intended behavior of the software. For instance, the AI might assert a certain output that is *technically* what the code does, but perhaps the requirement was different—which, as long as a human is in the loop, can actually help to catch a misunderstanding in either the code or the test.

Intelligent Debugging

Debugging often involves tedious searching through logs or stepping through code to locate the source of an error. Chapter 5 showed you how AI can act like a smart debugging companion. Some current AI tools can take an error message and problematic code as input and return an explanation and a code change to fix it.

For a glimpse of how AI-assisted debugging workflows may evolve, consider an AI system that monitors your program's execution, and when a crash or exception happens, it analyzes the stack trace and variable states to pinpoint the likely cause. Instead of just giving you an error message, it might say:

> The application crashed because userProfiles was null when calling getEmail(). This suggests a missing null-check when loading user profiles.

Further, the AI could suggest a fix:

> A possible solution is to initialize userProfiles if it's null or add a condition before calling getEmail(). Would you like me to apply this fix?

Future debugging AIs could integrate directly with runtime environments, catching issues in real time. They might even predict issues *before* they happen by analyzing code paths:

> This function might throw a DivisionByZero exception if called with y = 0; consider handling that case.

This is similar to static analysis but powered by the AI's learned knowledge of countless codebases and error patterns, making it potentially more insightful or flexible.

Predictive Maintenance and Refactoring

As requirements change over time, code becomes outdated or suboptimal. Maintenance involves activities like refactoring (improving code structure without changing behavior), updating dependencies, and optimizing performance. AI can assist in each of these areas:

Refactoring

A future AI could identify code smells (like duplicate code or long functions) and automatically refactor them. For instance, it might detect that you have similar chunks of code in three places and recommend abstracting them into a single helper function. Or it could transform a deeply nested set of loops into a more readable form. Since the AI has seen many examples of "good" code, it can suggest stylistic improvements (*https://oreil.ly/XWXC_*) to keep the codebase clean and maintainable. We might one day have a mode in our editors where the AI continuously refactors code in the background, with the developer reviewing and approving changes.

Updating dependencies

A future AI service might monitor your project's dependencies (such as libraries and frameworks) and automatically generate pull requests to update them to newer versions, including any code changes needed to accommodate breaking changes. For example, if a new version of a web framework changes the API, the AI could adapt your code to the new API. This would save developers the repetitive work of reading migration guides and fixing version issues.

Performance tuning

Maintenance often includes improving performance as data scales or usage patterns shift. AI can play a role by analyzing performance profiles and pointing out inefficiencies. For example, an AI might notice that a certain database query in your code is taking a long time and suggest adding an index or rewriting the query. It might identify that a loop in your code is making redundant calculations and propose a cache. This is akin to having a performance expert always keeping an eye on your application—proactively detecting inefficiencies like redundant loops or suboptimal data structures.

The AI might run in a staging environment, simulate heavy loads, and then feed you a report: "Under high load, Module X becomes a bottleneck due to Y. Consider refactoring using approach Z." In essence, the AI not only finds issues but also educates the team on better patterns.

AI-Driven Design and User Experience Personalization

Beyond the code and logic, AI is set to influence *how we design software and how users experience it.* Good software isn't just correct under the hood; it's also intuitive, accessible, and satisfying for users. AI will continue to develop new ways to create better user interfaces and tailor experiences to individual user needs.

Generative Design Tools

Today's AI design tools use techniques from generative adversarial networks or transformers to produce UI mockups from descriptions. A product manager can describe a feature in natural language:

> We need a mobile sign-up screen with a welcome message, a playful illustration, and a form for name, email, and password. It should have our brand colors and a friendly look.

An AI design assistant can take this description and generate several candidate UI designs in seconds, complete with layout, placeholder text, and even styled components. The designer or developer then picks the closest one and refines it.

In the future, these tools could be integrated directly into design software or even coding environments so that the line between "designing" and "coding the UI" blurs. The AI might directly output HTML/CSS or Flutter code for the design it generates, making it immediately testable. This would speed up the design iteration cycle tremendously. Instead of sketching by hand or in software, you'd collaborate with an AI that proposes designs based on best practices and vast training data of what users find appealing or usable.

Even in the creative process of design, an AI could be a muse. When a designer is brainstorming a color scheme or an illustration style for an app, an AI tool could generate a mood board of colors or even create custom iconography on the fly. For instance, they might tell the AI:

> I need a logo that combines the ideas of code and music.

It would produce a few sample logos mixing symbols of coding (like curly braces) with musical notes. While a professional designer might ultimately handcraft the final asset, the AI's suggestions can spark ideas and accelerate the exploration phase. In essence, AI can fill the role of a quick prototyper and creative partner that broadens the designer's palate of options.

It's important to note that in design and UX, human judgment is paramount. Aesthetic taste, understanding of human emotions, brand identity—these are things an AI can approximate but not inherently possess. Thus, AI in design is a tool to enhance human creativity, not replace it. It can handle the grunt work of producing variants and processing user data, freeing designers to focus on empathy and creative decisions.

For developers, AI-driven design means that the traditional handoff between design and development might become more fluid. Developers could generate UI code with AI in collaboration with designers, or vice versa. It also means frontend developers might spend less time tweaking layouts pixel by pixel and more time ensuring the design aligns with functionality and is implemented accessibly. They might also work

---

on creating the hooks for personalization—writing code that allows the AI to choose between layout A or B based on user data and ensuring both layouts are performant and solid.

In a future of vibe coding, you might "vibe design" as well: just describe the vibe (pun intended) you want for your application's look and feel, and AI will help materialize it. The result is a holistic AI development process—not just writing backend logic or database queries with AI assistance but crafting the whole product experience in partnership with AI.

AI for UX Research

Another aspect of design is understanding user behavior. AI can analyze usage data from your application (with privacy considerations in mind) to highlight where users struggle. For instance, an AI might detect that many users hover over a certain icon expecting it to be clickable, and it's not—indicating a UX improvement opportunity. Or it might notice that users from a certain demographic consistently drop off at a particular step of a workflow, suggesting that step might not be intuitive for them.

In the future, AI could even simulate user interactions (using models of user behavior) to predict UX issues *before* real users encounter them. This "virtual UX testing" could catch things like overly complex navigation or unclear labels during development, when they're easier to fix.

Personalized User Experiences

Personalization has been a buzzword for a while—in the sense of providing different content to different users based on preferences or history. AI can take personalization to the next level by fine-tuning software behavior and interfaces for each user in real time. For example, an app's AI could learn that a particular user tends to navigate the app via search rather than menus. The AI could then adapt by making the search bar more prominent for that user or even preloading search results it expects the user might want given the context (like a human assistant anticipating their boss's needs).

Another scenario would improve accessibility: if the AI detects a user is using screen-reader technology (and thus is perhaps visually impaired), it could automatically switch the application to a high-contrast, larger-font mode with optimized screen-reader labels, even beyond what the static accessibility settings might do. Essentially, software can become *adaptive*.

Imagine an ecommerce site that rearranges its layout on the fly—some users might see a grid of products and others a list with more details, depending on what seems to engage them more. These changes could be subtle and continuous as the AI experiments and learns—somewhat like how A/B testing works but on an individual level and autonomously.

The Evolution of Project Management with AI

Software development isn't just writing code and making designs; it's also planning, coordinating, and making decisions—the domain of project management and team leadership. AI's analytical and predictive capabilities can greatly assist in managing projects, from allocation of tasks to risk management and decision support. Here's how AI could reshape the way we plan and execute software projects:

Task allocation

Managing a team involves knowing each developer's strengths, weaknesses, and current workload, then assigning tasks accordingly. An AI project management assistant could analyze various data points—code commit history, areas of expertise (perhaps gleaned from which parts of the codebase a developer has worked on), even personal productivity patterns (some people code more effectively in the morning, others late at night)—and recommend who should tackle a new task.

For example, if a new feature involves database work and the AI knows Alice has done a lot of database-related tasks successfully and isn't overloaded, it might suggest assigning the task to Alice. Moreover, the AI could predict how long the task might take by comparing it to similar tasks in the past and considering the individual's velocity. This helps project managers set more realistic timelines and avoid overburdening any single team member. Over time, such an AI could learn to balance the workload like a skilled manager, ensuring that no one is idle and no one is overwhelmed.

Scheduling and sprint planning

AI can assist in breaking down high-level goals into actionable items. You might feed the AI a feature request or a user story, and it could suggest a list of subtasks required to implement it. Essentially, it could produce a draft plan or a work breakdown structure. During sprint planning (in Agile methodologies), the AI could analyze the backlog and, given the team's past velocity, suggest which set of tasks fits into the next sprint.

It could even highlight dependencies between tasks, ensuring the plan is logically ordered:

Task B should be done after Task A, as it builds on that functionality.

For long-term roadmapping, AI tools might simulate different scenarios:

If we prioritize Feature X now, the model predicts we risk delaying Feature Y by 2 weeks due to overlapping resource needs.

Having these simulations and data-driven insights can help human managers make informed decisions on priorities.

Risk analysis and management

Risk management often involves anticipating what could go wrong—delays, technical hurdles, integration issues—and planning mitigation efforts. AI is well suited for pattern recognition, so it could analyze historical project data (within the company or even industry-wide, if available) to identify risk factors.

For example, the AI might flag things like:

- Projects involving a switch in technology stack have a 30% higher chance of running over schedule based on historical data.
- We have slipped in integration testing phase in the last three projects; likely a risk for this project as well.

With this, managers can preemptively allocate more time or resources to those phases. Another angle is monitoring current progress: an AI system could watch the rate of task completion, the rate of bug discovery, etc., and send alerts if it senses trouble:

The team is closing tasks at half the expected rate this sprint; possible blockers need attention.

Essentially, AI can be an ever-vigilant project auditor, spotting issues before they escalate.

Decision support

Project management involves many decisions—like whether to cut a feature to meet a deadline or whether to invest in refactoring instead of adding new features. AI can't make these decisions because they involve business and human factors, but it can provide data to support them. For instance, if debating a refactor, the AI might report:

If we refactor module Z, based on complexity metrics and team input, it could reduce future development time on related features by 20%. It might add a two-week delay now but pay off in six months.

While these numbers would be estimates, having an objective analysis helps stakeholders weigh trade-offs more concretely.

Another example might be deciding whether to adopt a new library or build in-house. The AI could scan documentation, community support, and known issues about that library and summarize its pros and cons, saving the team hours of research.

Natural-language status queries

Stakeholders or managers could one day query an AI in natural language about project status:

How is the payment integration feature going? What are the blockers?

The AI, having parsed ticket updates, commit messages, and test results, might answer:

> The payment integration is 70% complete. One blocker is a failing test related to currency conversion, which two developers are currently debugging. If resolved by tomorrow, the feature is on track for completion by Friday.

This kind of accessible status reporting can improve communication, especially in large teams or teams with nontechnical stakeholders. The AI basically becomes an omniscient project assistant that knows the nitty-gritty details and can summarize them as needed.

Emotional and team health insights
This is a bit speculative, but AI could also gauge team morale or stress by analyzing communication patterns (respecting privacy and boundaries, of course). For example, an AI might detect that code review comments are becoming terse or Jira tickets are getting a lot of "reopen" actions—possibly indicating confusion or frustration—and gently alert a project lead to check in on the team's well-being. In remote or distributed teams, where such signals are harder to read, an AI that monitors the "digital mood" could be valuable. Of course, this would have to be handled delicately and transparently to avoid feeling invasive.

In all these ways, AI acts as a force multiplier for project managers. It handles the heavy analysis and routine suggestions, allowing human managers to focus on what they do best: making judgment calls, motivating the team, and handling the human side of collaboration. Good project management is as much art as science; AI can strengthen the science part (data, predictions, analysis) so that the art (leadership, vision, adaptability) can shine. Developers should welcome these enhancements too: a well-planned, well-monitored project means clearer goals and fewer nasty surprises. It also means less time in status meetings or updating spreadsheets—since the AI takes care of those details—and more time doing creative development work.

How Autonomous Agents Could Change Software Engineering

We're still in the early innings of this technology, but it's moving fast. It's worth pondering the longer-term implications and how things might evolve in the next few years. Here's a vision of the future of software engineering in the age of autonomous coding agents, drawing from current trends and some informed speculation:

AI agents will become a standard part of the dev team
Just as using source control or CI/CD is standard today, having AI agents participate in development could become routine. It might be normal that, every morning, you check an "AI assistant board" showing tasks done overnight by agents—

the code reviews will be waiting for you when you log in. There's already a hint of this today, with agents running "while you sleep." Engineers might commonly delegate a batch of tasks at day's end for the AI to attempt by next morning. The mindset of what a "developer's job" is will shift: less about typing out boilerplate or doing rote updates, more about defining problems, integrating solutions, and guiding the AI. You might say, to be a bit fanciful, that developers become more like product managers for AI developers—they specify what needs doing and ensure that it meets requirements.

Multiagent collaboration will be more common

Right now, each agent largely works in isolation on a task you give it. But the future could see scenarios where multiple agents with different specialties collaborate. One agent might be great at frontend tasks and another at backend tasks, and you give them a coordinated task (or maybe they even *figure out* how to split it). Alternatively, an agent could explore multiple solution paths in parallel—what Kojo calls *multibranch exploration*.

Imagine you give a complex problem to an AI and it spins up three subtasks with different approaches or architectures, then chooses the best one—or even asks *you* which direction you prefer. This could dramatically reduce the time it takes to evaluate different implementations (something that currently might take multiple engineers prototyping over days). Of course, orchestrating that is a nontrivial task, but it's not out of the question as agent frameworks become more advanced.

Intelligent checkpointing will let AIs ask humans for help

Future agents may be smart enough to ask for guidance proactively at decision points. This isn't just speculation: there's active research happening on uncertainty estimation and self-reflection for LLMs, with early signs that models can be trained or prompted to recognize when they're unsure and ask for help rather than forge ahead. For example, an agent might reach a point where two libraries could be used to implement something and instead of guessing, it pauses (much like a junior dev might) and asks you:

> I could use Library A or B for this—do you have a preference?

There's a growing belief in the industry that adding this kind of "intelligent checkpointing" makes agents feel more trustworthy, like collaborators rather than black boxes. It also aligns well with how humans work in teams—knowing when to ask instead of bluffing. While it's still early, we're starting to see more models that support this kind of behavior through techniques like tool-use reflection, planning with uncertainty thresholds, and making explicit affordances for user feedback midrun. Intelligent checkpointing requires the agent to know its own uncertainty, which is a challenge, but researchers are working on AI self-awareness, including confidence.

Agent UX will improve

As we offload more work to agents, we'll need better ways to keep track of what they're doing. Kojo proposes an *agent inbox*—a unified view of what tasks agents are working on, what's been done, and what needs your attention. This could be a dashboard showing all running agent tasks along with their progress ("3/5 steps completed" or "awaiting review") and results.

Instead of the current mix of logs and PRs, a clear interface to manage agents will emerge. Perhaps IDEs will have an "Agents" sidebar listing active tasks and a feed of updates. You might also get notifications:

- Agent X has finished task Y and opened PR #123.
- Agent Z needs input to continue.

This infrastructure will be important to scaling up usage without losing overview. After all, no one wants 10 silent bots doing who knows what with no central control.

Agents will integrate with issue trackers and CI systems

I foresee a tighter loop where an issue in your tracker (Jira, GitHub Issues, Linear) can be addressed by an agent from end to end. In fact, CodeGen's Linear integration already hints at this.

The workflow might be as follows:

1. A PM files a ticket with specs.
2. A developer (or tech lead) approves it for AI.
3. An AI agent picks it up, does it, and attaches the PR to the ticket.
4. A human reviews and tests the fix and closes the ticket.

This could make the development process more continuous. Similarly, CI systems might invoke agents automatically when certain checks fail. For instance, if a security scan finds vulnerabilities, an agent could attempt to upgrade the vulnerable library or refactor the risky code and then open a PR with the fix. Or if code coverage drops below threshold after a PR, an agent could generate additional tests to raise it. Think of it as *automated maintenance*.

As a concrete example, Dependabot currently opens PRs to update dependencies. Not only could an AI agent open the PR, but it could also adjust any code that broke due to the update, run tests, and ensure it's all good—basically a supercharged Dependabot.

Model improvements will narrow the 30% gap

The major AI models themselves (GPT-4, Gemini, Claude, and the like) will continue to improve their code understanding and generation. As they get more capable, that "last 30%" gap might shrink. We might see agents that hardly ever miss an obvious reuse or edge case, because the model has been trained on even more scenarios or has better reasoning.

With better models, agents will make fewer mistakes, require less oversight, and possibly handle more complex tasks. That said, software is inherently complex, so I suspect there will *always* be some gap for human judgment. Maybe it becomes the last 5%–10% rather than the last 30%.

I also expect models to become more efficient, making it feasible for those worried about data privacy (or cost) to run local or self-hosted agents. Open source coding models might catch up, to the point where you can have an on-prem agent that's nearly as good for many tasks as the big cloud agents.

Agents and tooling will become more specialized

We might see specialized coding agents for different domains or roles. Imagine a "BugFixer" agent that you point at a failing test or error log and it zeroes in on the bug, a "PerformanceGuru" agent that focuses on profiling and optimizing hot spots, or a specialized agent for writing documentation and code comments from an existing codebase.

By specializing, agents could incorporate more domain-specific knowledge or tools. We might see an agent that integrates with game engines to help with game dev tasks, or one that's great at data-engineering pipelines. A team of narrow AI specialists could parallel the distribution of expertise within human teams, where some devs are known for frontend work and others for infrastructure. You could have AI teammates like DocsBot, TestBot, RefactorBot, and SecurityBot, each tuned for those purposes. In fact, Cursor already has something called BugBot for automated PR reviews, which is a step in that direction. BugBot doesn't write code; it comments on PRs with a focus on bug risks, like a static analysis on steroids.

Developers will undergo a cultural and skill shift

If agents handle more routine coding, the skill sets of developers will shift more toward design, architecture, and oversight, as discussed in Chapter 4. Soft skills, like clearly communicating requirements (to humans and AIs alike), become even more important. Code reading and review skills may well become as essential as code writing skills. We might also place more emphasis on testing: since tests are a critical way to verify AI outputs, being good at writing test cases (or guiding AI to write them) remains valuable.

Essentially, the "human 30%" will concentrate on the higher-level critical thinking and quality-control aspects of software development. I suspect we'll also see changes in how junior developers ramp up. Maybe they'll start by managing an AI agent on simple tasks before writing a ton of code themselves, which could be both good (they can deliver value quickly) and challenging (they need to learn the fundamentals and not treat the AI as a crutch). It's an exciting time for those willing to adapt, but it may be uncomfortable for those who prefer the old ways. As I noted in Chapter 4, a big part of "future-proofing" your career in this AI era is embracing these tools and emphasizing your uniquely human strengths.

New roles and processes will emerge

We might see the rise of roles like "AI Wrangler" or "Automation Lead" in engineering teams—people who are particularly skilled at leveraging AI agents, designing workflows around them, and maintaining their configurations. It's analogous to how "build/release engineers" emerged when build systems became complex, or "DevOps engineers" as infrastructure automation grew. Similarly, audits to check that AI has not introduced any insecure patterns might become standard in code reviews.

There may be more emphasis on testing culture to provide extra confidence: perhaps every agent PR will have to include tests (written by the agent or a human) to be considered for merge. If AI agents are writing a lot of the code, maybe human engineers should write more of the tests (or vice versa) to ensure independent verification.

In essence, the future with background coding agents looks like one where developers orchestrate and verify, while AI agents execute and implement (see Figure 11-1). Software engineering could become more about supervising a fleet of automated coders and less about doing every step manually. This could unlock massive productivity, reduce the boring grunt work, and even allow teams to tackle technical debt and maintenance tasks they never had time for before. (Imagine clearing out all those minor bugs and inconsistencies because now you can just tell an AI to handle them!) It might also lower the barrier to prototyping new ideas: you could have an AI draft a whole prototype app, then just fine-tune it yourself. We may also get to explore more solutions before settling on decisions, since AI can generate alternatives quickly.

However, our industry must integrate these changes carefully. The human element—with its creativity, intuition, and ethical judgment—remains irreplaceable. AI can amplify our abilities, but it can also amplify mistakes if unchecked.

My vision is optimistic: used wisely, autonomous coding agents will make developers *more* productive and allow us to focus on the truly challenging and interesting parts of building software, ultimately leading us to build better software faster. Achieving that means cultivating good practices and being aware that our role as developers and engineers is evolving.

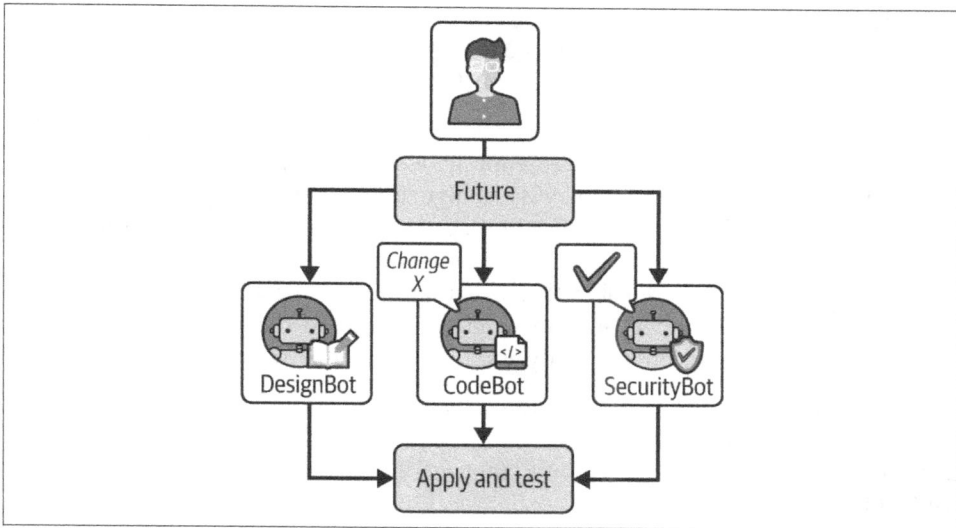

Figure 11-1. Multiagent AI collaboration architecture: developers orchestrate specialized AI agents for testing, design, coding, and security to collaboratively develop comprehensive software solutions.

The Future of Programming Languages: Natural-Language-Driven Development?

One of the most intriguing questions about the future of vibe coding is how it will shape programming languages. If we can "just tell the AI what we want," will we even need traditional syntax and languages? Will English (or any human language) become the new programming language? This section explores the possibilities.

We've already seen signs of natural language functioning as code in tools where you describe a task in plain language and the AI writes the code. If this trend continues, we might shift more of the programming effort to specifying the *intent* and *requirements* rather than the implementation. Future development environments could allow developers (or even nondevelopers) to write something like this:

> Every hour, check our database for inactive users, and send an email reminder to any user who hasn't logged in for 90 days, using template X. If the email bounces, mark the user as 'invalid email' in the database.

The AI could take this specification and translate it into the appropriate code (like setting up a cron job or scheduled function, writing the SQL queries or using the ORM, or calling an email API). Essentially, the programmer's role becomes more about policy and behavior description.

This doesn't mean programming languages will vanish overnight. Instead, what might happen is a *layering*: natural language for high-level orchestration and existing programming languages under the hood for fine-grained control.

One reason programming languages exist is because natural language can be ambiguous. If we remove formal languages entirely, we risk miscommunicating with the machine. AI might bridge this gap by disambiguating based on context and by asking clarifying questions, but there's likely a limit; certain complex algorithms or optimizations might still require very specific instructions that are easier to convey in code than prose. Thus, it's conceivable that programmers of the future will need to be bilingual in a sense: fluent in human language to talk to the AI, and fluent in the underlying technical concepts to verify and tweak what the AI produces.

We might also see the rise of *domain-specific natural languages*—constrained forms of English (or other languages) that AIs can reliably understand, tailored to software domains: for example, a "requirements language" for writing use cases that the AI can convert into tests or code.

Even if they don't go all the way to full natural language, AI's influence will likely bring programming languages to higher levels of abstraction. In the past, we moved from assembly to high-level languages and from manual memory management to garbage-collected environments, each time raising the level of abstraction. AI could allow us to define abstractions on the fly. Think of this in terms of "programming with intent," as discussed throughout this book: you specify a goal and the AI figures out how to achieve it, possibly writing lower-level code as needed.

Another possibility is *hybrid* languages that blend natural language and code. For example, a future language might allow code like this:

```
// Create a list of customer names from the orders, excluding duplicates

// and sorted alphabetically, then print it.

list<Customer> customers = orders -> map(order -> order.customerName)

                                  -> unique()

                                  -> sort()

                                  -> print();
```

In this pseudo example, the comment in English is almost executable by the AI. Maybe, in the actual environment, you wouldn't even need the lambda syntax; the AI could infer from the comment what you intend and fill it out. Or maybe the language would have constructs that look like English but are formal enough for the AI to parse. Think of it as an evolution of comments and pseudocode into actual code, with AI interpreting the intent behind them.

Coding is already becoming more conversational. Instead of writing a complete program, you start a dialogue with the AI:

Prompt: "I need a function to calculate loyalty points for customers based on their purchase history."

AI: "Sure. Do all products count equally, or do some products give more points? And how should time factor in (e.g., recent purchases versus older)?"

Prompt: "Electronics give 2x points compared to other categories. And purchases in the last month give a 10% bonus."

AI: "Understood. Here is the function implementing that… *[AI presents code]*. Shall I also generate tests for different scenarios?"

Prompt: "Yes, and also make sure it handles the case of no purchase history gracefully (should return 0 points)."

In this scenario, programming is a back-and-forth in natural language with the AI, which writes the code and asks clarification questions. This is akin to pair programming, except the pair partner is an AI. We already see early versions with ChatGPT plug-ins and Copilot Chat, etc. In the future, this could become the dominant mode for creating software: a conversation that progressively refines the software, which is much more fluid than writing a strict static text file from scratch.

Even if much of coding becomes natural language–driven, understanding how code and computers work will remain important. Calculators and spreadsheets didn't eliminate the need for a mathematician or accountant to understand arithmetic. You need to know when the AI's output is *off* somehow. If the AI misunderstands an English instruction, a skilled developer might switch to pseudocode or actual code to pin it down. So while the trivia of syntax might become less crucial (no need to remember the exact order of some API's parameters if the AI can fill that in), algorithmic thinking and debugging will still be vital. The languages might change, but the underlying logic and problem-solving skills persist.

However, the barrier to entry for programming is already lower. Nondevelopers and domain experts can directly create simple applications by conversing with AI through vibe coding. This democratization is exciting: more people can create software solutions without deep programming knowledge. The professional developers will then tackle the harder problems, integrate those citizen-developed scripts safely, or build the platforms that allow such interactions.

Even as AI helps us code in natural language, AIs themselves might evolve new "languages" that are somewhere in between. Perhaps new programming paradigms will emerge that are inherently AI-friendly—meaning they leave space for the AI to fill in blanks, for instance, a language that allows partial programs with placeholders that an AI can resolve ("[Optimize here for speed]") or with fuzzy logic that the AI can refine into deterministic logic.

In the end, what's likely is not a complete replacement of programming languages with English but a fusion of the two: more expressive power for developers and a more intuitive way to tell computers what to do. As Andrej Karpathy aptly puts it (*https://www.youtube.com/watch?v=LCEmiRjPEtQ*), "Maybe the future of programming isn't about writing perfect code anymore. Maybe it's about perfectly explaining what you want." The essence of programming—thinking clearly about a problem and specifying a solution—remains. The form of the specification, however, will evolve to be more natural, with AI as the translator that turns our high-level intentions into low-level execution.

This future holds great promise: faster development, more accessibility, and the ability to create increasingly complex systems by focusing on *what* we want to achieve rather than the nitty-gritty of *how to type it out*. As always, each leap in abstraction has led to an explosion in creativity (high-level languages enabled software that assembly could never have scaled to). Natural-language-driven development could unleash another wave of innovation, with vibe coders at the forefront, literally *talking* new worlds into existence through software.

How Vibe Coding Is Reshaping the Industry

Throughout this book, several fundamental principles and ideas have emerged:

Intent over implementation
> Vibe coding shifts the focus from writing step-by-step code to expressing the intent or desired outcome and letting AI handle the implementation details. This changes how we approach problems: we think more about *what* we want to achieve and less about *how to type it out*. It's a higher-level way of thinking about software development.

AI as a collaborative partner
> Rather than a tool used in isolation, AI in vibe coding is like a pair programmer or an assistant. It's interactive and iterative. We saw how important it is to guide the AI (through prompt engineering), to review its output, and to combine our strengths with the AI's. The future isn't "AI replacing programmers" but programmers working alongside AI for greater productivity (*https://oreil.ly/0uP00*).

Ethics and responsibility
> We emphasized that with great power (of AI) comes great responsibility. Mitigating bias, ensuring fairness, keeping processes transparent, and maintaining accountability are all critical. The industry is recognizing that relying on AI without guardrails can cause issues, so best practices around testing AI outputs, documenting AI involvement, and addressing legal questions (like IP rights of AI-generated code) are becoming part of standard procedure.

AI goes beyond code generation

AI's role extends to testing, debugging, design, project management, and more. This holistic integration means the entire software lifecycle is accelerated and enhanced by AI. Tools will increasingly support these phases—some already do, like AI test generation in IDEs or AI-based project scheduling tools.

Skills are evolving, but fundamentals are evergreen

Programmers who embrace the previously mentioned practices will find that their skill set is evolving—shifting to include prompt engineering, AI oversight, data analysis, and high-level design alongside traditional coding and algorithmic skills. The core problem-solving mindset remains crucial, but the day-to-day tasks look different.

Yet certain fundamentals hold: understanding your problem domain deeply, writing clear specifications (prompts are basically specs), maintaining rigorous testing and validation, and focusing on user needs. AI doesn't change these; if anything, it amplifies their importance because any ambiguity or lack of clarity can be magnified by AI's ultrafast execution.

This new paradigm of vibe coding is reshaping the industry in practical ways. Teams that adopt AI tools report significant boosts in productivity: developers can complete features in less time, or handle more complex projects with the same resources. It's also lowering entry barriers: less-experienced developers can achieve more with AI guidance, potentially leveling up faster. On the flip side, it's pushing experienced devs to expand their horizons and avoid getting complacent with old workflows.

Companies are starting to hire not just for programming knowledge but also for "AI literacy"—the ability to leverage AI tools effectively. Job descriptions might soon include familiarity with AI coding assistants, just like they include familiarity with version control or cloud platforms today. Being a pioneer in vibe coding thus offers a career advantage.

Importantly, vibe coding democratizes programming to an extent. More people—including those who aren't traditional software engineers—can participate in software creation by describing what they want. This could lead to a flourishing of software tailored to niche needs, created by domain experts with the help of AI (with professional developers focusing on providing guardrails, platforms, and polished core components for them to use).

It's an inspirational time. We stand on the brink of a transformation that we as developers get to shape. Think back to the early days of computing: those who embraced the personal computer revolution ended up creating the world we have now. Today, AI in programming is a similar inflection point. Embracing it means being part of defining how software is built for decades to come.

Summary and Next Steps

The future of programming is not something that will just happen to us—it's something we will create. Each of us in the developer community has a role to play in how vibe coding and AI tools are adopted, regulated, and advanced. This is a call to action for you as a reader and practitioner:

Experiment

Don't wait for all the answers to be given to you. Go out and try vibe coding in different contexts. Use AI to build something quirky and new. Push the boundaries of what these tools can do. Maybe you'll discover a novel use case or a limitation that no one has documented yet. Each experiment, whether it succeeds or fails, contributes knowledge to the community.

Share your findings

Write about your experiences or at least discuss them with peers. If you find a technique that works brilliantly, publish it. If you encounter a pitfall, warn others. In this rapid evolution, community knowledge sharing is how we all keep up. You could save someone days of debugging by posting that solution you found to an AI quirk, or spark someone's creativity by sharing a cool AI-assisted project.

Contribute to tools

If you have the inclination, contribute to the development of AI tools themselves. This might mean contributing code to open source AI frameworks or simply giving detailed feedback to tool makers (many of whom are very eager to hear from users about what to improve). By helping shape the tools, you directly influence how the future will look. Many AI coding assistants today have come a long way because developers like you tested beta versions and provided insight.

Advocate for positive change

Within your organizations or communities, advocate for using AI to improve productivity and also for training people to use it properly. Encourage managers to allow time for learning AI tools or to update policies that might forbid them out of misunderstanding. Show how it can be done securely and beneficially. The more success stories emerge of AI augmenting teams positively, the more the industry will lean into it.

Keep a lifelong student mentality

Adopt the mindset that we are all students in this new era. Stay humble and open-minded. The juniors of tomorrow might come in knowing AI tooling natively (like how today's new grads might have grown up with more exposure to coding than some older folks did). Be ready to learn from anyone, regardless of experience level, because this is new to everyone in some way. If you keep that student mentality, you'll always find growth and avoid the trap of thinking you've figured it all out.

Balance enthusiasm with prudence

Be enthusiastic about what's possible—your excitement will inspire others. But also be the voice of prudence when needed, ensuring that excitement doesn't lead to careless use. For example, champion AI-driven development but also push for unit tests and code reviews on AI outputs. This balanced approach will make vibe coding sustainable and respected.

Mentor the next generation

As you gain mastery, help newcomers. Vibe coding lowers the barriers to entry, meaning more beginners might dive into programming. They'll need guidance to learn solid fundamentals that AI might abstract away. By mentoring them, you ensure that the next generation of developers doesn't become overly reliant on AI without understanding. You'll be passing on the torch of good software engineering practices, now enhanced by AI.

The exponential change we're seeing is a rare opportunity. Think of previous technological leaps, from the Industrial Revolution to the internet boom—those who engaged with them shaped entire industries. We are at such a juncture with AI in software development. It's not just about keeping your job or making it easier; it's about having a say in how technology evolves and how it impacts society.

By reading this book, you've shown you're a forward-thinking person. Now, I encourage you to take that forward thinking and put it into action. Every line of code you write with AI, every prompt you engineer, every colleague you teach, every policy you influence—it all contributes to the future of vibe coding.

In closing, remember that at its heart, coding has always been about creation and solving problems. Vibe coding, powered by AI, is an incredibly powerful new medium for creation. Embrace it with optimism and curiosity. Use it to build things that matter. And as you do, keep the human element at the center—our creativity, our judgment, our values.

The future of programming is being written right now, not just in code but in how we choose to integrate these AI partners into our work. It's an exciting, uncharted path, and each of us gets to be a pioneer. So step forward, experiment boldly, share freely, and lead with the best of human intellect and spirit. By doing so, you won't just be adapting to the future—you'll be actively *shaping* it.

Happy vibe coding, and I'll see you in the future you help create!

Index

A

accessibility, future improvement with AI, 209

actions and reasoning in ReAct prompts, 57

adaptability and learning, importance of, 87

AI (artificial intelligence)
  autonomous AI coding agents, 71
  coding assistance, 3
  coding spectrum, 4
  combining multiple models to maximize strengths, 195-197
  confidence far exceeding its reliability, 68
  as first drafter, 72, 73
  going beyond code generation, 221
  midlevel engineers using, 88
  as pair programmer, 72, 75
    best practices for, 75
  practicing problem solving and debugging without using AI, 91
  real-time collaboration with in full stack development, 133-135
  as validator, 72, 76
  where AI still struggles, 33

AI pair programmer versus AI assistant developer, 192

AI patterns, learning from, 164

AI-assisted engineering, 3
  differences from vibe coding, 10
  structured approach with AI partner, 7-10
    code migration or refactoring, 8
    expectations, 9
    generating full mini-application or feature from detailed specs, 9
    goal of high-quality code, 9
    workflow, 7

when it should take precedence, 32

AI-augmented development, future of, 205-223
  automated test generation, 205
  how vibe coding is shaping the industry, 220
  intelligent debugging, 206
  possible changes by autonomous agents to software engineering, 212-216
  predictive maintenance and refactoring, 206
  project management, evolution with AI, 210-212
  shaping programming languages or possible natural-language-driven development, 217-220
  shaping the future of vibe coding, 222-223

AI-based coding tools
  generating convincing but incorrect output, 68
  incapable of producing new abstractions or strategies, 68
  integrating testing suggestions, 105
  situations in which they struggle, 68
  tasks they excel at, 67

AI-generated code, understanding, 97-107
  code readability and structure, 100
  debugging strategies for, 101
  developer's role, reviewing, refining, and owning the code, 106
  majority solution not most appropriate solution, 99
  refactoring code for maintainability and ownership of, 103
  unit, integration, and end-to-end testing, importance of, 104

AI-human collaboration, optimizing in full stack development, 134
algorithms
    junior developers' understanding of, 91
    performance optimization in AI-generated code, 158
ambiguous references in prompts, 42
Angular, 121
    tips on, 126
Anthropic's Claude language model, 21
APIs
    backend/API development patterns with AI, 126-130
        API documentation and testing, 130
        implementing endpoints, 126
        multistep operations at endpoints, orchestrating, 128
    failed calls, error handling on frontend, 133
    integrating in web application frontend using AI, 125
    junior developers implementing new endpoint following patterns, 90
    outdated, checking for use in AI code, 101
    penetration and fuzzing tests on, 151
    testing error handling in AI-generated systems, 155
    in web application backends, 121
architect and editor, senior engineers and developers as, 82
architecture
    foundational texts on, 161
    midlevel engineers learning system architecture, 88
    solid architecture needing human oversight, 88
    using architectural patterns to encourage modularity and avoid sprawl, 160
Artifacts feature (Claude), 28
async agents, 188
    (see also autonomous background coding agents)
    coordination paradox, 200
async/await functions, 159
attributions for AI-generated code, 177
audits
    periodic security and performance audits of codebase, 169
    security, 137
        (see also security)

authentication
    asking AI to whip up user logging system, 6
    creating REST API for with Cline, 20
    improper, in AI-generated code, 145, 146
author of AI-generated code, 173
authorization, improper, in AI-generated code, 145
autonomous AI coding agents, 71
    using VSCode with Cline, 20
autonomous background coding agents, 187
    about, 187
    best practices for effective use, 202-204
    challenges and limitations, 199-201
    comparison to in-IDE AI assistants, 192
    how they could change software engineering, 212-216
    how they work, 188-192
    major players in, 198-199

B

backends
    backend/API development patterns with AI
        business logic and validation, 127
        database integration, 127
        implementing endpoints, 126
        using frameworks or boilerplates, 127
    hardening for service converting CSV files to charts, 117
    integrating with frontend in web application using AI, 132-135
        aligning frontend and backend contracts, 132
        real-time collaboration with AI, 133
    testing error handling in AI-generated systems, 155
    web application, 121
background coding agents, 187
    (see also autonomous background coding agents)
Bandit (security scanner), 149
bcrypt, using to hash and compare passwords, 147
bias in AI output, 37, 178-181, 184
bidirectional translation (ChatGPT), 28
big ball of mud architectural antipattern, 161
blue-green deployments, 168
Bolt.new, 111
boundaries between system components, managing, 84

handling frontend complex logic with AI guidance, 125

Composer mode (Cursor), 21

concurrency, 91, 159

concurrent agent operations, managing, 203

configurations, insecure, in AI-generated code, 145

consistency and standardization in coding, 36

constraints
  including in prompts, 42
  mentioning in contextual prompts, 55

constructs, AI-specific, overrelying on, 162

context
  Claude's understanding of broader context, 28
  context window size in vibe coding, 18
  Cursor's project-wide context, 23
  global context suggestions by Windsurf, 24
  leveraging in AI-assisted coding, 14

context window, 51

contextual prompting, 54

control over AI-generated prototyping, 112

conversation, stateful, versus one-shot prompting, 60

conversational interfaces, generating complete applications through, 111

Copilot, 192
  lawsuit against, 174
  reactive nature of Copilot-style assistants, 193

copyrights, AI-generated code and, 172, 173
  possible copyrightable material, 174

cost optimization, 88

credentials
  hard-coded, in AI-generated code, 144
  management of for deployments, 168

credentials, hard-coded, in AI-generated code, 144

critical thinking and foresight, 85

cross-site scripting (XSS) in web apps, 145

CRUD (create, read, update, delete) operations, 30
  feature prototyping and CRUD applications, 31

CSS
  AI generating, 109
  AI integrating CSS library, 114
  AI outputting CSS styling, 115

Cline generating complete CSS/HTML page example, 110
  handling for web application frontend using AI, 124

CSV files, converting to charts, AI-assisted prototyping of, 117

cultural biases, 178

Cursor IDE, 21, 111, 187, 190
  background coding agents, 198
  background coding gents, 189
  code generation by, 21
  editing existing code, 22
  Gemini's integration with, 27
  using effectively in professional workflow, 22

D

dashboards
  internal company dashboard built using AI, 138

data bias, 179

data consistency rules (database), 132

data partitioning and replication, 88

data protection laws, 181

data structures, 91

databases
  design and integration in web application using AI, 130-132
    checking AI-generated queries, 131
    database queries, 131
    using an ORM, 130
  integration in web application backend using AI, 127
  query optimization for AI-generated code, 159
  in web application backends, 121
    transactions in, 129

date formatting, using AI for, 73
  mismatches in AI-generated components generated in isolation, 157

de minimis, 172

death of the junior developer, 90

debugging
  of AI-assisted code, 10
  of AI-generated code, 101-103
  by autonomous coding agents, 193
  effective prompts to AI for, 44
  intelligent debugging using AI, 206
  junior developers practicing without AI, 91

lack of skill development in caused by AI
coding, 71
as timeless engineering skill, 86
using Cursor, 23
decision support in project management, 211
deep reasoning models, 25
DeepSeek model, 25
defaults, insecure, in AI-generated code, 145
deletes
cascading deletes in databases, 132
demo-quality trap, 72
democratization of programming, 7
dependence on AI coding tools, problems
caused by, 71
dependencies, 121
background coding agents installing, 188
checking for unvetted libraries or license
risks, 184
Cline installing, 20
in React useEffect hook, 126
updating, using future AI, 207
dependency management and updates, security
vulnerability in AI-generated code, 146
deployments
best practices for reliable deployment,
167-170
before and during deployment, 167
ongoing practices after deployment, 169
design
AI-driven design and UX personalization,
207-209
AI for UX research, 209
generative design tools, 208
personalized user experiences, 209
design-to-code process, acceleration using
AI prototyping tools, 111
learning system design, 88
UI and UX, midlevel engineers venturing
into, 89
developers
considered as authors of AI-generated code,
173
cultural and skill shift in future resulting
from use of autonomous agents, 215
developers as editors, code reviews formal-
izing, 166
evolving AI-generated prototype toward
production, 115-118
how they're actually using AI, 69-76

common failure patterns, 70-72
practical workflow patterns, what
actually works, 72
innovations resulting in more growth and
opportunities for, 95
junior developers thriving along with AI,
90-94
communicating and collaborating, 94
developing eye for maintainability, 92
developing prompting and tooling skills,
92
focusing on testing and verification, 91
learning the fundamentals, 91
practicing problem solving and debugging without AI, 91
seeking feedback and mentorship, 93
shifting mindset from consuming to creating solutions, 94
reviewing, refining, and owning AI-
generated code, 106
roles evolving, not disappearing, 81
development
AI-assisted, 4
AI-assisted engineering permeating entire
lifecycle, 8
AI-powered tools dramatically accelerating,
5
faster cycles with AI-assisted coding, 36
plan-first development with AI support, 8
Devin, 190, 193
as AI teammate, 198
(see also AI)
DevOps
background coding agents integrating with
tools, 194
midlevel engineers mastering, 85
vibe coding woven into, 72
diffs, 190
discrimination resulting from AI usage, 184
diverse teams, hiring, 180
Django, 127
documentation
adding while evolving prototype toward
production, 116
produced by AI for web application backend API, 130
providing for AI-accelerated codebase, 163
Doe v. GitHub, Inc. class-action lawsuit, 174
domain expertise, building, 85

domain mastery and foresight, cultivating, 83
domain-specific natural languages, 218
domains, software-engineering-specific, 85

E

ecommerce site by solo developer, built using AI, 138
edge cases
    AI introducing unusual edge cases, 157
    brainstorming for prototype using AI, 116
    checking AI's handling of, 98
emotional and team health insights, gauging using AI, 212
end-to-end tests
    writing for AI-generated code, 105
endpoints
    implementing for backend API, 126
    multistep operations, orchestrating, 128
engineering
    switching from rapid prototyping mode to disciplined engineering, 117
engineers
    future-proofing your career with durable engineering skills, 95
    midlevel engineers, adapting and specializing, 84-90
        building domain expertise, 85
        cross-functional communication, 87
        focusing on code review and quality assurance, 86
        learning new tools and adapting to change, 87
        learning system design and architecture, 88
        learning systems thinking, 87
        managing systems integration and boundaries, 84
        performance optimization and DevOps, 85
        using AI, 88
        venturing into UI and UX design, 89
    senior engineers and developers, leveraging experience with AI, 82-84
        being the architect and editor in chief, 82
        cultivating domain mastery and foresight, 83
        honing soft skills and leadership, 83
        mentoring and setting standards, 83

using AI as force multiplier for big initiatives, 82
environment, specifying in prompts, 42
error handling
    revealing sensitive information in AI-generated code, 146, 147
    testing for AI-generated systems, 155
errors
    finding and fixing in AI-generated code, 101-103
ESLint and security plug-ins, 149
ethical implications of vibe coding, 171-186, 220
    bias and fairness, 178-181
    intellectual property considerations, 171-176
    transparency and attribution, 177-178
EU's AI Act, 177
exceptions (unhandled) in AI code, 100
execution of code and commands by autonomous coding agents, 193
execution stage, autonomous coding agents, 189
expectations of AI-assisted engineering versus vibe coding, 10
experimentation
    enhancement by AI-assisted coding, 36
    vibe coding encouraging mindset of, 16
Express routes, 126

F

failure modes and recovery procedures, 88
failure patterns with use of AI-assisted coding, 70
    demo-quality trap, 72
    two steps back pattern, 70
failures
    learning from, 170
fair use, 173
fairness in AI-generated output, 178-181
fallbacks in AI-generated code, 162
features
    ease of adding using AI, 119
feedback
    feedback loop with AI in prompts, 43
    feedback loops with autonomous systems, 203
    junior developers seeking from team members, 93

few-shot prompting, 50
fidelity of AI-generated prototypes to input or intention, 112
first drafter, AI as, 72, 73
force multiplier, AI as, 84
foresight, using to steer AI, 83, 85
formatters, 156, 160
formatting
    ensuring consistent code formatting in AI code, 100
frameworks
    modern framework utilization by AI coding assistants, 31
    using in web application backends, 127
frontends
    integrating with backend in web application using AI, 132-135
        aligning frontend and backend contracts, 132
        real-time collaboration with AI, 133-135
    refactoring for prototype service converting CSV files to charts, 118
    testing error handling in AI-generated systems, 155
    testing for AI-generated web applications, 136
    web application, 121
    web application frontend development patterns with AI, 123-126
        framework-specific tips, 126
        handling complexity with AI, 125
        implementing components from descriptions, 124
        integrating APIs and state management, 125
        styling and layout, 124
full stack flow with AI (example), 134
full-text searches, coding agents defaulting to, 189
functionality you didn't want in AI code, 98
functions
    AI defining multiple functions when one is expected, 100
    performance optimization in AI-generated code, 158, 159
    refactoring in AI-generated code, 103
fundamentals
    evergreen nature of, 221

importance of learning by junior developers, 91
future of AI-augmented development (see AI-augmented development, future of)
future-proofing your career with durable engineering skills, 95
fuzz testing of AI-generated code, 151, 155

G

Gemini, 18
    choosing between Google's Gemini, Anthropic's Claude, and OpenAI models, 29
    multimodal coding capabilities, 27
    support for multiple AI models, 26
gender bias, 179
generator versus reviewer asymmetry, 194
GitHub CodeQL, 149
GitHub Copilot, 187
    lawsuit against, 174
    living in the editor, 194
GitHub's Copilot for Pull Requests, 166
glue code and integration, using vibe coding for, 31
goals of vibe coding versus AI-assisted engineering, 11
Google Gemini (see Gemini)
Google Jules, 198
    (see also Jules)
Google LLC v. Oracle America, Inc. (court case), 173
governance and process in responsible AI, 185
GPT-4, OpenAI's ToS for code, 173
gray areas in intellectual property issues with AI-generated code, 176

H

Helmet middleware, 152
hooks in React, 126
HTML/CSS
    AI generating, 109
    Cline generating complete HTML/CSS page example, 110
    generation by AI design tools, 208
    UI Layout AI generating, 197
HTML/CSS page
    creating using AI assistant, 110
human contribution, maximizing, 81-96

as power tools meant for power users, 96
thriving on examples and correlations, 45
training on vast corpus of programming
knowledge, 36
load balancing, 88
load testing, 155
logging
incorporating and using in tests of AI-
generated systems, 156
optimizing practices for security purposes,
152
Lovable, 111

M

maintainability
ensuring in AI-accelerated codebases,
160-164
considerations while prompting, 160
follow-up practices, 163
working with code output, 162
junior developers developing eye for, 92
refactoring AI-generated code for, 103
testing for AI-generated systems, 156
maintenance, predictive, using AI, 206
majority solution effect, 99
memory
optimizations for performance in AI-
generated code, 158
memory management, 91
mentorship
junior developers seeking from team members, 93
senior engineers mentoring and setting
standards, 83
metaprogramming, 55
midlevel engineers (see engineers)
minimum viable product (MVP)
building quickly with help of AI pair programmer, 30
web application MVP, 139
model cards, 183
models (AI), 25-26
adapting your tone in prompts to, 49
categories based on approach and strengths,
25
choosing right model for your needs, 29
choosing right model for your task, 25
combining multiple models to maximize
strengths, 195-197

differentiating models by task type, 196
human-AI hybrid teams, 196
using an orchestration system, 196
context window size, 18
future improvements to, narrowing 30%
gap, 214
knowing limits of, 59
major models in coding landscape, 26-29
ChatGPT, 28
Claude, 27
Google Gemini, 27
multimodel approach in development, 29
practical tips for any model, 26
providing updates to compensate for training cutoffs, 151
updated models with security focus, using,
152
variable output quality in coding, 36
modes of operation (Windsurf), 24
modularity, encouraging in AI code, 160
MongoDB, 127
monitoring, setting up in AI-generated systems, 156
multimodal processing (AI models), 25
MVP (see minimum viable product)

N

natural-language coding environments, 12
natural-language project status queries, 211
natural-language-driven development, 217-220
nondeterminism in AI systems, 156

O

object-relational mappers (see ORMs)
observability, setting up for deployments, 168
off-by-one errors, 100
one-shot prompting, 50
stateful conversation versus, 60
open source
and class action lawsuit Doe v. GitHub, Inc.,
174
information about norms, sources of, 172
not synonymous with public domain, 172
open source AI models, 25
OpenAI
models, 25
support for multiple AI models, 26
OpenAI models

project management, evolution with AI,
 210-212
prompt antipatterns, avoiding, 60-63
 ignoring AI's clarification or output, 62
 inconsistency in prompts, 62
 missing the question, 61
 overloaded prompts, 61
 vague prompts, 60
 vague references, 62
 vague success criteria, 61
prompt engineering, 39
 fundamentals of, 40
prompting techniques, 49-58
 advanced prompting, combining techniques
  and handling complexity, 58-63
  knowing model's limits, 59
 chain-of-thought prompting, 51, 53
 contextual prompting, 54
 metaprogramming, 55
 one-shot and two-shot prompting, 50
 ReAct, 57
 role prompting, 53
 self-consistency, 56
 zero-shot prompting, 49
prompts
 ambiguity in, leading to ambiguity in code,
  37
 checking AI's interpretation and implementation of, 98
 considerations for maintainability of AI
  code while prompting, 160
 effective communication with AI, 39
  comparison of two prompts, 46-49
  iterative refinement and feedback loop
   with AI, 43
  specificity and clarity in prompts, 41
 junior developers developing skills in, 92
 prompt artists versus AI orchestra conductors, 12
 prompting AI as form of communication,
  94
 prompting and code generation, responsible
  AI, 184
 refining in iterative prototyping using AI,
  113
 understanding, 14
proof of concept, 109
property-based testing, 155
prototyping

AI-driven, tools and techniques, 109-120
 addressing challenges in AI prototyping,
  119
 concept to prototype, iterative refinement, 112-115
 evolving prototype toward production,
  115
 prototyping tools, 111-112
 rapid prototyping with AI assistants,
  109-111
enhancement by AI-assisted coding, 36
feature prototyping, 31
PRs (pull requests), 165
 autonomous coding agent PRs, 201

Q

quality
 demo-quality trap with AI coding, 72
 variable output quality of AI models, 36
quality assurance
 AI tools enhancing efficiency and effectiveness of, 76
 maximizing benefits of AI and human capabilities in, 76
 midlevel engineers focusing on, 86
 process for AI-assisted projects, unusual
  edge cases and, 157
question, missing in prompts, 61

R

race, gender, and age, variables in algorithms,
 179
racial biases, 179
RAG (retrieval-augmented generation), 23
rate limiting or throttling mechanisms to prevent brute force attacks, 147
React, 121
 tips on, 126
ReAct (Reason + Act) prompting, 57
readability of code
 AI-generated code, issues with, 100
reasoning, deep reasoning AI models, 25
refactoring
 of AI code after testing, 156
 of AI code for maintainability, 103
 continuous refactoring of AI-accelerated
  codebase, 162
 requesting for AI-assisted code that could
  be simpler, 166

About the Author

Addy Osmani is a senior engineering leader at Google, where he works on developer experience, performance, and AI-powered software development tools. He has 25 years of industry experience building web technologies and has authored multiple books on software engineering best practices.

Addy has worked extensively with AI-driven developer tools, testing and evaluating emerging platforms like Cursor, Cline, Copilot, Bolt, v0, Lovable, and Claude Code. His writing on AI-assisted software development has influenced thousands of developers, and his leadership at Google Chrome has helped shape the future of web performance and AI-augmented developer workflows.

This book distills his deep expertise in software engineering and his hands-on experience with AI-powered coding assistants, offering developers practical strategies to integrate AI into their daily workflow and adapt to the rapidly changing landscape of software development.

Colophon

The birds on the cover of *Beyond Vibe Coding* are wallcreepers (*Tichodroma muraria*), a species native to inland cliffs and mountain peaks across Europe, the Middle East, and Asia. In flight, wallcreepers are said to look like large butterflies, but they are difficult to spot at rest against rock faces. The wings have rich red coloring with black and white feather tips, while the bodies are mostly blue-gray. Breeding males have black necks.

Adult wallcreepers are about 6 inches long and weigh about 0.6 ounces. They raise a single brood each year, laying clutches of three to five eggs in cup nests of moss and grasses wedged into rock crevices. They are insectivores.

The IUCN Red List of Threatened Species lists the wallcreeper's conservation status as "Least Concern." Many of the animals on O'Reilly covers are endangered; all of them are important to the world.

The cover illustration is by José Marzan Jr., based on an antique line engraving from *Lydekker's Royal Natural History*. The series design is by Edie Freedman, Ellie Volckhausen, and Karen Montgomery. The cover fonts are Gilroy Semibold and Guardian Sans. The text font is Adobe Minion Pro; the heading font is Adobe Myriad Condensed; and the code font is Dalton Maag's Ubuntu Mono.

O'REILLY®

Learn from experts. Become one yourself.

60,000+ titles | Live events with experts | Role-based courses
Interactive learning | Certification preparation

Try the O'Reilly learning platform free for 10 days.

www.ingramcontent.com/pod-product-compliance
Lightning Source LLC
Chambersburg PA
CBHW061403210326
41598CB00035B/6077

* 9 7 9 8 3 4 1 6 3 4 7 5 6 *